Personal trust investment management

C.F.A. Monograph Series

Personal trust investment management

Proceedings

C.F.A. RESEARCH SEMINAR
May 4-6, 1967
Charlottesville, Virginia

C.F.A. Monograph Series

1968
RICHARD D. IRWIN, INC., Homewood, Illinois
IRWIN-DORSEY, LIMITED, Nobleton, Ontario

First printing, August, 1968

To

E. LINWOOD SAVAGE

1907–1968

Staunch advocate of the professionalization of the financial analyst.

C.F.A. Research Seminar

on

PERSONAL TRUST INVESTMENT MANAGEMENT

Seminarians

FRANK E. BLOCK, C.F.A., *Vice President,* The Citizens and Southern National Bank, Atlanta, Georgia.

RICHARD M. BURRIDGE, C.F.A., *Vice President,* The Northern Trust Company, Chicago, Illinois.

JAMES A. CLOSE, C.F.A., *Senior Vice President,* Merchants National Bank & Trust Company of Syracuse, Syracuse, New York.

HULL P. DOLSON, C.F.A., *Senior Vice President,* The First National Bank of Oregon, Portland, Oregon.

M. HARVEY EARP, C.F.A., *Vice President,* Mercantile National Bank at Dallas, Dallas, Texas.

PATRICK J. JAMES, C.F.A., *Vice President,* The Chase Manhattan Bank, New York, New York.

JOSEPH Y. JEANES, JR., C.F.A., *Vice President,* Wilmington Trust Company, Wilmington, Delaware.

WESLEY F. JONES, C.F.A., *Vice President,* Security First National Bank, Los Angeles, California.

EDMUND A. MENNIS, C.F.A., *Senior Vice President,* Republic National Bank of Dallas, Dallas, Texas.

C. RODERICK O'NEIL, C.F.A., *Vice President,* Manufacturers Hanover Trust Company, New York, New York.

WILLIAM A. STENSON, C.F.A., *Executive Vice President,* The Bank of New York, New York, New York.

ALEXANDER J. V. THELEN, C.F.A., *Vice President*, Citizens Bank and Trust Company, Charlottesville, Virginia.

DAVID D. WILLIAMS, C.F.A., *Vice President*, National Bank of Detroit, Detroit, Michigan.

Seminar Committee

Frank E. Block, *Chairman*

M. Harvey Earp

Edmund A. Mennis

Joseph Y. Jeanes, Jr.

Moderator

MYRON J. SPENCER, *formerly Associate Dean*, Northeastern University, Boston, Massachusetts.

Representing the C.F.A. Research Foundation

M. DUTTON MOREHOUSE, C.F.A., *Manager*, Brown Brothers Harriman & Co., Chicago, Illinois, *President of the Board of Trustees*.

Representing the Institute of Chartered Financial Analysts

E. LINWOOD SAVAGE, C.F.A., *Vice President*, New England Merchants National Bank, Boston, Massachusetts, *President of the Board of Trustees*.

C. STEWART SHEPPARD, Professor of Business Administration, Graduate School of Business Administration, University of Virginia, *Executive Director*.

C. RAY SMITH, Associate Professor of Business Administration, Graduate School of Business Administration, University of Virginia, *Administrative Director*.

G. J. MACFARLANE, *Research Assistant*.

Foreword

The object of the C.F.A. Research Foundation is to foster studies directed toward the practical needs of the financial analyst and the portfolio manager in areas not presently or adequately covered by available texts. Publications of the Foundation are to be made available to the public in an impartial manner. We are indebted to the institutions and individuals listed on the following page who provided the initial financial support for the underlying administrative organization and work of the Foundation.

This publication represents a record of Seminar proceedings, and as such the manuscript has not been submitted to the Trustees of the C.F.A. Research Foundation for approval of its content prior to publication.

M. DUTTON MOREHOUSE
President, Board of Trustees
C.F.A. Research Foundation

CONTRIBUTORS TO
THE C.F.A. RESEARCH FOUNDATION

Institutions

Appco Foundation (Abbott, Proctor & Paine)
The Bank of New York
Bolton, Tremblay & Company
Brown Brothers Harriman & Co.
The Citizens and Southern National Bank
The Detroit Bank & Trust Company
Donaldson, Lufkin & Jenrette, Inc.
Drexel Harriman Ripley Incorporated
Duff, Anderson & Clark, Inc.
Duff and Phelps, Inc.
F. Eberstadt & Co.
Lionel D. Edie & Company Incorporated
Fidelity Management & Research Company
E. F. Hutton & Co. Inc.
Investors Diversified Services, Inc.
Loeb, Rhoades & Co.
Loomis, Sayles & Company Incorporated
Merrill Lynch, Pierce, Fenner & Smith Inc.
Naess & Thomas
National Bank of Detroit
New England Merchants National Bank
Paine, Webber, Jackson & Curtis
Republic National Bank of Dallas
Salomon Brothers & Hutzler
Smith, Barney & Co. Incorporated
Union Commerce Bank
H. C. Wainwright & Co.
White, Weld & Co.
Wilmington Trust Company
Dean Witter & Co.

Individuals

Leonard E. Barlow, C.F.A.
George S. Bissell, C.F.A.
Philip P. Brooks, Jr., C.F.A.
Harold A. Dulan, C.F.A.
Andrew P. Ferretti, C.F.A.
Joseph F. Glibert, C.F.A.
George M. Hansen, C.F.A.
Charles A. Hoskin, C.F.A.
A. Moyer Kulp, C.F.A.
David S. Loveland, C.F.A.
Gilbert H. Palmer, C.F.A.
Robert H. Perry, C.F.A.
Don Rose, Jr., C.F.A.
Charles W. Walker, C.F.A.
Sidney R. Winters

Preface

The C.F.A. Research Foundation was created in December, 1965, to foster research in the areas of financial analysis as related to securities investment. The first research project selected for support by the Foundation's Trustees was one proposed by the Institute of Chartered Financial Analysts, of which I was president at the time.

The Institute was formed in 1959 by the Financial Analysts Federation (now composed of 41 constituent societies having over 11,000 members) as a major step forward in its program of professionalizing the financial analyst. Beginning in 1963, examinations designed to test individual competence and skill in fields of knowledge pertinent to the practice of financial analysis as related to securities investment have been conducted. The Institute has awarded 1,829 charters and at present over 4,000 candidates are registered.

In addition to conducting examinations and awarding the professional designation *Chartered Financial Analyst,* the objectives of the Institute include the maintenance of professional and ethical standards, the fostering of higher educational standards in the field of financial analysis, and the stimulation of research. Specifically, the last two of these objectives are spelled out in the Institute's Articles of Incorporation, as follows: "To guide and encourage the continuing education of persons engaged in the professional practice of financial analysis and, to this end, to promote and encourage research and the preparation, publication, and dissemination of educational materials in the fields of knowledge pertinent to the professional practice of financial analysis."

Among pertinent "educational materials" available, one of the greatest deficiencies is acknowledged to be in the institutional portfolio management area. In endeavoring to fill this gap it seemed logical to try to take advantage of the experience and skills of active professional portfolio managers. The problem: how to transfer their accumulated knowledge to the printed page? We, the trustees, know they were too busy to do very much writing. We thought they might be willing to sit around a table and talk. While we were not sure we could persuade the individuals to spare the necessary time, we were encouraged by the fact that we had a large number of C.F.A. portfolio managers to call upon.

An individual's participation in the C.F.A. program implies his willingness to contribute to the continuing education of financial analysts, and his interest in actively trying to improve investing and analytical techniques.

Frank E. Block, C.F.A., vice president of the Citizens and Southern National Bank, Atlanta, Georgia, accepted the assignment of chairman of the Project Committee, and deserves a large part of the credit for the seminar's success. Assisting him in all phases of the organization and conduct of the seminar was the Committee composed of M. Harvey Earp, C.F.A., formerly vice president and trust investment officer of the Mercantile National Bank of Dallas (now associated with Burnham & Company); Joseph Y. Jeanes, Jr., C.F.A., vice president, Wilmington Trust Company; and Edmund A. Mennis, C.F.A., senior vice president and chairman of the Trust Investment Committee of the Republic National Bank of Dallas.

Through the efforts of the Project Committee an outstanding group of senior trust investment men assembled in Charlottesville, Virginia, in May, 1967, and enthusiastically discussed personal trust investment policies for two-and-one-half days. The areas to be covered were carefully outlined in advance by the Project Committee, but the seminar discussions were entirely spontaneous.

The experience acquired in the conduct of this seminar should facilitate similar projects covering other types of institutional portfolio management, the administration of research and portfolio management departments, analytical report writing, the use of economic research in investment decision making, and other pertinent areas.

E. LINWOOD SAVAGE, C.F.A.
President (1966–1967)
The Institute of Chartered
Financial Analysts

Table of contents

Introduction to the seminar

by Frank E. Block, C.F.A.

Early in 1966 I was called upon by an old friend, Dutton Morehouse, to accept the charge of holding a Seminar on Personal Trust Investment Management in the hope of producing a useful monograph on the subject. Dutton is President of the C.F.A. Research Foundation, and one of the godfathers of the whole C.F.A. program. My acceptance was based on the belief that I would be able to find someone else to do all of the work.

There was little difficulty in selecting the right men for the Seminar Committee. Dr. Edmund Mennis and Harvey Earp were old friends and fellow associate editors of *The Financial Analysts Journal*. Ed is chairman of the Research and Publications Committee of the Institute of Chartered Financial Analysts, and an expert on the relation of corporate profits to economic fluctuations. Harvey is chairman of the Financial Analysts Federation Education Committee, had managed the F.A.F.'s Rockford Seminar, and had written on legal problems of trust investing and on general investment matters. I knew Joseph Jeanes also through the Institute's Research and Publications Committee and admired him immensely. He is an unbelievably hard worker, with an organized mind and a special insight into the very human problems of trust investing and business organizations.

I did not miss my mark in selecting my fellow committeemen. Each accepted, and each excelled in his dedication to the success of the project. In avoiding work or inconvenience for myself, I imposed outrageously on each of them.

It would be difficult to overstate the contributions of the staff of the Institute. Stewart Sheppard, Ray Smith, and Jerry MacFarlane are masters in the care and feeding of C.F.A.'s, but their real accomplishment was in bringing some sort of order out of the deluge of disordered comments of the most articulate seminarians I have come across.

The seminarians were selected by Dutton, Stewart, Lin Savage (then the president of the Institute), and your committee chairman. That they played their part well is perfectly clear to us, and should be obvious by their positions, and by the significance of their remarks. One could not have found a more articulate and dedicated group of fanatics. The committee was delighted with them.

In order to keep the dialogue under some sort of control, Myron J. Spencer of Northeastern University was selected to keep us from wandering too far afield from the appointed topics for discussion.

In designing the monograph the staff of the Institute and the Committeemen joined in a good deal of debate on the relative merits of two approaches.

The first was to take the conversation exactly as it came out on the taped transcript and to let the reader feel that he was a part of the seminar itself. The second viewpoint was to extract the best ideas, put them in decent, if not inspired, English, and organize the material along the lines of the original outline (a common practice in the editing of seminars).

The first approach made a most readable, but badly disorganized, presentation of both the wisdom and the inanities of vigorous debate. While all of the main topics would be touched upon, the emphasis would be on the controversial areas. On the other hand, there would be no explanation of the significance of what was being said for the benefit of the uninitiated reader.

The second approach was to emphasize organization, precise or even intelligent rhetoric, and a host of other benefits. This would not, however, retain any of the flavor, the readability, nor the plain good fun of participating in the Seminar.

Our conclusion was the usual compromise. To the degree possible, we have left the dialogue exactly as it was spoken, excepting those instances where minor modifications were necessary due to meaning. Roughly, a half of the transcript has been cast out. Summaries replace the substantive items eliminated.

Since the reader cannot have a copy of the tapes, he will just have to imagine the tone of voice when an outraged seminarian exclaims "ridiculous" at some viewpoint which he holds in low esteem.

Conversational semantics have not been probed deeply by students of general linguistics. In conversation, people speak in a most informal and careless manner. In the heat of the debate, sentences break down into a shower of ideas, expressed as fragmentary phrases. No one cares about rhetoric when there is a point to be gotten across. One must read the words of the seminarians with a consciousness that they were not giving speeches, but rather engaging in the popular indoor sport of "shop talk."

The other half of the compromise was to make occasional adjustments in the chronological order of the dialogue, where transposition seemed mandatory, and to add bridging paragraphs (presented in a different style of type) either for clarification or amplification of a point under discussion.

Thus, we have sought the best of both worlds, but beg the indulgence of the reader for our compromise between order and liveliness.

One might pose the question: "Why were personal trust investments chosen as the first topic to be covered by this series of seminars?" The answer is a simple one. Very little of merit has been written on the subject of trust investing. The typical investment textbook devotes perhaps a paragraph, or a page or so, to the subject. Often the text material is accompanied by a tabular summary of recent date, revealing that bank trustees invest, say 25 percent in government and tax exempt bonds, perhaps 25 percent in corporate bonds, 45 percent or so in common stocks, and a sprinkling in real estate, mortgages, preferred stocks, and miscellaneous assets. This sort of statistical slander quite reasonably leaves the reader with the impression that trustees consider equity investment to be slightly risky, if not downright reckless, and that "good old bonds" are the safe place for a trustee to put money.

Happily, the reader will discover, as he progresses through this monograph, that today's professional trustees don't think that way. The public is misled by an assorted collection of statistics that include vast sums of money invested for, say: the State Highway Department—Construction Fund #27; for Veterans Administration Guardianships; for those trusts which must be invested in "legal securities"; for escrow accounts; for public retirement funds which may be restricted largely to fixed income securities; etc. The point is that absolutely no information can be derived from the aggregate statistics that are published as "Assets Held by Trust Departments".

Textbooks and public statistics alone cannot be blamed for the general misapprehension of trustors about the alleged ultraconservatism of a modern trust investment organization in handling personal trusts. The truth of the matter is that most busy trust investment men would much prefer to talk, rather than to write, and that they really prefer to talk among themselves, in pleasant but private surroundings. The typical trust man making a presentation before a mixed audience is quite likely to feel the shadow of his legal counsel cast across his 3-by-5 notecards. As a result he is quite careful to say nothing that is controversial or that might be considered a contradiction of accepted trust law and practice. Thus, wherever we turn, we find the literature on personal trust investing to be distressingly sparse, somewhat misleading, and very much noncommittal.

I suppose that all of the trouble started with some very well-intentioned jurists who had to face problems in the times they knew, but with an unfortunate lack of foresight. We find it quite easy to criticize their decisions with today's bountiful stockpile of hindsight.

The most famous of legal cases on trust investing is *Harvard* v. *Amory,* which dates back to 1830. This is the case that propounded the famous Prudent Man Rule, requiring that a trustee observe how men of prudence invest their money, not for speculation, but for income and safety, and that a trustee should go and do likewise. This case was followed by another, *Marshal* v. *Frazier,* in which the court refined the Prudent Man Rule to the extent of saying that a trustee should observe how the prudent man invests money *for others,* and do likewise. These cases provided the foundation for "Prudent Man Laws" in the majority of our 50 states.

It is stimulating to look backwards, and imagine what was a sound investment and what was speculation in the 1830's. There were practically no common stocks around. Land produced whatever the good Lord chose for that season. Safety and income were to be found in high quality bonds and well-selected mortgages. Presumably, financing a whaling ship, or a prospecting party to traverse the unknown vastness of the far West, would constitute raw speculation. This is hardly today's investment environment.

The only trouble was that each court decision was based on earlier court decisions, since common law is based on precedent. A relentless procession of decisions developed over the ensuing 130 odd years, without much recognition of the changing nature of investing, the increasing availability of high quality investment opportunities, the emergence of inflation after World War II, and a host of other circumstances which changed entirely the mix of sound investment choices. Cases which were decided originally as matters of *fact,* were subsequently quoted as matters of *law,* and the legal tomes were soon filled with a conglomerate of good, bad, and indifferent rulings which bore little relationship to the realities of investing today. They certainly failed to recognize the development of the professional investor.

We cannot say that any of the legal decisions are wrong. Yet, we can not avoid a moral obligation to approve nothing less than the best investment practices, and we must suffer whatever legal consequences befall those who try to do what they believe to be right.

With this background in mind, the Seminar Committee set forth as its objective to seek the *best* ways of personal trust investing, leaving the inhibiting influence of legal consequences to someone else to worry about later on.

The Seminar Committee prepared a rather extensive outline on the subject matter hopefully to be covered in two-and-a-half days of discussion by our group of eminent investment seminarians. At one point, the outline ran to 54 pages, and touched on every controversial topic the committee could think of. The final decision was to reduce it to a brief outline of a few pages, with the benign confidence that wherever there were dedicated trust investment men, there would be plenty of controversy. The preparation of the longer outline was not a total loss, in that the committeemen learned from their preliminary work the areas that must be covered if we were to be successful in our project.

One idea was held foremost in our thinking. This was to avoid the sort of compromising pap which had occasionally been published as the consensus of other eminent groups of trust men. The student of trust investment matters has doubtlessly discovered some of these pamphlets, which read like a nicely edited version of the investment chapter from *Scott on Trusts* (an excellent summary of the legal decisions on trust investing). This, we did not want. In order to avoid it, we paid particularly close attention to the selection of a group of seminarians who were known to be both articulate and knowledgeable. A second point of considerable importance was our assurance to the seminarians that their individual comments would be identified neither by name nor by organization, so that each would be able to return to his desk with assurance of continued gainful employment and no nasty little notes from the chairman of the board.

The format of our Seminar was rather simple and straightforward. The program consisted of five half-day sessions, each session dedicated to a specific phase of trust investing. To kick off each subject, a committeeman or a seminarian was called upon to make a brief presentation of the various topic headings of the outline for that session. His remarks were generally a recitation of one or more viewpoints which might deserve consideration, although the speaker did not necessarily agree with all of the viewpoints he presented.

This was merely the impetus of the dialogue, and was designed primarily to remind the seminarians of the topics to be covered during that particular session. The fascinating thing was the way the seminarians passed by the less controversial topics with little or routine observance and hurried on to the areas of meaty controversy between a traditional conservative view of trust investing, as opposed to the rational, innovating, and more aggressive approach which is the practice, or the dream, of most professional trust investment men today.

Any fears we might have had that we would run out of conversational material were pretty well demolished before the first coffee break. No excuse was found for hiding investment timidity behind a curtain of legal or traditional constraints. The theme was clearly, "Use our best judgment as professional investors, and if our attorneys can't defend us for following the spirit of the law's requirement of prudence, then professional investment men in the trust business will simply have to go elsewhere to exercise their abilities." At that point, presumably, they will be considered to be the "prudent men," whom the implicitly nonprudent trustee is supposed to mimic.

I suppose the point of all of this is that *in today's investment environment the professional investor is the prudent man*, to whom the ancient courts made reference. It is the typical successful businessman who is the novice in today's tough investment markets. Uncle Louie may be a very successful Ford dealer, but he has no idea of the sophistication which has developed in the investment discipline. He has no computer to test out his valuation models or to make a spectral analysis of his portfolios. He can't measure the effectiveness of diversification, simply because he's never even heard of co-variance. He has no time for field trips, nor would he know how to ask the right questions. His analysis of financial statements is likely to be primitive, and his ability to make earnings forecasts based on carefully prepared economic projections and a real depth of knowledge of industries is clearly limited. In short, Uncle Louie's chances of beating a professional *at the same level of risk* are about one in a million.

The Seminar Committee believes sincerely that important concepts were expressed which challenge past practices in personal trust investing. The stature of the seminarians is such that their views cannot be taken lightly. They represent institutions handling trust assets, ranging from a few hundred million dollars to a substantial number of billions. At a guess, the seminarians and the seminar committeemen are responsible for investments of at least $40 billion or more. They were selected because they enjoy national reputations in their profession, both as practitioners and as scholars. At times they unanimously expressed views which were contrary either to a traditional trust investment viewpoint, or to opinions widely held by laymen on how professional trustees invest.

CHAPTER ONE

Trust investment philosophy: the Prudent Man Rule

In managing personal trust investments, the professional trustee must work within the framework of statutory law. Most states have Prudent Man statutes of a similar nature.

The following excerpt from a typical Prudent Man statute formed the basis for much of the discussion in the first session of the seminar.

In acquiring, investing, reinvesting, exchanging, retaining, selling, and managing property for the benefit of another, a fiduciary shall exercise the judgment and care under the circumstances then prevailing, which men of prudence, discretion, and intelligence, exercise in the management of their own affairs, not in regard to speculation but in regard to the permanent disposition of their funds, considering the probable income as well as the probable safety of their capital.

While this broad statement has the advantage of encompassing almost all possible situations, it has the disadvantage of being subject to a wide range of different interpretations.

In order to establish a basic framework for the initial session, the seminarians were asked to assume that they were sitting as the investment policy committee of a brand new trust department. This department had opened no accounts; therefore, the discussion was devoted mainly to a general philosophy of trust investing.

This session of the seminar set the pattern for subsequent meetings. Each was initiated by a few introductory remarks on the topic to be covered. In some cases, a seminarian was asked to introduce the subject, while in others the preliminary remarks were made by one of the seminar committeemen. In each case, the remarks followed a general outline the committee had prepared.

Naturally, the seminarians were somewhat cold at first. No one knew exactly what was expected of him. The room seemed full of strangers, and the two microphones on the table looked a bit ominous.

Fortunately, a quarter of an hour or so was spent in welcoming speeches, comments about the seminar outline and the procedures to be followed, and reassurances that the identities of the seminarians would be well hidden.

The reader will sense some restraint on the part of the seminarians during the early part of the session. As the conversation warmed up, however, controversy began to develop, and the self-consciousness disappeared. Some of the debates initiated in this session pour over into the next chapter of the monograph.

The discussion that follows in this chapter revolves primarily around those policies trustees would consider prudent under prevailing economic and social conditions. The seminarians recognized that the legalistic and traditional interpretation of the concept of prudence required an individual trustee to conform to the conventions established by the majority of trustees. It was observed, however, that such a conventional approach precluded an individual trustee from reacting promptly and intelligently to changing circumstances.

Diversification remains a cornerstone of prudent fiduciary investment policy. However, there has been a significant change in the modern trustee's application of this principle of diversification in that increasing emphasis must be placed on selectivity and specific account circumstances. The seminarians expressed greater concern about a situation of overdiversification than they did about a situation of undue concentration. The conclusion in view of the many factors to be considered in administering individual accounts—tax consequences, stability and outlook for the securities held, time horizon, and so on—was that it was difficult, if not impossible, to establish specific rules of diversification for personal trust investment policy.

NICK:[1] It would be difficult to begin any discussion of trusts without talking about the Prudent Man Rule and what it means. We know that we must be prudent men, and that we must be prudent trustees. Unfortunately, guidelines relating to prudence are rather hazy because many court decisions concerning trustees were made in the 1930's, but since that time very little specific trust law has developed on the subject.

---

[1] Pseudonyms are used in this transcript to avoid identification of the seminarians and committeemen. For purposes of further concealment of actual identities, these pseudonyms have been rotated on a random pattern.

It is difficult for me to define prudence. Perhaps we might approach the problem by discussing various elements which enter into the concept of prudence.

Item one: A concept which I have found difficult to define is investment quality. What do we mean by quality? Is it determined by the volatility in the earnings of a company? By the predictability of those earnings? If so, within what limits of volatility? 50 percent, plus or minus? 10 percent, plus or minus?

Item two: Should we use absolute or relative standards? That is, should we have one set of criteria for industrial stocks, another set for utilities? Or should we use different criteria for each industry? If we have one set of criteria for steel, is it proper to have another set of criteria for drug stocks?

Item three: What are the standards for diversification? What is acceptable diversification? What would be the minimum amount of diversification? What would be the range, in other words? Do we really understand each other when we talk about diversification? Do we mean stock/bond ratios? Do we mean diversification within the bond sector? Do we mean diversification within the stock sector? Do we mean by class of bond? Do we mean the maturity of bonds? Or geographical diversification?

Item four: Does our time horizon contribute to prudence or imprudence? Does the same time horizon apply to the bond sector as to the stock sector? Is the bond sector a more permanent investment, or a less permanent investment? What is the minimum acceptable time horizon? Is it 6 months, 5 years, 30 years, 100 years? Over what time period should we set our investment policy?

Item five: Are turnover guidelines practical? How much turnover is too much? Specifically, is it 10 percent of the account, 20 percent of the account, 100 percent, or 200 percent of the account?

The last item: Should we establish performance objectives? If so, how should these performance objectives be set? Of course, this really encompasses most of what I have been discussing.

I admit to complete inadequacy in making a factual definition of some of these points. To begin at the beginning, what is "prudent"?

NED: We might start off with that. I think a lot of these things need to be defined so that we will all be using the same definitions.

GUY: Is prudence to be decided in a complete vacuum? For whom are you trying to be prudent? This worries me, because there are certain instances where you are dealing with extremely wealthy people who have a large current income, whose children have a large current income, and whose complete objective in setting up these trusts is growth. This is increasingly the case, particularly in the larger accounts.

On the other hand, you may have an account which has a low tax cost basis, or maybe an account in a high tax bracket. Then, too, you may have accounts where the outside resources of the people must necessarily be taken into consideration. Can you judge the prudence of an investment entirely without reference to the whole picture? And is this not true also of diversification? If you have a trust with an income of $20,000 or $25,000, you would certainly say that some investment in IBM might be perfectly logical. Maybe a fair amount of it. In contrast, in a very small trust, unless the objective is very clearly defined to be growth, you would think several times before buying a very low-yielding stock.

VAN: You are saying that prudence is the ability to accept risk?

GEORGE: Prudence is conditioned by the ability to accept risk in any particular case.

GENE: It seems to me that you are trying to equate prudence with the concept of suitability.

GREG: Isn't prudence something that applies to every account? Accounts vary, and certainly prudence can have various meanings in accounts with different size, income, and other characteristics. I don't think you can get away from the fact that in every portfolio you are looking at, unless you have a trust instrument that has some special provisions, you are going to be judged on the basis of whether or not you are prudent in that account. It may be a $5 million account, which gives you lots of latitude, or a small $50,000 or $100,000 fund. It seems to me the element of prudence exists in all funds as far as the trustee is concerned, because legally he is going to be measured by the application of prudence to a specific account.

If an instrument limited you entirely to bonds, or entirely to stocks, or to certain classes of issues, that's apart from the general rule.

GUY: If you are limited to bonds, you can still be prudent. You might be able to make some use of convertibles.

NED: May I define prudence as, "the intelligent application of investment media in a given investment environment to meet the objectives of an account"?

VAN: You removed the legal qualifications. You are not looking at it, in that definition, in a legal framework.

NED: That's right.

VIC: Well then, what is an imprudent investment? Would you define it as one that is going to get you in court?

KEN: An imprudent investment is handling the money in a way that's not suitable for the account. If you take too much risk for the beneficiaries involved, you are imprudent. If you bought a $100,000 house when all you can afford is one that is one-third as expensive, then you have acted imprudently. Imprudence in the investment area is just like imprudence in any other area in your life.

VIC: Yes, but are there any standards, or are they all personal judgments? What might be prudent to you might seem imprudent to me. This is the problem I think we are wrestling with. Words like "prudence" and "value" are essentially subjective words. They mean different things to different people. Are there any objective standards of prudence or value that we could all accept?

GENE: Hasn't the legal standard always been that if one man takes an action and he happens to be the only person in the investment business doing that particular thing, then he is imprudent? But an action is not an imprudent act if the majority of people in the business are doing it? "Prudent acts are the acts of prudent men." Therefore, if you have a large number of men acting in a certain way, may you assume that their actions are prudent?

NORM: That is in the original Prudent Man decision.

NED: It makes no provision for the brilliant man who does the unusual thing.

KEN: Like that first share of Xerox. (*laughter*)

GENE: It certainly would be wonderful if Ned's definition of a prudent act were one we could all follow. Obviously, we can't.

VIC: Does a prudent investment for a trust officer differ from that of investment people in general? In other words, why should a trustee be at the end of the line in buying Xerox, or the airlines? Does some other type of investing institution have to blaze a path before you can say, "Other people are doing it and, therefore, we can"? Doesn't that mean that trust investment is always toward the end of the procession? Does the Prudent Man approach force us to avoid innovation?

GENE: This has always been the problem. Trust people have tended to follow rather than lead. They have been afraid to do things simply because other people haven't been doing them.

KEN: I certainly don't agree that we are followers, that it is imprudent to lead. I don't think it is imprudent to lead, but it may be *considered* imprudent to lead.

NED: If you lead, you are running a risk as the law stands today.

NICK: Isn't a prudent man one who acts in a logical fashion? If your action is based on a solid premise, following sound logic, then it would seem to me that you have a defensible position regardless of whether or not others have taken that action before. We got into a discussion of this last night with Ned. He sampled certain other institutions to find their general philosophy. We decided that we really didn't know whether his sample was broad enough, whether his cases had been picked in order to get the end result he desired, or whether he talked primarily with people who were of his same frame of mind. It seems to me that this raises a very serious question in regard to the feasibility of such surveys.

GIL: All I've heard so far is that prudence means different things to different people, and it means different things with respect to the variety of objectives. Of course, we knew that to begin with. Do we have a chance of deriving from this discussion any definition that would answer the original proposition: What is prudence? Is there an objective standard?

GEORGE: The point I was trying to make was that there are elements of prudence aside from the legal aspects. Shouldn't the element of judgment be a critical factor in defining prudence?

GLENN: I think, too, there is an element of consistency in applying judgment to accounts. I can't rationalize diametrically opposed applications of policy to accounts of a similar nature.

GARY: New York State did not have a Prudent Man Rule for a long time and still does not. There was a committee trying to get ammunition to justify to the legislature the fact that trustees should be allowed to be more "imprudent" by buying more common stocks. (*laughter*) It's only recently that they have been permitted to put 35 percent in common stocks.

One thing the committee did was to take a look at what other investors with similar goals were doing. One part of the job was to look at college endowments. There, the objectives were to invest money for the preservation of the principal involved, to get a reasonable income, and to get protection against inflation. These are pretty much the objectives of many trust accounts, except that endowments are tax-free institutions.

Every college in the country with an endowment over $10 million was contacted and data compiled on them. It turned out that the colleges, by and large, were investing larger percentages in common stocks than were trustees for the country as a whole, even where the trustees had full discretion.

Take the University of Rochester as a classic example. With a portfolio of several hundred million dollars in common stocks, they had only 36 different issues at the last annual report. I remember that a year ago 70 percent of their portfolio was in three common stocks—Xerox, IBM, and Eastman Kodak. Of course, the performance has been wonderful.

VIC: We may define prudence as what other prudent men do with their investments. We have said that if we can't find other institutions or other trust people taking actions similar to ours we might well be considered imprudent. In hindsight, we would say that a prudent investment is one that works out well, and that it is an imprudent investment if it doesn't work out well. No one ever challenges you, or hauls you into court, regardless of how imprudent you might appear to be by foresight, if by hindsight the results are favorable.

KEN: As C.F.A.'s, shouldn't we try to get the phrase "professional judgment" into prudence somewhere? It never has been, but that doesn't mean that it shouldn't be. We are looking back on what the Prudent Man Rule has been, not at what it should be. I think we've got to offer a voice in changing this concept to include professional judgment.

NORM: What does professional judgment mean to you?

KEN: We, as professionals, have a much greater ability to analyze securities than the legally defined "prudent man" has. And we thereby assume the responsibility of being evaluated as professional trustees.

NORM: You are referring to our facilities, I assume.

KEN: And our experience. I think I am better able to decide on investment ideas than my wife is, although she is very prudent about a lot of things. Her marriage, for example. (*laughter*)

NORM: I'll repeat my question.

VIC: I think you have an extraordinarily good point here. You are asking: "What would happen today if we were to set out to rewrite the Prudent Man Rule?" If we could arrive at a definition, this would truly be a contribution.

NORM: I see one thing wrong. You are thinking in terms of the facilities of a large bank. How far down the scale in size and facilities can you go and still be professional? In other words, can a private trustee ever be professional?

GEORGE: If he has the skill in this area, yes.

KEN: He might not be as broadly professional, but in individual cases he can be equally professional.

NORM: You see what I am driving at?

KEN: Without the sources of information?

VAN: Those are readily available. You can get all the dope you want on most securities.

VIC: Is it a question also of the time you can devote to it?

NORM: These are all implied in your use of the word "professional."

NED: Well, yes, the man who is an insurance salesman, and is also the trustee for his nephew, doesn't have the time, although he might be smart enough. But he's in a much more difficult position even than the one-man trust department with a good correspondent bank that provides help and additional information.

NICK: Of course, Ned, in this regard I think it is well established that professional trustees are held to a different standard than individual trustees. I assume that we are only talking here about professional trustees. This is the group in which we are interested.

NORM: Corporate trustees?

NICK: Professional trustees. People who represent themselves as being professional trustees, whether they be corporate trustees, or a group of attorneys, or whatever. As I understand it, if you represent yourself to be a professional trustee you are therefore held to a much higher standard than some other type of individual.

GUY: I would think the higher standard would be applied if you, as an employee of a brokerage firm, were trustee for your sister's money. You are a professional trustee, even though you get no compensation for it, because you are informed. You have access to information. You live in a financial atmosphere that is conducive to investment judgment.

GEORGE: In the eyes of the law, isn't any trustee a professional trustee?

NED: No. The law says that if you hold yourself forth as having special skills, and advertise yourself as a trustee, a higher standard of investment behavior is required of you than of a person who does not hold himself forth as having those skills.

KEN: Shouldn't we object to that? Shouldn't we get something in the record to let everybody know what is so important about this professional judgment?

GEORGE: If the individual misappropriates funds, or does not manage funds properly, he is punished in the same way as professional trustees are punished. It is his responsibility to get proper counsel—

proper professional advice. If he doesn't do it, he is responsible for the resulting loss, which he may have to repay personally. There's no court in the land that would let him out of the door. This comes right back to individual discretion, which gives you pretty broad latitude in reaching a decision.

GREG: Let's look at prudence within the framework of a model Prudent Man statute. The key phrase in such a statute would describe the proper trust investment posture to be one ". . . which men of prudence, discretion, and intelligence, [would] exercise in the management of their own affairs. . . ."

Remember that we are talking about investing, reinvesting, purchasing, acquiring, selling, and managing property for the benefit of another. Not for oneself. For the benefit of another. A trustee shall exercise judgment and care. Those are also key words. Certainly you wouldn't take out judgment. What does judgment mean? Judgment means reasoned thought. There is nothing wrong with this definition, because that is what it is.

GENE: The best definition of judgment is simply reasoned thought.

NED: It wouldn't be good judgment to make a decision without seeking adequate information, so I think judgment implies that in some way or other you build a source of information.

GREG: I think this question of information should be discussed in connection with some other words and phrases. There are several of them that I want to mention. "Care" is kind of hard to define, but certainly it means thinking as well as acting.

GUY: Don't you think care also implies that you continue to check up on your decision?

GREG: That's a further factor. Still, that's "thinking," following through. It's acting, as a follow-through process. A second point is "under the circumstances then prevailing." You might say present circumstances. This means at the present time. This rules out hindsight. Where it states "circumstances," what does it mean? It means the trust circumstances. It means the economy and business circumstances. Under "trust circumstances" it includes age, beneficiaries, the economy, business circumstances, interest rates, and so on.

Another point is, "which men of prudence, discretion, and intelligence, exercise in the management of their own affairs." Now what does prudence mean? My best definition is "careful management." Maybe it is professional judgment, but the word "judgment" is already there.

NED: In today's context, these men of prudence almost of necessity have to be professionals. In fact, we have few nonprofessionals who can meet this definition.

GREG: The degree has certainly risen so that the level of responsibility is considerably higher. "Discretion" is the second word after prudence—"which men of prudence, discretion"—and this means the freedom and authority to make decisions and choices. It is your decision to sell some stock, or to hold it. And under "intelligence," I guess it's hard to pin that one down, but part of it is the ability to learn or understand from experience—the use of the faculty of reason in solving problems. Now these definitions may be general, but they describe what we do. We do exercise the faculty of reason in solving the problems of whether or not to sell a stock. Then there is the phrase "not in regard to speculation." Let's put that in focus. I think two things are included in that statement—one is quality and the other is price.

NED: Let me challenge that just for one moment. Government bonds are considered good quality—"trust investment quality," by almost anyone's definition. Yet, I can speculate in them! I can put 5 percent down and buy an issue on which a rights offering may come up next week. If I guess right, I might double my investment in a few days. The thought I am trying to inject here is the matter of application. Doesn't the time horizon become part of this question of speculation? In other words, are we trying to make a fast buck at high risk? We can wipe out that 5 percent margin real quick! Time and the risk element become a part of speculation.

GREG: That brings up another point, which is, "not in regard to speculation, but in regard to permanent disposition of their funds." I submit at this point that there is no such thing as a permanent investment. Nevertheless, I think the words are used to emphasize the opposite of a temporary investment, or disposition of funds for trading purposes. I think we are distinguishing between a trading function and a trustee function in investing, when we say "the permanent disposition," not meaning "permanent" per se.

VIC: This would not preclude your having, let's say, a portion of the account in Treasury bills for later investment?

GREG: I wouldn't think so. The word permanent must mean something closer to a process of *continuing* investment rather than buy and hold forever.

VIC: Well, there's no argument about that. I just wanted to get it on the record.

GREG: Then we come to "probable income." In that connection, we look at the past, the present, and the future.

Finally, there is "the probable safety of . . . capital"—not actual safety but probable safety, which takes into consideration the past and present and a look into the future.

VIC: When you say safety of capital, Greg, would you include the concept of maintaining purchasing power?

GREG: Yes.

NED: Greg, let's go back to "probable income." This dates back to 1830, *Harvard* v. *Amory*—a time when there were no common stocks in which to invest. Investments were basically bonds and other fixed income securities.

GUY: There was also no income tax.

NED: If we were rewriting this definition today, wouldn't we say "consideration of probable overall return." You know, income plus appreciation over a period of time.

GREG: But we do have life tenants and remaindermen. For example, in a $100,000 trust fund under a will, where the life tenant shares only in income, I think we would emphasize "probable income." The basic "overall return" may be secondary if a charity gets the remainder, or some cousin. But this gets into questions of the intent of the testator.

GUY: In interpreting "under the present circumstances," there may be certain limitations on the desirability of income. In some cases you may not want income above a certain amount because of tax rates. On the other hand, there are many instances in which income is absolutely necessary.

GREG: All that is said is that probable income and probable safety should be considered in relation to the case in hand.

NED: The phrase "probable income and probable safety," is old-fashioned language, I think.

GEORGE: Ned, should we get back to discussing what we mean by professional judgment? Isn't this what we are really concerned with? I would like to give an actual illustration. In 1952, an officer in a dynamic growth company established living trusts for his two children with two different banks. He gave cash and stock of his own company. He gave broad powers in the agreement. The only condition was that, before the program was established a reasonably exhaustive study should be made of his company's stock to clarify the attractiveness of the stock as an investment. This is all that was stated.

A very favorable report classified it as an attractive stock for investment. The grantor said, "You go ahead . . . you do what you want to." One of the banks decided to hold on to the stock. The other bank thought it the better part of wisdom to diversify immediately. The performance at the end of 1965 in the bank that held the stock was 400 percent better than in the other bank. Now, who was prudent and who was imprudent?

GREG: I don't think there is any question but that prudence means careful management. The Prudent Man laws, as far as trustees are concerned, refer to the prudent man as any individual who carefully manages his property. Now, that doesn't mean that he can't buy issues down the line quite a long way from that stock if he has enough capital to warrant it. Certainly, there isn't just one pattern of quality. There are all kinds of variations. As trustees, we must remember that most states are governed by the Prudent Man Rule.

GENE: How would you answer George's question? Which bank was prudent?

GEORGE: I should like to make further observations on this. These are living trusts, and the stock went in the trusts with a tax cost of one fifth the actual market value. I'm sorry, I should have quantified that.

VIC: How large a percent of the trust——

GEORGE: Well, 50 percent of the trust was stock, the rest was cash. The only request made was that the stock be reviewed. He didn't tell the trustees what to do. But he wanted them to establish a precedent at that particular time, and then to do as they saw fit as they went along.

GLENN: And one of the banks never did sell any of the stock?

GEORGE: That's right. Not up to 1965. If it has done it since then, I don't know.

VIC: How large was the total fund?

GEORGE: Oh it was about $220,000. At the time it was started $110,000 of it in the stock, the rest in cash.

VIC: A beautiful case of the misconception of risk and reward. Looking back with perfect hindsight, the rewards were substantial for the bank's taking the greater risk. I think that one of the problems which we all face in investments is that 99 percent of our attention is focused on the reward, and we rarely worry about the risk. If it works out, fine; if it doesn't work out, then you are in court.

GEORGE: You have other points to keep in mind. The tax aspect is very important, very important. When you net it out, the low tax cost created a substantial handicap if the stock were to be sold. There would be a state and a federal capital gains tax. This is a very interesting and delicate case. I don't know how many of you run into this in your own particular fields, but we have several trusts of this type that have been set up by executives of corporations. They leave securities in this fashion for their youngsters at very low cost. Sometimes, the companies are very outstanding. In many cases, they aren't, but the question is still: What should a prudent man do? He analyzes the security. He concludes it is an outstanding investment. I know about a————[paper company] holding, which came into a trust that had a cost of 25 cents a share and was selling for 30. Well now, what do you do? Can you pick securities? Sure, prudence requires that we be careful. But careful in what way? How? When? This gets down to the point of just what sort of judgment we have. How is that judgment to be evaluated, by the investor [trustor] and the courts?

GLENN: To look at it another way, under no circumstances should we have a fixed percentage of the total account in any one asset. I don't think it is necessary to say that we are prudent as long as we don't have more than 5 or 10 percent of the account in one security. As you suggest, the tax factor, the age of the beneficiary, and other factors, have a bearing on the matter of prudence.

NED: On the question of concentration, it's basically a question of risk. This is true also of diversification. Diversification can only protect you against certain things. Diversification can't protect you if there is a drop in the stock market, because even though you are broadly diversified, about half of the movement in stocks is due to movements in the market itself. Diversification doesn't solve all of your problems, but if you are concentrated 50 percent in a low-quality cyclical stock, the risk that you are taking is a great deal more than it is in the case of, say, IBM. If you had done a thorough study of IBM and found it to be an attractive company of prime quality, that's one thing. If you had done a study of the cyclical stock and found that it is attractive at the current price, but that it is a high-risk situation because of its standing in its industry, then what?

VIC: I think that a better example is General Motors, which is a fine quality company yet one much more exposed to cyclical fluctuations in earnings and price than IBM. You might argue that over 10 or 15 years it will grow at X percent a year, but you are certainly going to vary around that trend much more than you will around IBM's. What do you do if you have concentration in General Motors instead of IBM?

VAN: If it's on your buy list, you hold it.

Vic: Yes, but the chance of General Motors being taken off, and then being put back on your buy list is a lot greater than the chance of IBM being on and off.

Van: Sure it is, but when it goes off your buy list then you can take your step toward diversification.

George: General Motors being on the buy list doesn't necessarily mean the same as having an IBM. I think that in the case of General Motors you know the background, the cyclical risks, that the rate of growth is probably not as good as, or maybe even lower than, the economy as a whole, and you probably haven't any idea of putting it in the same category with IBM.

Guy: I would agree with you. It seems to me that the objectives of most of the trusts of this kind are long-term growth. You can argue that the growth of General Motors would be less than that of a dozen other stocks, including some utility stocks, over a 10- or 20-year period.

Nick: Let me pursue the point you made earlier, in light of what we have said, in order to get to specifics. I assume from what has been said that if I felt, after having analyzed the facts in a logical and consistent manner, that I wanted to have 100 percent of an account in IBM or General Motors, this would be entirely prudent. Is this correct?

George: No.

Ken: It would be correct if your judgment about IBM could be that good. The reason you have more money in IBM than you have in a low-quality cyclical stock is because you are surer that your judgment is right on IBM.

George: A prudent man wouldn't put 100 percent in anything, no matter how good he thought it was going to be. The case that I brought up is important because it is an actual case, and we face it every day. This is the case in which a person gives you specific assets, and he lets you render your judgment. In a case like this in the state of New York, for example, you can have as much as 30 percent of the price taken away by capital gains taxes. Thus, you are putting far less dollars back to work. With that kind of a handicap, I think that it is an entirely different situation from trying to bet on your judgment that you're going to be 100 percent right on IBM, or Xerox, or anything else. No prudent man would ever do that.

Nick: But what limits are you going to put on me? If it were 80 percent, would that be all right?

Greg: Isn't it part of the "circumstances then prevailing"?

NICK: How much can I put in IBM if, in my judgment, it met all your criteria? Why can't I put 75 percent in IBM?

GREG: We are talking about today's circumstances, but we are also talking in relation to a specific set of circumstances surrounding an individual or account. This is where "today's circumstances" become a problem. You have to think of them in the light of the circumstances in this particular person's case. Maybe income is important, maybe it isn't. Maybe the capital gains tax is a factor that weighs pretty large. The growth factor is very large in IBM, so you might conclude to stay with the entire holding, even though it may be 50 percent of an account. Recognizing that a concentration of 50 percent isn't good normally, it might still be justified under the prevailing circumstances.

NICK: Aren't there some limits? Let me just drive on this a little more. My concern is that any time I get into a borderline case with my committee, the committee always wins. Where do I go to get help in this regard?

GUY: This is like saying you won't buy a stock at more than 50 times earnings. Conceivably, there could be a set of circumstances where you would be willing to do this. I think all you can say is that you are *unlikely* to buy a stock at 50 times earnings.

Maybe a company that is inherently diversified should be discussed. It carries less risk than a highly specialized company. IBM versus Xerox. 3M verus Xerox. All you can say is that a prudent man would probably be very much more unlikely to leave everything in Xerox than, say, 3M.

NED: Here again, we take the "risk–return concept" and say that by diversifying we can reduce certain risks. We can't reduce the risk of an industry going down. We can't reduce the risk of the stock market going down, but we can improve the return-to-risk of the whole portfolio by a certain amount of the right kind of diversification. I cannot give an absolute answer on the degree of diversification, such as, "no more than one percent in any one stock," or anything of that sort. I don't think there are any fixed rules, because the degree of diversification depends on the type of stocks that you're talking about.

NICK: Is there an extreme limit? We know the absolute limit is 100 percent; now, is the extreme limit 90, 80, 70, 60, 50? Is there some limit on which we can agree?

GLENN: I don't think there is any percentage limit we can accept as a standard. We pointed out earlier that account circumstances vary so widely—matters such as age, other income, tax factors—that it seems to me that your standard of prudence is very closely related to the account. I'd suggest that in George's example neither trust officer was particularly prudent. One of them cut the stock down to 5 percent of the account, while the other let it run, starting out at 50 percent up to 80 percent. Maybe there is some place in between these percentages that would represent prudence.

KEN: You are then saying that the decision should rest on two things —the account and the individual stock.

VAL: What about your timing? That's the most important consideration it seems to me, because 30 years ago you would have been a brilliant investor if you had left all your money in Du Pont. If you still retained all your money in Du Pont, you would be merely talented.

NICK: I'm confused. You imply that there is some percentage to be held in mind, but everybody here says no to 100 percent.

KEN: I didn't say no to 100 percent. I haven't strong enough convictions, I wish I did have, about a particular stock. If I did, I would like to think that I would be willing to hold 100 percent of an account in that stock for a limited time horizon.

GEORGE: Would you hold 100 percent in a stock if your convictions were strong enough?

KEN: Yes.

GEORGE: Starting fresh with cash, would a prudent man put 100 percent——

KEN: No! That's the point.

NICK: Then, what would be the percentage?

KEN: Last fall, for example, the premium you had to pay for the outstanding growth stocks that you wanted to own long range was relatively small. In a period such as that, I would like to concentrate my buying in a very small number of names—six, seven, eight, ten names, even in a million-dollar account.

VAN: We are keeping this within the framework of common stocks. There are other investments, and prudent investors often put 100 percent of their funds into one enterprise, into one business. I don't think that's any different from investing in common stocks. I don't see anything wrong with having 100 percent of an account in a common stock if your professional judgment indicates that's a prudent and reasonable thing to do.

GENE: If you feel you can really discriminate between that stock and all other stocks.

VAN: I think it would be a rare instance, but people invest that way every day.

GEORGE: I was involved in a court case in which I had to testify as to the wisdom of owning a 68 percent position in a common stock which had been held for a number of years, fortunately to advantage. I was asked by the judge what, in my professional judgment, constituted proper diversification. I hadn't thought the question out, as I had to answer it rather rapidly. I said, "individual commitments from 5 to 10 percent, industry 20 to 25, depending on my view of the industry outlook and the economy at that specific time, subject to change at any given time in any of these conditions."

KEN: And you sell the winners when they become more than 10 percent, and keep the losers!

GEORGE: What makes you think *you* are right? That is *my* professional judgment.

VAN: Well, what makes you think *you* are right?

KEN: Those are the upper limits that you have grown up with.

GEORGE: That's right. In the eyes of the court, my professional opinion prevailed.

KEN: Sure!

GEORGE: That's the point I am getting at. That's why I think it is so important that we, as a group, try to evolve something that can be looked upon as representing professional judgment.

GIL: Thus far, we have come to the position where we might agree that since prudent behavior is not defined in the Ten Commandments the only definition we are going to get will result from the distillation of professional judgments. But then we get hung up on the question of what constitutes professional judgment. The points that Greg has enumerated give us at least a chance to come up with something that will be generally acceptable. Obviously, we can't get any agreement here in terms of precise limitations.

KEN: Analyze the 10 most successful accounts that any of us have in our trust departments, and I'll bet the diversification limitations are violated in every one of those 10 accounts.

GIL: This really confirms the point I have just made.

NED: Analyze the 10 worst while you are at it.

KEN: I would bet they were overly diversified.

NICK: Let me read you one sentence out of the Trust Manual. It says, "As a rule of thumb, not more than 20 percent of the principal of any account should be invested in securities or other obligations of any one issuer or obligor. This guideline should not be applied to accounts wherein the principal is small, under fifty thousand dollars, however."

KEN: That comes from a nonprofessional investor known as the Comptroller of Currency. (*laughter*)

NICK: Are we saying that a professional investor would not concentrate his funds as much as the nonprofessional? Are we willing to say that?

GIL: Do we want to accept this?

NICK: George says 10 percent would be his rule, right?

GEORGE: Yes, it would, and I follow it.

NED: I think that in an aggressive account we would be more than 15 percent in IBM.

GUY: I would be willing to do that.

NED: Maybe not at today's prices, but normally.

GEORGE: You are never going to be called on to back up your judgment on the Prudent Man Rule until you make a mistake. There is no question about that. In general, mistakes arise when you start with cash, rather than in an old account full of stocks that you have to keep because of capital gains tax problems, and in which concentrations may be higher. This is a very common problem.

Many executives—those who exercise stock options—transfer shares to trusts for their children. These are received at a very low cost—that's a handicap—and it is going to be an increasing problem with passing of time.

KEN: I don't think you can make generalizations.

NICK: You have to assume that you have a cash sum of money.

GEORGE: Here again we may ask: What is professional judgment? How could we define it in terms acceptable to us and to the courts?

KEN: Let us take another look at diversification. In a very large account, how much diversification would you have? What is the limit? Would you have 100 names in a $50 million account, or do you have only 20 names?

NED: I think most of us are in the process of trying to reduce the number of names very substantially. Thinking in trust institutions is shifting very rapidly to a more selective approach rather than to an overdiversified approach. We have found that when we have 100 names we are going to do exactly what Standard and Poor's 500 does. No better, no worse. Professionals expect to do better. We are not going to be satisfied unless we do better than the market as a whole.

We are becoming more selective. I think this is due partly to the fact that we've got more faith today in our security analysts' abilities to pick securities than we had 50 years ago. We are saying about them, "All right, they know how to pick winners, and so we are going to bet on our boys because we believe in them." In trying to reduce the number of stocks, we still hold enough of the remaining stocks so that if they perform well they will really mean something to the account. If you have only 1 percent of an account in a stock, and it performs well, it still doesn't mean anything to the account. If it doubles, the account increases by only 1 percent.

Besides, we know that our top 10 stocks will outperform our top 100 by a large margin.

KEN: George, I would like to hear your suggestions on this because you represent some large funds. Do you get up to 100 names in some of your funds? 90? 80?

GEORGE: In very large ones you do. A few years ago, if you followed our line of discussion you wouldn't have purchased an airline. Their total market valuation was very low. The market for each issue was thin.

GENE: You are saying, then, that if you wanted to establish a position in the airlines you had to buy more than one.

GEORGE: Yes. You had to buy more than one. As a matter of fact, we became horrified in some cases. At one time, we made an evaluation and found that we owned a very large percentage of the airlines in this country. It scared the hell out of me. (*laughter*)

CHAPTER TWO

Trust investment
philosophy:
general policy

This chapter continues the discussion of general investment policy for a trust department. However, discussion shifts from the legal and traditional restraints to questions of just what does and what does not represent sound investment judgment.

It becomes clearer that it is not possible to quantify investment policies. The investment world is dynamic. Arbitrary maximum and minimum limits that might seem sensible today may turn out to be disastrous tomorrow. In addition, because of the wide variety of objectives of individual accounts broad policies can be useful only as guidelines and are applicable only to the average account—whatever that may be. Each trust account has its own peculiar aims, conditions, and limitations. Thus, it appears that what is needed is the right set of attitudes rather than the right set of numbers.

The discussion ranges over a wide list of policy topics, including risk, trust investment quality, diversification, turnover, time horizon, speculation, the usefulness of market analysis, and certain aspects of the concept of permanency.

The question of permanency, which was touched on in the previous chapter, is broadened a bit. While the seminarians did not contradict their earlier view that permanent investment was not a buy-and-hold approach, but more a matter of the continuous investment process, the discussion also brought out the view that while a trustee invests **for** the long term he invests **in** the short term. It was also suggested that despite the longer-term objectives of an account the trustee should seek to accomplish the account's objectives in every time period.

Generally, the seminarians expressed little faith in pure technical analysis of the formalized variety, but considered it to be good investment judgment to apply the sort of market analysis that is based upon economic, political, and psychological factors. Short-term price and volume action of the stock were considered to be valid both as signaling devices and as aids in the timing of investment changes, but little support was offered to the Dow theorists, point and figure chartists, and the like.

NICK: What are we as a trust committee going to say to our investment department? What limits are we going to put on our investment department? This is the open question in broad general policy terms. Coming back to diversification, are we simply going to say to our investment department that the policy of our institution is that we shall act in a prudent manner? Is this what we are going to charge our investment department with? Or, are we going to be more specific and say that, as a policy of this institution, we will not commit new funds to the extent of more than 20 percent of a trust account in one security. I think, to deal with such questions, we have to keep the posture of a trust committee trying to set some guidelines for our investment department. Now, obviously, there are many variations, and we could discuss them endlessly, but, I repeat, what are the limits we are going to set on our investment department? Or are we going to set *any* limits? Are we merely going to tell them that we expect them to act in a prudent manner?

KEN: Why can't we set finite limits, then be willing to modify them in exceptional cases?

VAN: Nobody would quarrel with that, after all the discussion we have had.

NED: We don't have an account yet in this hypothetical trust department, so we haven't any specific problems. We could set some generalized policies and say, "All right, men, these are the rules. If you break a rule you had better have a good reason in the file." Then we could rattle off the investment philosophy—that is, whether we are going to be aggressive or conservative in our investment approach. And by conservative I am talking about a traditional and highly legalistic approach. I think these are the broad questions that someone has to decide. I guess these issues normally have been decided by merely noticing what has evolved in the department over the last 20 years, and that becomes the broad policy. But wouldn't it be better somewhere along the line to put the whole thing in writing?

GREG: It seems to me that each account has its own policy. Broad guidelines are fine, providing you have a lot of loopholes and open doors. We like to look at each fund having new cash for investment, and then determine the program that the investment department thinks is best, using the judgment of the committee as they view the suggested program as a whole. If all other things considered seem proper— product mix, levels of quality—we approve the suggested program for that account.

I think that in the light of the economy at any given time there certainly can be some broad guidelines, but you have to be awfully careful that you don't get some beneficiary who is going to say, "You said you'd do *this* generally for accounts, and you didn't do that with mine." Then you're on the hot seat. This is the one problem of trying to stay clean and yet give some leadership to your group. You can do it by checking each case when it comes through and confirming the variations in policy. We have overall thinking that we'd apply as far as product mix goes. We have guidance lists, as you all have, with a broad number of issues of securities from which to draw.

To establish broad policy, I suppose one of the things that should be on our record is that there are *ranges in quality*. I don't want to get into the subject until you're ready for it here. In my book, there is a wide range in quality. Furthermore, there is greater latitude in quality in a larger fund than there is permitted in a smaller fund. You have some degree of deviation.

Picture a wealthy individual who is a prudent man. With his $10 million, he has room to put a million into real estate. I might call it speculation, but it can be developed into a profitable investment. There is a lot of that done in my state.

With respect to the ideal mixture of securities, there are some general things you head toward. Maybe we should try to evolve these general factors. Our general thinking in trust accounts is 65 percent equity position, but it may vary. Some accounts will be 70, others will be 60 percent.

GEORGE: Why?

GREG: To recognize the purchasing power concept and to recognize some reserve position, backlog, and strength. In some accounts the equity position would be 100 percent, but the holdings must fit that account. I don't think you would have a broad policy of 100 percent.

GUY: In a relatively small trust where the resources are limited, you would give more emphasis to stability, to income, and to other things. In larger trusts, the taxation factor is particularly important. You would be willing to modify your philosophy as the size of the trust increases. This may be true regardless of the objectives of the account.

NICK: I'm not talking about the exceptional case. I think rules will always have exceptions. What I am struggling with is this problem of a trust committee asking, "What is the limit of professional judgment?" Everybody seemed to agree that you wouldn't have 100 percent in one stock no matter how good you thought the stock was.

GEORGE: Do you have to have numbers to define professionalism?

NICK: No, not necessarily. If the subject matter is vague, and if all we can do is say that there are no guidelines, then so be it. We then have to use vague terms, such as, "we won't speculate," "we will be very prudent," "we will use good judgment." Now, nobody can quarrel with that. We can all wave the flag and go from there.

KEN: Yes, but we need to be more specific.

GEORGE: What constitutes good judgment?

GIL: You are really going to have to come up with an earthshaking answer. Perhaps you will have to quantify the unquantifiable.

GENE: Are we putting the cart before the horse? We are going to talk about many of these things over the next couple of days. Should we have something like this come at the end of our seminar, instead of at the very beginning when we are all struggling with definitions and terms, and where we are trying to understand one another's thinking?

NICK: Do you think that through the use of these terms in our discussion these terms will become more clearly defined?

GLENN: Have we established in our discussion so far that diversification is in itself no test of prudence?

GENE: Well, we have many words such as quality and diversification, which are completely hazy to everybody.

GEORGE: Let's each one of us put down on paper what we think constitutes investment judgment. I think this should be separate and distinct from investment philosophy. How would we want to be judged?

GENE: George, by this do you mean what an investment decision should be based on?

GEORGE: That would be one of the facts that should be considered in proper investment judgment.

During the final session of the seminar, the various definitions of investment judgment were discussed briefly and are summarized in the following review.

GIL: I would like to begin with the comments on investment judgment that were submitted. The uniformity is remarkable. There is a certain common thread that runs through all of the definitions. The first important point is that prudent investment judgment is what you think it is. (laughter) The second element involves some degree of intelligence backed up by professional experience, using all the information available in order to reach an investment decision. That's really the theme that runs through all of these definitions: an intelligent, well-trained individual with a measure of experience, using all the inputs available to him in order to reach an investment decision. Some of you were very careful to add, "in a fiduciary capacity."

NED: I think here our concept of prudent investment judgment is perhaps a challenge to the legal point of view.

GIL: Nick made some reference to the time horizon problem in his initial presentation. We didn't do much with it, so, Nick, maybe you would reopen this discussion.

NICK: What is the prudent trustee's time horizon?

KEN: May I lead off? Then you can all chop off my neck. I assume we are talking about common stocks, but I suppose that my view would be true for any investment. I think the proper time horizon for a trustee is to take as long a view as possible with due regard for what might happen over the short term.

GLENN: Like losing the account. (*laughter*)

GREG: We are only now forming the trust department. Let's not lose our accounts before we get them.

GLENN: If your time horizon is too long, you might lose them.

KEN: Well, I could give a specific example. When we buy our old favorite IBM, we buy it as a long-range investment. Nevertheless, we have to buy it in the framework of its market price and of the outlook for the company at that particular time. These influences affect our near-term objectives, even though they have a lesser influence on our longer-term objectives.

NED: Does the near-term outlook of the company give you much information about the quality of the company?

KEN: That's another subject. I don't know what you are talking about when you say quality.

NED: When we talk about quality, aren't we really talking about companies that will hold up very well over the long term?

KEN: I don't know; that's another subject.

NICK: Coming back to the time horizon problem, trustees are conventionally permanent investors. OK. What is permanent? If you buy U.S. Steel on a cyclical swing, is that permanent investment?

GENE: No, but it is a valid investment. Take General Motors. Do you think its price has fully discounted a hypothetical decline in auto sales? Is there anything invalid in buying a stock on that basis?

VIC: Doesn't the time horizon vary with the stock, even when you are making a permanent disposition of funds? You are saying that given information under the circumstances now prevailing you are not buying a stock in anticipation of some short-term development. Rather, you are making a commitment until the conditions are different from what they are now. At that point, you might be disposed to sell it. You don't have a time horizon measured by the clock or the calendar. You really have it measured by the expectations of the earnings of the company.

VAN: Wouldn't you include price in there?

VIC: Yes, the price comes in there in the sense that essentially you are investing in the business at the current price. Now, conditions can change in one of two ways. Something can affect the conditions of the company, the earnings factor. Or something else can affect the price. One of these will change your attitude about the stock, and therefore you may want to sell it. It seems to me that is a reasonable way to look at the question of price.

GENE: You can't be thinking in terms of the life of the stock when you buy a stock. You are buying it because you like the company and because you feel you want to be a partner in that particular business. You would be a partner in that business until such time as you felt it wouldn't be worthwhile any more.

NED: We have challenged what in some states is known legally as the rule of permanency, and waded right on through it without blinking our eyes. Are you all aware of what we have done? (*laughter*)

GREG: We often hear many expressions such as "three to five years." There's no way you can tell. I think the definition Gene made is an excellent one. Constant review should determine the continuation of the holding.

VIC: Then this leads to another point. I'm thinking of a turnover question, which is directly related. This is a kind of time horizon. It would seem to me that you could not set any rigid turnover definition.

GENE: That goes right back to professional judgment.

VIC: In other words, you can't say that X percent turnover is acceptable. It could be high or low, depending on what the conditions are. And it is not imprudent to have a high turnover.

KEN: Right. Or low turnover.

GENE: I think it would be a sign of imprudence to have a low turnover.

NICK: I think it can be stated that there is no imprudent turnover figure.

VAN: Right.

GENE: Turnover is a symptom. It isn't a cause.

KEN: It's a reaction, not an action.

GIL: If you define time horizon as you have just defined it, then you can't develop a specific definition chronologically for turnover.

GREG: If for some reason or other you haven't made any changes in a portfolio, let's say for a period of an entire year, the client gets the review and his assumption right there is that you haven't even followed the account.

KEN: Well, I happen to feel that it is a good discipline to make some change when an account is looked at because it is a rare trust indeed, of any size, that has exactly what you should buy with your money at that time.

GIL: What do you mean by good discipline, Ken? How are you defining that?

GENE: It's a pruning mechanism that forces you to be constantly reviewing, and kicking out the worst items, and replacing them with something better.

GEORGE: Would you make changes just to make changes when you review an account?

GENE: Of course not.

KEN: No.

VAN: None of us do that. (*laughter*)

GENE: I would question, though, this concept of having no limit on turnover. In the first place, we do have tax considerations, and if you say there should be unlimited turnover, that would imply that taking short-term capital gains is a desirable thing.

KEN: All of those things have to be taken into consideration.

GENE: That is one of the impediments to making changes in personal trust accounts, but if you can justify a change, then you ought to do it. Even if in that particular year it led to a high turnover.

KEN: I want to get away from putting any finite limits on turnover.

VAN: I understand, but I think there is some danger in just saying that unlimited turnover is acceptable.

GENE: Account considerations must be weighed, of course. Some people don't like to sell stocks. Then you should be much more cautious about putting a stock in an account which you feel you would want to sell at some time; a stock that has to be sold successfully.

VAN: That, then, is putting our understanding of turnover on the same basis as that of a broker, is it not?

GENE: What do you mean?

VAN: Well, I think there is more incentive for turnover in a brokerage house than there is in a trust company because of the commission. If you say an unlimited turnover is a reasonable or prudent thing, you are losing sight of some of the trust responsibilities.

GENE: If your judgment indicates that you ought to make a change, then you should.

GEORGE: Our incentive is based on judgment.

KEITH: That's right.

GENE: We know that it is a cost to the account to make a change. This is a factor that we would weigh.

GEORGE: How much weight should be given the tax considerations?

KEN: Depends on the age of the person.

NED: I think I should challenge Ken on his statement that we should have no turnover guidelines. If we happen to turn over an account 100 percent one day, from the outside it would appear that we were doing what you might call day trading. Yet, it is conceivable that there could be a justification on one day for believing that a major shift should be made, that the account needed complete revision, as a result of some dramatic event—the President died, or something dramatic happened. On this day, our judgment is that we should not be in these securities. We should be in other securities. I can conceive of events happening where you would have very rapid turnover. But I think each change would have to be a decision that stood on its own, as opposed to "I think these stocks are going to go up today, and I am going to buy them now and sell them tomorrow."

GENE: Could I suggest a guideline in terms of turnover? We should tell our account men that we will be very surprised if there isn't some turnover in an account during the course of a year, without trying to quantify the amount of turnover in any way.

KEN: Accounts should be reviewed often enough so that some turnover would result logically.

GENE: That's right.

GLENN: I just want to ask whether it would clarify this question if we stood back a moment and reviewed our posture as trustees as against that of an individual acting for his own account. Leaving aside the professional ability and experience involved, are we in the same position as the broker acting for himself, regarding this matter of turnover? Does being a trustee make our policy different from that of an individual? I think it does. I think this is what is traditional trust thinking as to turnover in an account. Our objectives are somewhat longer range. Our objectives permit less risk-taking than theirs. Lord knows I am not a conservationist as far as estates are concerned, but——

GREG: You are less opportunistic——

GEORGE: Are there any accounts that aren't interested in making money?

KEN: Is this performance something new?

GEORGE: Yes.

GLENN: I guess what we are getting to, then, is a matter of risk. Yes, all our accounts are interested in making money, and all our accounts are interested in keeping up with the rising cost of living.

GREG: If income is your prime objective in an account, and there are many of these accounts, you are not going to make the performance in high-yielding bonds or stocks that you will in low-yield stocks. You may get some performance, but income and appreciation just don't go together.

KEN: That doesn't mean that you won't make switches to improve income.

GARY: I think the answer to Glenn's question is that as professional investment men we should expect to have two things. First, smaller diversification than the layman investor. We can select securities better than he can. Second, we can have a higher rate of turnover because we can spot changes in the investment spectrum more accurately. I think that we should have both a higher rate of turnover and less diversification.

NED: During the course of a year, at least two or three industries become so attractive that we decide that we should invest in those industries, either because the stocks go down in price or the outlook has changed for the better. Knowing that at least a few times a year these developments are going to take place, it seems to me that most accounts are going to have some activity every year including income accounts. I would not expect to see many accounts that had zero activity during the course of a year, simply because we are going to commit an awful lot of our accounts to the stocks of attractive industries.

GEORGE: This is very interesting. Lots of trusts last for many years, are long standing.

KEN: Suppose the gal's 85 years old!

GEORGE: Well, no, say it's a trust that runs from one generation to the next where you don't have the problem of anyone's dying, but could have very low tax cost basis. Would you make a lot of changes? This is a very interesting point.

GENE: It definitely makes it harder, because of capital gains taxes.

GUY: This is certainly true, particularly if you are reasonably satisfied with the companies held.

GARY: In many of your personal trusts, the tax cost bases—to the remaindermen—are going to be the tax costs of the trust. Right? Somebody is going to have to pay the taxes sooner or later.

GUY: But why is this your problem as a trustee? I am perfectly willing to write off a cost of existing securities, but is it our problem that remaindermen get these stocks at very low costs? Isn't this their individual headache? They could give them to charity and write them up in that fashion.

GLENN: In a course in investment management, we defined investment securities as those we think will perform well enough to overcome that tax liability.

GEORGE: I just talked with an investment officer of one of the old banks who came to see some of our people, including me, on a very important matter. They had recently reviewed all of their trusts because they found out that there had been some graft by some of their people. They had over 100 accounts that had oil holdings representing as high as 70 percent of the funds. The range was from 40 to 70 percent. They knew nothing about these holdings. They had held them all these years. No one complained until now. Now what do you do? The interesting thing is that the cost was very low. All of a sudden, there seemed to be some reason for universal concern about the oil industry. The trustees were finally raising questions themselves.

GLENN: I guess you would have to face up to the fact that they haven't done an adequate job.

GEORGE: I couldn't tell him that. (*laughter*) But, seriously, that's the kind of thing I'm getting at.

KEITH: We have accounts like that of our own.

GEORGE: I am certain we all have, because this was an extremely popular industry a few years ago, and all of a sudden things changed.

GIL: Well, gentlemen, when we started this discussion our starting point was the time horizon question and the turnover question. Have we exhausted this?

GLENN: I want to restate something. I think there is a risk inherent in trading in an account, if you want to use that expression, or having too frequent moves in an account. I think we are undertaking an element of risk that perhaps might not be appropriate for an individual.

GENE: Is it a risk to the account, or is it a risk to the managers?

GLENN: I think to both.

GENE: He is equating trading with very high turnover.

VAN: This doesn't mean it is going to happen.

GENE: Wouldn't it be silly, Van, to create a constraint that would mean you wouldn't exercise your best judgment? If you set a limit on turnover, that is exactly what you have done.

GUY: Is this really saying that if there is unlimited turnover, or if there is absolutely no turnover, it is somewhat a reflection on the ability or the judgment of the people who are doing the investing?

KEN: Well, that follows.

GREG: Not necessarily. Good investment judgment—I just wrote this down, so I don't know what it sounds like—"good investment judgment includes an investment follow-through on consideration of sales and purchases." Now this does not limit you to a year. An investment follow-through can be anytime—tomorrow, next month, 10 years. If for some reason an item should be sold, that sale could be made with purchase of an item that had better prospects. This is turnover, but turnover within the framework of judgment.

GENE: I really feel that one of the difficulties in getting people to make enough changes is that the account man does run a bit of a risk when he shifts from a stock where he's got a big profit. You look at the cost of the new holding, and you look at the market, and you-know-who —the boss—could complain. You switch, and your new book cost is the money that you got from selling the old investment. It isn't the original amount of money that was put in the old holding. Thus, the new stock could show an immediate loss. If the account man is wrong, then he gets all sorts of feedback—that is, criticism.

KEN: Because the nature of this personal trust business has always been looking backward rather than forward.

GENE: I'm not speaking of getting sued. I mean just the relationship between the account manager and the higher-ups.

GUY: You've got to be right twice. This is the real problem. You've got to be right on your sale and right on the reinvestment.

GENE: So it means that you are using careful judgment. If your judgment indicates that you should do something, you should do it.

KEN: But you've got to be right twice.

GENE: Every day you have to be right about that stock.

GLENN: Don't misunderstand me in my view. I think that trust investment officers, for years, have been conservationists. They've been content to sit with their blue chips and watch them move along at 3, 4, 5, 6 percent a year. Now all of a sudden we are becoming quite conscious of the fact that we don't exercise enough active management, and we haven't made the effort to improve the securities in accounts that we should have. I wouldn't like to see us run to the other extreme where we have to show a great deal of activity, where we have to get into this stock and get out of that stock in order to be judged competent managers.

VAN: Right! I don't think our definition of turnover should be the same as that of a broker, because we should have some distinction between our definition of what is a reasonable turnover as against any other type of investor.

KEN: We should say at the outset that we will not turn over stocks for any reason other than investment judgment. On the other hand, where investment judgment dictates, we will not be constrained by any percentage turnover.

NICK: Let's summarize along this line, as far as the turnover question is concerned. Number one: turnover, in and of itself, is no indication of investment prudence or imprudence. Number two: if there is any significance to the question of turnover, it is the absence of any turnover. That is the point that should be watched most carefully.

GENE: Well, I think either extreme. You begin to really take a close look at the way choices were made, and just what the decisions were based on. If turnover was zero, or if it was very high—either way.

GIL: This sort of goes back to something Ken said a minute ago. Maybe I can get you to expand on that a little bit. The implication was that if you just sit on a particular asset, day after day, that you have made a decision.

KEN: The same decision as to buy it.

GIL: Well, now how often do I have to make that appraisal?

GENE: It literally is day to day. Theoretically, if you hold ———— [a blue chip oil] you buy it each day. Another mistake. (*laughter*)

GLENN: What it comes down to is that you make a mistake if you hold your oils, but you don't make a mistake if you hold IBM. This is hindsight again.

VIC: I think we are all foursquare against speculation, but I am not quite sure that we know what we are foursquare against. What is it? I can remember one of the questions in one of the C.F.A. Study Guides— What is the difference between investment and speculation?

This gets into the area of permanency. In other words, presumably speculation is not permanent investment; we know what it is *not*. What is it? Can anyone give an acceptable definition of speculation?

GENE: To me, speculation is making investment decisions on the basis of your evaluation of the buying and selling pressures that will affect the price of a particular stock. I contrast that with making investment decisions on the basis of your economic and other evaluations of the company as a partnership interest which is going to either prosper or not prosper.

NED: That brings up another approach. Is it a speculation when, in order for the transaction to be successful, you have to sell it successfully within a reasonably short period of time?

GLENN: If the time horizon is too short, it is probably a speculation. Is this true?

GUY: Is this necessarily true? Suppose we have knowledge of a new chemical process, for instance. A major breakthrough. Maybe it is in the very early state of production. Is it still a speculation, even though you may have a several-year time horizon?

NED: There I think we are talking about the quality of the company and the risk inherent in the company. Let's take the example of IBM. I think most of us feel that we could buy IBM and have the feeling that we were going to hold it indefinitely into the future, and that it would be a successful investment operation. If we decided we wanted to buy ———— [a speculative stock] today, we would probably have to have a successful sale—some price in sight, that is, before the company goes broke.

Maybe that is not a good example. But perhaps you wanted to own I.T.&T., and you decided the way to do it was to buy American Broadcasting with the hope that the merger would go through. You'd figure you were buying I.T.&T. about 10 points under the market. A single event becomes the criterion of success for that operation. Is it not somewhat speculative? Whether it is the market itself, a merger going through, or a new product clicking, or———

KEN: You could go a step further. Is buying IBM at close to 50 times earnings a speculation relative to buying it last fall at under 30 times earnings?

NED: The risk is certainly higher at 50 times than it was at 30. Also, buying bonds with yields at 2.5 percent is a lot more risky than buying bonds with yields above 5 percent, because, historically, yields have been above 5 percent only a couple of times in the last 100 years.

NICK: But is that a helpful criterion?

VIC: Well, you are broadening out the definition of speculation, and you wouldn't accept Gene's definition.

KEN: I think Gene's definition is pretty good myself.

GENE: You mentioned a merger, Ned. If you knew a merger was going to go through, and you bought the stock on that basis, is that a speculation?

NED: If you knew it was going to go through, and there was a very high degree of certainty, I would say that it is not a speculation. If there was a high degree of uncertainty——

GENE: You would add to what I said, then. The degree of variability of the knowledge on which you made an economic evaluation would add to or detract from the speculative aspect of the decision. There is some speculation if you bought a stock and you really had no way to evaluate whether a particular chemical process was going to work out or not, particularly if you had to pay a high price to share in it.

VIC: Must all trust department investment be based on so-called fundamental analysis? Is there no place in trust department operations for anything called technical analysis? Would you accept that?

GENE: No, I wouldn't. In my opinion anybody who buys a stock is speculating to some extent, since it will not have been a successful investment unless the price goes up.

VIC: I would challenge the statement that a stock must go up in order to be a successful investment. If you have an account that is income-oriented, and you buy a stock that yields 6 percent, you don't expect it to go up. You can argue that ——— [a stable blue chip income stock] at a 6 percent yield, let's say, would be an appropriate investment, although you never expect the thing to go up.

GEORGE: I don't think that is a fair assumption. It would go up if it stayed at the 6 percent yield limit because the dividend grows.

GENE: Well, if you buy ——— [a blue chip high-yield oil stock], and you never get any change in the dividend over the next 10 years, I don't think that you really would say it was a successful investment. You could get just about the same yield on bonds with a higher degree of certainty.

GIL: Is it fair to say that what you are driving at here is a difference between risk and uncertainty? If you are able to calculate a risk, even though that risk may be high, the investment is not speculative? In contrast, if you are venturing into something where there is no calculable risk, you are dealing in an area of uncertainty, and that is speculative?

GENE: Yes. I guess you might say that if the risk can't be quantified, the investment must be speculative.

GLENN: If there is an uncalculable risk, it is speculation.

GARY: Then your judgment is all wrong.

GENE: That's right. You are unable to make a judgment.

VIC: Gene, back to technical analysis. You said you were going to expand on where it fits in trust investment.

GENE: I was just going to say that an analysis of the price/earnings ratio, which is nothing more than an evaluation of whether a stock is overly popular or underly popular, may be just technical analysis.

VIC: I wouldn't say price/earnings ratios are not a part of fundamental analysis. Technical analysis, as I understand it, is pure price analysis.

GENE: Right. Well, I believe that pure price analysis has very limited, if any, application to making trust investments.

VIC: OK.

GEORGE: I think it can be definitely said that in many cases where you have a broad choice of investments you can use some type of technical approach to indicate which of these investments might be the more popular one.

GENE: I am very confident of one thing that you said: You can use technical analysis in making a decision that will help you to be right half the time.

GIL: Where did you get that figure, Gene?

GENE: Because it would be very hard to be wrong more than half the time. (*laughter*)

GEORGE: How do you associate these observations, Gene, with conditioned judgment? All of us are conditioned to be sensitive to the market. Sometimes, we decide something should be done. We really can't adequately define why.

GENE: It's right. We know it is right. The market is telling us something. I think these are valid influences to deal with—point and figure work, or the 200-day moving line, and that sort of thing.

GEORGE: I don't know that it is either one of those. It is just some innate feeling or sense.

GIL: Nick wants to argue in behalf of the technician.

NICK: I am not sure that I should. This may get off into a long discussion, but the question is simply whether or not there is a relationship between price and value in the short run. I remember a very interesting all-night conversation at the Rockford Seminar last year with Ezra Solomon. Solomon was talking about the long run. Well, anything under 10 years is a short run to Ezra, and as an academician he certainly can defend that position. But, I don't know how practical this is to us, having the problem from year to year of answering for our actions. Consequently, while you buy *for* the long run you buy *in* the short run if you make the proposition that over the short run there is a basic distinction between prices and fundamental value. It seems to me that you are coming back to what George said a minute ago. You say, on the one hand, "this technician stuff is a lot of nonsense." Yet, on the other hand, we implicitly use some sort of technical approach in our own minds. We simply don't put it down on paper, because it is very difficult to defend.

NED: Are you saying that what is traditionally called market technician work—such formalized things as the Dow Theory, point and figure charts, volume, short interest, and all these other indicators—is just nonsense? Aren't we all, to a degree, market technicians? Hasn't every one of us at some time said, "I don't like the way the market looks."

NICK: Right. What are you saying when you say that?

NED: You say, "I have observed a lot of things about the market, and I have reached a conclusion about the market." I think all of us do this.

VIC: I would say there is one further step, if nobody else will stand up for the technical approach. I would say that most of us who do analysis from a fundamental point of view and reach a decision to buy XYZ stock at a certain price, then take a look at the chartbook and review the volume and price activity. Has the stock had a rapid rise? Is it in a declining trend? We may call our trading department and have them get a feel of the market. Are there any blocks floating around? I think we will all take this last step before we finally say, "OK, I am going to go ahead and buy it." I think most of us do this.

GEORGE: Don't charts run in the nature of a fever chart that a doctor uses? You are getting the position of a security at that particular time as part of your analysis.

VIC: And another step. How many of us have noticed the action of a stock? We have noticed the price has been rising rapidly and steadily for two or three months. We haul in the analyst and say, "I don't know what has been going on, but you had better take a look at it."

GEORGE: That's what I was going to ask you. (*laughter*)

VIC: Isn't this a technical approach? I just want to be doubly sure we don't take the technician out, cut his throat, throw him on the city dump, and forget about him.

GLENN: I think when we stand here and see, for example, that ———— [an oil stock] sits where it is while the market keeps taking stock at this level, and it gets out of kilter with the rest of the market, we will conclude that it is the time to turn the analyst loose again to go back and take another good hard look at ————. I think this initiative is probably technician's work.

NICK: Should we distinguish between technical and market analysis? I think what we might think of as technical analysis in the historical sense—the flags, head and shoulders, and all that stuff—we might not consider useful. On the other hand, all of us are engaged in market analysis. This is an analysis of the relative position of one industry versus another, the market psychology, the effect of international events, and so on. This, to me, is market analysis as opposed to formal technical analysis theories.

GIL: You are offering this as a suggestion, aren't you, on the general issue that Vic has raised about speculation?

NICK: Yes. Using market analysis, it seems to me, would be good judgment. All of us as professionals probably do this. All I am saying is that it would be very bad for a fundamentalist to analyze a company and decide that it is a good company without knowing whether it is overpriced or underpriced in terms of market attitudes. Some fundamentalists completely ignore or forget about price, just as the technician supposedly ignores fundamentals.

GEORGE: No customer has to be told Du Pont is a good company. He knows it. You've got to tell him when to buy it and when to sell it. This has been my experience. I find that the more I have gotten away from basic research, the more of a market analyst I became. I've been forced to become price-oriented to keep from going to sleep on a stock for the very reason you just pointed out. I think the technical aspects do have a place because of the emphasis you put on it and how you relate it to your basic research work.

GENE: I think the classic definition of quality is the ability to withstand adversity. This has always been thought of in *financial* terms. In other words: Is the company going to be able to make it through a bad period?

There is a new kind of adversity that has affected every trust account. A new way to define a blue chip, or a new way to define quality, involves the real adversity that companies are faced with today. This is *change*. This is the basic concept of quality that we try to get across. Is the company able to adapt itself to change?

KEN: Does it have control over its own destiny?

GENE: Right.

GLENN: At least, quality shouldn't be limited to what others are doing. I think that whether other institutions are interested in the stock is important from the standpoint of breadth of the market and market support, but I certainly think we should be able to make a group decision that the stock is prudent to buy regardless of the fact that the number of institutional holders may be 3 and not 300.

VAN: I don't see anything wrong with the old-fashioned definition that quality is the ability to withstand adversity. Implicit in that is the ability of management to innovate and control its own destiny.

A lot of people focused on one sort of adversity—the business cycle —while the other adversities were largely ignored. I was just trying to bring them into some sort of perspective. Rightly, or wrongly, what the market is saying today is that economic adversity may not be anywhere as near as big a problem as it used to be.

VAN: Adversity does not need to be defined in terms of economic cycles.

GENE: Yes, right.

GEORGE: Before we go any further with this point, would there be any advantage to evaluate, in this discussion, the qualitative measurements that are given by the rating agencies? You would be surprised at the weight they carry in court.

VIC: I'm not sufficiently familiar with how they derive them. George, do you know? Rattle off the four or five measures. I must confess that occasionally looking at them I wonder what hat they pulled them out of. There are various standards that they use for both stock and bond ratings. I am not so much concerned about bond ratings, but the stock ratings I wonder about. I am just wondering how we as an organization should really try to use them.

GLENN: Bury them.

GEORGE: Pardon?

GLENN: We should attempt to bury them.

GEORGE: We use them.

GARY: Many of the stocks are not rated.

GEORGE: Most are, except for some of the finance and savings and loan companies. These people have quantitative standards which they use, but we have discovered that the intangible aspects are growing in importance.

VIC: We have discussed one intangible. We have said that quality is the ability to withstand adversity in financial terms. Then, a few minutes later, we brought up the economic issue. If economic adversity today is not as much of a problem as it was 10 years ago, you are also saying by implication that stocks that are considered quality today would not have been considered quality 10 years ago.

KEN: I think you want to look at quality two ways: Gene's way for your pessimistic side—in other words, your lower level of quality. Then you must make your quality judgment of the ability of the company to move ahead. That's the ideal company to have—one that can withstand financial adversity but that can also make progress.

VIC: Would you elaborate further by saying that there isn't a rigid dividing line but a quality spectrum?

GUY: There's a tremendous gray area. No two people agree.

KEN: We agree on the ability to move ahead.

VIC: And also, quality is not related to price or a stock's valuation in the market. Quality is related to earnings in the company.

GUY: Correct.

GIL: Well, then, we generally agree on this.

KEN: I think we also ought to mention something about the complete lack of worry about balance sheets that now exists among young analysts. Somewhere in this discussion, we should decide that there ought to be a look at the balance sheet before deciding about the quality of a company.

NICK: What Gene is saying is that you should be almost completely balance sheet-oriented to prove that the company will not go out of business.

GENE: No, there are many things besides the balance sheet. You imply there is a strong balance sheet, but there are plenty of weak companies with a strong balance sheet.

KEN: Like ———— [a former blue chip which had great financial strength] 20 years ago. That was considered a quality company, but it has not been in terms of its ability to move ahead.

NICK: But in terms of survival, it certainly has survived.

GENE: Quality is a lot more than surviving.

NICK: Along this same line, what about the volatility of the company's earnings? Is this a consideration in quality?

GENE: I would differentiate between predictability and volatility. We can deal with a company where we think we can predict the earnings, even though they may be very volatile. Like a copper company.

GIL: Well, this is significant. What definition of quality are we going to end up with?

GEORGE: Maybe we are getting down to qualitative measurements.

NED: Let me throw out something on which I had a great battle with one of my security analysts. He wanted to buy a company that had been losing money, had a weak balance sheet, huge financial problems, and lousy management. They had just put some new management people in, and no one could know for sure whether they were any good or not. I told him that if he ever got into a law suit for using it in a trust account he wouldn't have a leg to stand on. He said, "Well, the present balance sheet and the past record of the company mean nothing if we can build a sufficient file on the future of the company. If we can build a strong case for the future of this company, and find reasons why it is going to do well in the future, the present and the past do not matter." What do you think of this argument?

KEN: He is talking the way a lot of people think in the market now. Everybody is looking for an opportunity for a turnaround. ———— [a blue chip electric utility] has no chance for a turnaround at all; therefore, nobody wants it at the moment.

NICK: Predictability of earnings is not a price factor at the moment.

GENE: Ned, the situation you outlined is not a predictable situation in terms of the kind of people who are involved and the problem that they face. If you really had a high degree of confidence in your ability to predict, and knew they had the contracts, and knew what their costs were going to be, you wouldn't have felt quite the same way.

NED: This one had a great number of question marks, and fabulous intentions. Multiply price by production, and sales would be so much.

GEORGE: Was this being recommended for a trust account?

NED: He wanted to use it in a trust account, but I wouldn't let him.

GENE: I think you very definitely were right.

NED: But the stock went up. (*laughter*)

NICK: Well, then could we have two criteria for quality? One is the ability to withstand adversity. The second is predictability.

VIC: The third is Ken's point—the ability to move ahead.

KEN: Predictability is an added plus factor.

GIL: Any other observations on this issue of trust investment quality? All right, then, I think we have just about exhausted the points you brought up, Nick.

NICK: May I take just one step back, and I hope it is a very short one. When we say safety of capital, we are all agreed here that we are talking in terms of purchasing power, not in terms of dollars.

ALL: Yes.

GUY: This is true as long as purchasing power continues to be a problem, but you can conceive a set of circumstances where it would be different.

VIC: I can't. (*laughter*)

GENE: If you lost money for the account, deflation wouldn't be a justification.

GUY: A few situations existed in the last half of the last century when there were periodic severe depressions that you don't have now. Then, you did not have either the Federal Reserve Board, or the kind of securities available for investment, or a lot of other things. I think the standards regarding trusteeship have changed.

NED: We all agree that there is a moral obligation, but there is only one court case that I have run across that actually implied that there was a legal obligation to protect against inflation. I have the impression that this trend will develop in future court cases.

GREG: I think you are right.

GIL: Now, of course, we are going over into the realm of some forecasting. Let's get on with the performance objectives, and see what we can do with it in the next few minutes.

NICK: The question here is twofold. One, is it proper for a trustee to have a policy of trying to exceed the performance of some leading average? If so, from what base? Question number two, over what time period?

VAN: I wouldn't relate performance to any individual average. I would relate it to the risk you are willing to accept within the account. In other words, if you accept an above-average risk you should get an above-average return. Your performance should be above average. That should set your objective.

GENE: How do you define risk?

VAN: Performance is certainly related to risk, but there are many accounts where you are under restrictions to assume below-average risk, and I don't think that your performance can be expected to match the popular averages because you are taking below-average risk.

NED: Well, we said on our quality consideration that we were going to buy above-average companies where the risk was small.

GENE: Does that mean that you are losing less in a year during which the average goes down?

KEN: Is there more than above-average risk in a large business such as——?

VAN: Well, you get into specific examples. I relate it to risk rather than to a popular average.

GIL: Van, are you saying, in effect, that once you've set your objective the ability to meet that objective is tied to whatever risks you would have to take? In that case, I can summarize this part of it in one sentence.

GLENN: Which is what?

GIL: The performance results can be measured by how near you come to the target. In other words, do you get to the target that you set for yourself, or do you not?

GENE: Which, as Van said, is the matching or beating of the averages.

VAN: I say, *if* you take above-average risk you should do better than the averages.

GENE: Well, do you think you have to take above-average risks—whatever the word risk means—to beat the average?

VAN: Yes, I think you do.

VIC: I wouldn't argue if you are talking of performance solely in terms of appreciation or depreciation in an account.

VAN: No, total investment return.

KEN: Last year, I could have beaten the average with no risk at all if I had put all my money in Treasury bills. I would have beaten them by a wide margin.

NICK: That would have been the thing to do.

VAN: You took a risk, betting that the market would go down. You bet heavily on it.

KEN: I went right back to my judgment, didn't I?

VAN: But you took a risk.

GENE: Ridiculous. Every time you do anything, you are taking a risk.

VAN: You can buy a broad list of 150 stocks, weigh them all equally, and do about as well as the popular average.

GENE: Another position is to have an account with exactly the same composition as the Dow Jones Average.

VAN: No, I don't think that is right, because I think we are talking about risk to the customer, aren't we? We aren't talking about risk of losing the account because we didn't do as well as the market.

VIC: Can I get back to my point again? And I want to make a mild exception. In taking this total investment return concept, it seems to me that accounts, broadly speaking, can have the objective of a total return or some concept of appreciation or enhancement in value. There are other accounts which have different objectives. Accounts may have an objective of conservation of principal. You have an obligation of X thousand dollars nine months hence, and that's your objective, and you shouldn't try to get any appreciation at all. You have other accounts where you have a minimum income requirement. You have to provide Mrs. Jones with 500 bucks a month. I don't care how you do it, but you've got to get that.

GENE: Those are the easy ones.

VIC: Admittedly, but the point I am making is that we can't say that we measure our performance against an average, or against a total investment return, in all cases. The performance really must be related to what you have set as your objectives.

GIL: But many customers state one objective but actually look for performance in terms of some other objective.

GEORGE: Should you make an effort to educate the income client and tell him——

VIC: We have instruments where the income distribution is specifically set in dollars.

GEORGE: We should look ahead into the future. What should we tell our income clients? It's a very important function.

GENE: It is possible to write a trust instrument so that you get around that.

GEORGE: That's right. What should we do as trustees?

GUY: Assume you are given a personal trust that somebody sets up for an old housekeeper who is disabled. It could go on for 15 or 20 years. You mustn't put it all in fixed-income securities.

GIL: I think, in a sense, you have put your finger on the heart of what this may mean to us at this point. What are the performance objectives when dealing with personal trusts? That's, after all, what we are talking about.

GREG: Doesn't the performance objective depend upon the individual case that's involved?

NED: The first performance objective is to meet the objectives of the account; and second to have superior investment performance, giving consideration to the risks taken.

NICK: Over what time period?

NED: *Every* time period.

GREG: Use the phrase, "giving consideration to the broad risks involved." I think you have money-rate risk and business risk in any investment. You have purchasing-power-of-the-dollar risk by not making certain investments, and you've got market risk. You have fundamental risk which requires analysis of the balance sheet. It seems to me that the broad term "risks" covers it.

CHAPTER THREE

The investment process: establishing topical policy

This and succeeding chapters move from the broad philosophical considerations of investment policy to the more pragmatic day-to-day problems that confront the investment manager. The present chapter deals with general policy considerations in managing investments.

The introductory remarks of the discussion leader outline rather clearly the areas to be covered and provide an overview of things to come. The remainder of this chapter covers three broad areas: examination of the economic environment, analysis of the market environment, and security selections within the environment as analyzed. The discussion tended to be choppy; therefore brief summaries are appended at the end of each major section. As the discussion progressed, some strong opinions and some challenging ideas were developed when the seminarians got down to the question of how they perform their daily tasks.

VIC: The preceding discussion was devoted to some of the broad philosophical aspects of investment policy, and the assignment I was given for this session was to talk about topical policy, or the day-to-day policy decisions that you make in an operating trust department. I would like first to review in very broad terms the investment approach that I suspect is typical of most of us.

It really falls into two parts. One I would call policy considerations. There are three considerations. First, this involves looking at the economic environment—the near- and longer-term outlook. Usually, the near term is the calendar year you are in or the one you are about to enter. The longer-term outlook considers the three- to five-year look. The second consideration is the market environment, looking at the stock market, the trends in the market based on both earnings prospects and the valuation of those earnings (the P/E ratio); then the money market environment, short- and long-term interest rates trends. The third consideration is the selection of securities—that is, the selection of stocks and bonds that are expected to perform favorably under the business and market environment that has been projected.

The second broad part of the investment policy approach is the consideration of particular portfolios—that is, establishing the portfolio objectives, the determination of the fixed/equity ratios, the diversification within the equity portion by industry or type of security, or within the bond section by type of bond and maturity and so on, and then the selection of the particular securities to go into the account.

Now that is a very broad outline. I would like to go through that again and pause at each point where I think there may be some areas worthy of discussion.

Let's take the broad policy considerations first. The first area I talked about was the analysis of the economic environment. In talking to many people in the investment field, I have the feeling that there are three separate ways of looking at the value of economic analysis.

One school says that such analysis is of limited value. In the first place, the cyclical fluctuations in the economy are of decreasing importance. Not only that, the stock market always leads the business cycle. Frequently, the market has its own independent cycles, and the amplitudes of business cycle changes are rarely related to the amplitudes of stock market changes, so really you don't have to bother about economic analysis.

The second school of thought says that economic analysis gives a picture of the business and investment environment. It tells you what kind of atmosphere you are going to be investing in. It has limited relationship to security selection, and you don't have to tie the two of them together. It merely gives you a feeling of where you are.

The third school of thought—and I suspect my prejudices may show in this area—says that in order for economic analysis to be useful it has to go beyond the broad aggregates, such as gross national product, industrial production, and the broad Department of Commerce profit series. Analysis really has to be focused on the fact that the link between economic analysis and investment is the impact of the economic environment on profits. And you have to focus on the impact of economic developments on profits in particular areas. Things such as taxes, prices, and costs and wages, and political and foreign developments have to be considered. I would also argue that the economic outlook must include not only the near term and the long term, but also some consideration of what the vulnerability, the downside risk, is in the economy over a three- to five-year period. Your objective must be to get an integrated outlook for industry and company profits. That's the main function of the economist or economic analysis.

The second broad policy consideration is analysis of the market environment. It seems to me, this is divided in two parts. One is general expectations about market prices—i.e., is the market going up or down, or is a particular stock going up or down in price? The second part has a different approach; it is concerned with expectations about values, i.e., price as related to earnings—P/E ratios.

In the broad policy area, the third division is that of security selection. There are about five subheadings under this section.

One is the approach to selection. Do you go into the stock area directly and select companies? The argument here is that if you structure yourself by industry you overlook the conglomerate company, or the one that doesn't really fit into any industry, so that your selection process should begin with particular companies.

Another approach is to select the industry and then the company. If you use this approach, frequently you will have the problem of how you aggregate companies to get some general concept of what's going on. One aggregation is by industry. Another is to aggregate companies by the relationship to some economic time series—GNP or something like that. A third approach would be from an earnings volatility viewpoint—that is, the cyclical stocks, the high growth stocks, the more moderate growth stocks—differentiating between IBM and the utilities, for example. Or regulated versus nonregulated companies, or looking at them from the point of view of the technological orientation of their sales. Or still another approach of aggregating would be by either historical or expected market performance.

The third point under security selection is the question of whether you confine your selection to the quality blue chips or expand it to new and unproven companies. We touched on that earlier, and I don't think we came to any conclusion about it. Particularly in those accounts which are large, to what extent do marketability considerations enter into your security selection?

Another factor under security selection is the risk consideration. I think there is a difference between the risk in an account and the risk in a particular stock. Risk may be defined either as some earnings or price variability, or it can be defined in terms of stocks having a cyclical risk or a foreign risk (either from foreign competition or through foreign subsidiaries), financial risks, competitive risks—you can think of a dozen qualitative risks of particular stocks.

And then, finally, on security selection how do you make price judgments on securities? Do you approach price as an absolute intrinsic value? Do you have a relative value approach, or do you mix them up and use a little of both? In price judgments should you make changes in securities on a price basis only? If the stock is a great company like IBM at 500 or 600 or some price, would you trim back your holdings just on a price basis alone?

Turning now to the second major sector that I talked about—portfolio considerations. The first consideration relates to the statement of objectives in a portfolio. Should the statement of objectives be in general terms? Such statements may be phrases such as the need for income, conservation of principal, appreciation. Or should you try to state the objectives in specific terms? Do you expect the portfolio to make a particular return—8 percent, or 9 percent, or 10 percent, or some percent a year? Can you quantify the loss exposure you are willing to take —the risk you are willing to take? Should you specify for a particular account what the performance time horizon should be? Will you be looking at the performance of this account every quarter as some will require you to do, or every year, or will you look at it over three to five years? What are you specifically trying to do? What are the objectives?

The second major portfolio consideration is the fixed/equity ratio problem. How large an equity percent can you have in a conservative widows and orphans account? How large an equity percent can you have in a performance-oriented account? Should you always have a reserve in an account? Can you use the concept of a maximum ratio of an account with some percent of maximum being your current position, which can be changed from time to time? Should you be fully invested at that maximum at all times? Are you speculating on changes in market prices if you keep a reserve? If you change your ratio, how often should you change it? By how much? And what are the factors that would make you change it? Should it be changed on a shift in expectations about business or about the market?

The third major portfolio consideration is one that we touched on earlier—the question of diversification. But the considerations here are on a topical basis. Should diversification be considered something that is permanent, or do you vary it in an account over time? Should your diversification be based on one assumption of the outlook—that is, should you invest in those areas you think have the greatest probability of doing well over the period ahead? Or should you try to diversify to cover several probabilities? Do you concentrate or do you *hedge* in diversification? Should diversification be adjusted for the size of the account? In other words, if you have a small account you might not diversify as much as in a large account because you don't like to buy odd lots. To put it another way, suppose your stocks are 15 percent of your total portfolio. Do you run the common stock portion of 15 percent as if it were 100 percent as far as equities are concerned?

The fourth major area in portfolio considerations is security evaluation, and this covers securities held as well as new money. I would argue that in valuing securities, when you combine them in a portfolio it is a good deal different than a collection of individual securities, because they all vary in quantity and tax status and risk exposure, so you have really a separate entity to look at. You have a separate risk evaluation to make. There is a risk in individual securities, but when you put five of them together you've got a different and probably lower risk mix.

How do you measure risk and return? Return presumably measures income plus appreciation expected, but what kind of a quantitative risk measure can be used? We talk about covariance. The concept is easy, but I'm afraid that the mathematical application of it is a pretty formidable job. Ned's definition of risk is the probability that the account will not meet its objectives. I think that is broad and simple, but having said that, how do you button it down?

In the problem of managing the bond portfolio, should you always hold bonds to maturity or can you trade them? Should your maturities always be diversified over a 20-year period, with a certain amount maturing every year or every couple of years? Or should you concentrate? Should you manage a bond portfolio at all, or should you buy it and hold it?

And then, finally, the tax considerations in an account—if you have a gain, should you realize that gain if the outlook for the market or the stock is unfavorable or if the stock is believed overvalued? Do you consider merely the stock or the alternatives that you would put the money in? Should you realize losses if a more advantageous use of capital is available?

Those are the subjects that I thought might give us something to talk about. (*laughter*)

GIL: Let's start off with the subject of economic analysis and its application to investment.

VIC: I'd like to make one point if I could. It seems to me that there is a deplorable lack of communication between the economics department of most banks and the trust department.

VAN: I take exception to that. (*laughter*)

VIC: By saying a deplorable lack of communication, I don't mean that they don't talk to each other! I mean meaningful understanding of what they can contribute to each other. That's what I mean by communication. The economist frequently doesn't understand what the investment man is looking for, and the investment man thinks that the economist is off on cloud eight most of the time. I would argue for an approach which really requires the economist to be investment-oriented and to be able to contribute inputs an investment man can use. It's not easy to find this kind of economist, but I think it is very valuable if you can get one.

KEN: You have to follow a very narrow road, though, because the economist may think he is smarter than you are, starting out, and if you teach him too much about the investment business he's going to take the ball, and he will set investment policy for you as far as you will let him set it.

GENE: That's right. I think you have to define very clearly what he is supposed to be doing. To me, his basic job, and what he is valuable for, is providing a support for your analysts, helping them to properly appraise the earning power, near term, for companies. This is a basic part of how you go about making investment decisions. We may not need his judgment in terms of price/earnings ratios or that sort of thing. His economic knowledge, which is sound and helpful, gives him no special insight into this other basic area of values and prices.

VIC: But he can make a contribution to the analyst in the earnings area. In my judgment at least, the one area in financial analysis that is woefully neglected is not the valuation area, where we have more literature than we have time to read, but in the problem of how you determine earnings and earnings trends. And if you are wrong here, I don't care how sophisticated your valuation technique is, you are going to get the wrong answer.

GENE: On the other hand, if you are right there——

VIC: ——you can use relatively crude valuation techniques and do a good job.

VAN: Well, I still take exception. Let's take the automobile industry as an example. I don't think the economist has been any help in appraising the outlook for the automobile stocks, as such, either on the down side or the up side.

VIC: That's stocks. How about the earnings?

VAN: He may have forecast correctly that profit margins were going to come under pressure, and demand factors were going to be such that fixed costs were going to become more difficult to cover. All those things. But the fact of the matter is that even in the face of these problems the automobile stocks have done extremely well.

VIC: Has your automobile analyst done any better?

VAN: The economist should give you an indication of direction of the trend.

GUY: He might be able to give you some idea of either the volume of sales or the trend of labor costs. This is the climate in which the industry operates.

VIC: Right. The ability of a price increase to stick, the chances of an excise tax being imposed or withdrawn—these are the kinds of economic information the economist can feed in.

GIL: It seems to me that the group may be challenging your last point here, Vic, that economic analysis must have as one of its objectives an integrated outlook for industry and company profits. If I understood Van, he would say that, in effect, you can't be sure you are going to get decent projections of this kind from most economists.

GEORGE: I think you can expect overall profits forecasts for companies as a whole or an industry forecast. Beyond that, I don't think it is the economist's function.

VIC: Let me explain, Gil. I don't mean that it is the economist who prepares the integrated profits outlook. This is done by the investment man, but the economist's work should be directed to enable you to reach this goal.

KEN: Let's get somewhere in this record that one of the great contributions of the economist, as I see it, is to keep everybody on the investment side posted as to what's going on in Washington, what they're thinking about, and the political climate.

NED: There's another area in which I think he can be particularly helpful. Once you have agreed that he is roughly right about the coming year, and everyone in the whole investment organization has accepted this, then you have a pretty good chance of not having your auto man predicting a 10 million car year and your steel man using 8 million cars and projecting a 40 percent drop in steel production!

VIC: That's the integration I am arguing for.

GENE: That's a basic part of running a research department.

NED: Internal consistency in the economic approach. We collect and prepare a consensus view on the economy, which 99 percent of the staff agrees with. Take that to the analysts and let the analysts with their own knowledge of the particular industries adjust it if they really feel strongly about particular segments, and make sure then that the ramifications for any investments are followed through. And then that becomes our consensus view, which we use as an economic framework for our research department.

VIC: Are you then in effect letting the analyst determine the economic outlook?

GENE: We let him have a voice in it. I don't believe it is right to just artificially impose a structure on the analyst. We give him a voice so that he has a little more willingness to conform to the finished product.

VIC: I would argue that this business of determining the outlook is really a policy function of an investment policy committee. The economist has an input and the analyst has input, but sooner or later the policy committee says, "This is our view."

GENE: That's right.

VIC: Unless you have this direction and agreement, you are not likely to get, as Ned pointed out, an integrated set of earnings assumptions.

GENE: But it is a help to us and a help to the analyst to give him a chance then to review this consensus, because the analysts are talking to market research people and the industry's economists.

VIC: If the economist is worth his salt, he certainly talks to the analyst to get his views.

KEN: The analyst can reflect the views of industry economists he talks to when he is out in the field.

GENE: That's right. Like the auto man. Industry economists have no ability to predict their own sales.

VAN: What do you do when the economist says automobile sales will be 10 million and your auto analyst thinks they are going to be 8 million? (*laughter*)

VAL: It seems to me one of the greatest uses of the economist is that he is always looking for trouble—either good news or bad news— and will tend to hold down overenthusiasm and provide balance. I think the typical analyst tends to forecast the continuation of the trend as he gets it from company management. And I think the greatest benefit of the economist is to once in a while inject the thought that maybe it isn't going to happen this way.

GENE: The analyst is just likely to say sales or earnings will be down a little. But when you sit down with the analysts, the economist is valuable because he might say, for instance, "the last time we had a 15 percent decline in auto sales, earnings were down 40 percent," or something like that. This helps the analyst to keep his perspective.

VIC: But take your question about what happens when a conflict has to be solved. It comes before us as a policy committee. The analyst and the economist make their appeals, and the policy committee thinks there will be 10 million cars, and right or wrong it is our responsibility to resolve the argument.

GEORGE: The policy committee should make the decision—after the analyst has given them his opinion.

GENE: Give him a chance.

GIL: You don't necessarily disagree, George, but you emphasize the fact that the analyst should be heard as well as the economist.

GEORGE: He should be heard, and taken very seriously, as it is his responsibility. If you wish to overrule him, that's something else again.

Although there were some differing views on just how the economist should be used, the group certainly agreed that economic analysis is an important part of investment analysis. Unfortunately, because of time limitations several other facets of the subject were omitted.

A most important question was in relation to the kind of economist who can be most useful in an investment organization. Too often the complaint is heard that the economist is too theoretical and after painting a broad picture of the outlook fails to relate the impact of economic developments on profits. Others complain that the economist's language is often too technical and can't be understood by an investment staff that may not be sophisticated in the jargon of the economic profession. There is little doubt that the selection of the economist is quite important, and the wrong man can add confusion rather than improve understanding.

A second point not covered was the use of an inside economist versus the use of outside consultants. Because of the size of many organizations, or the many other functions an economist is called on to perform in a bank, outside consultants are often employed to provide an economic input directly oriented to the needs of the investment operation.

There was little doubt in the minds of the seminarians that economic analysis will be of growing importance in investment analysis, but each organization will have to evolve its own approach, depending on size, economic understanding of its staff, and the economic talent available.

GIL: The next point in Vic's breakdown is analysis of the market environment. We had two approaches here—general expectations about prices and expectations about values in terms of P/E ratios.

VIC: I think that there is a difference in talking about price changes and talking about changes in the evaluation of earnings. I would guess that probably most of us lean to the second rather than the first.

KEN: What's the difference?

VIC: In discussing prices alone you are talking about whether the stock market is going to go up, down, or sideways. You are talking essentially about the pattern of the S & P or the Dow or some such market average without relating it to earnings. I would say that just talking about price and price trends in the market isn't really meaningful unless you take a look at the earnings.

GIL: Perhaps that would be a little bit better if you said general expectations about price indicators of some sort. Confusion arises over the term "prices."

GENE: Which do you feel should be weighted most heavily in making a decision about the stock?

VIC: Earnings.

GENE: I agree.

GEORGE: Rather than the price/earnings multiple?

GENE: I can prove that over any extended period of time the company with the best earnings has done the best in the market. There's no question about that, regardless of price/earnings ratio.

KEN: But the market psychology is heavily weighted in terms of price/earnings ratios at some times and less at other times. Except in speculative markets, the valuation methods are valid.

GENE: Well, that is year to year. There has been such a high correlation between the companies that have been able to show the best growth in earnings and companies that perform better in price than the averages that it is hard for me to see where we would improve our performance by giving a lot of weight to P/E ratios.

KEN: Well, we all remember some studies that showed that low P/E stocks did very well at certain times.[1]

GENE: Right. What they said is that if you say the market is predicting the earnings trend of companies by the price/earnings ratio, so that a high P/E is a predictor of above-average earnings performance and a low P/E is the reverse, then the market is right two times out of three. In other words, two out of three high P/E stocks actually outperform the median stock. One out of three does not, but that one third kills you. They are assuming that you have no ability to discriminate on the basis of the real earnings outlook.

KEN: In other words, you can pick the high price/earnings ratio stocks and really justify them, but the low price/earnings ratio stocks will give you pleasant surprises.

GENE: Right, if you have any ability to do that.

NED: Of course, the thing that ruins you on that one third that doesn't work out is not only the earnings decline but the drop in the P/E ratio.

GENE: We went back over the Compustat[2] tapes and selected 800 to 900 companies per year; we had to drop others out for various reasons. We divided the earnings into four quartiles in terms of change year-to-year and then figured out what percentage of each quartile of those stocks outperformed the median price change per year. From 1960 to 1965—six years. I will just read the top quartile performance yearly. For the first year, 73 percent of the stocks outperformed the median price. For later years, it was 71 percent, 76 percent, 82 percent, 77 percent, 87 percent, for a combined average of 78 percent. Now this is on over 800 observations per year. What percentage of the stocks that fell in the bottom quartile in earnings changes outperformed the median price—13 percent, 22 percent, 21 percent, 19 percent, 20 percent, 18 percent, averaged out 18 percent. And quartile by quartile, I'll just give you the averages for the six years—78 percent, 64 percent, 39 percent, 18 percent.

---

[1] See "Recent Study of P/E Ratios," by Nicholas Molodovsky, and "Recent Studies of P/E Ratios—A Reply," by Paul K. Miller, Jr., and Thomas E. Beach, *Financial Analysts Journal*, May–June, 1967, pp. 101–10.

[2] Compustat is a service of Standard Statistics Company, which puts on machine tape the income and balance sheet figures of leading corporations grouped by industry and regularly brought up to date.

KEN: So all you've got to do is accurately predict earnings.

NORM: How far ahead?

GENE: One year. But the ones that really do well for you are the low P/E stocks that report surprisingly good earnings.

VIC: I would argue that there is an additional use of P/E ratios. There are in certain areas of the market certain trends of P/E ratios, certain groups of stocks when you use a method of aggregating them, that have interesting market patterns. A good example is the long swings in the utility stocks. Their P/E relative to the market swings from two or three multiples above the market, then comes down below the market, and then goes up again. These trends last three or four years. But I think these swings can give you either an assurance or some concern about whether you want to invest here. In the meantime, the earnings are moving along at 6 percent a year, come hell or high water.

VAN: How about the problem that existed in the late '50's though when earnings were flat for the total economy for four or five years, and yet you had a terrific increase in stock prices due entirely to rising P/E multiples?

VIC: Yes. 1955 through 1960.

VAN: That was a fairly extended period of time when earnings were not the determinate. It was the price/earnings multiple.

KEN: The market as a whole more than doubled during that period of time. Even with earnings flat.

VAN: I don't think you can just say categorically that it is always earnings. I think an analyst should be better on earnings than on P/E's.

GEORGE: I don't know anything else we could expect from an analyst. That is their primary function.

VIC: This is a really important point. I think that there is a general consensus around here that earnings are more important than valuation techniques, yet I think the emphasis in the literature is the other way around.

GIL: That's right.

GENE: It is very enticing to think that you can find some way to hit P/E and hit it right, and the formulas that have been derived are essentially attempting to forecast P/E's. Since I feel that P/E is a reflection of the popularity or lack of popularity of a stock I really question whether anybody can forecast it.

NICK: Gene, how large a sample do you have to have before your probability begins to work?

GENE: Well, for instance, in our list, which is, if you take the industrials, 140 stocks, if you had done nothing but make your stock selections on the basis of our estimates of earnings you would have done very substantially better than the market in 1966.

NED: Would you have found yourself all of a sudden with 80 percent of your money in the airlines?

GENE: No. The top quartile of earnings of 140 stocks is 35 stocks. All 35 obviously cover lots of industries, give you diversification, although not traditional diversification.

NED: Might it not be that out of those 35, 25 were in 4 industries or something like that?

GENE: Well, I could look at that, Ned, but I am sure that is not so. Obviously, every stock we have in the office equipment industry was in the top group. But we feel that to make a good investment decision you've got to review lots of alternatives, so we are not weighting our list of things that we look at by any particular formula.

NICK: It would not concern you, then, that you have no representation in the utility group?

GENE: Right.

NICK: Nor would it concern you that you didn't have diversification in the traditional sense?

GENE: That's right.

NICK: In other words, you buy 35 stocks and the diversification can fall where it fell.

VIC: Hold it now. Could you wind up, therefore, as the logical result of this, with all of your securities in one industry?

GENE: It could happen.

KEN: It wouldn't though, as a matter of fact.

GENE: There were oils, office equipment, and electronics. There were drugs——

GEORGE: A broad list.

GENE: Sure. It left out whole broad segments of the economy that we were tickled to death to leave out.

KEN: That you wished you didn't own.

GENE: We are all looking to buy good growth at a low P/E. If you can do that, then you are doing the best possible job. On the other hand, a high P/E is many times equated with high risk.

GEORGE: One of the most interesting performances was ——— Airlines with a low P/E in 1962. That stock performed better during the next 3 years than in any similar period you could pick for the last 16 years.

GIL: Well, either Gene or George, would the statistical data you had indicate that prices tended as a rule to rise disproportionately after an earnings turn——

GEORGE: Dramatically.

GIL: Always disproportionately?

GEORGE: Absolutely. Airlines went from 3 to 90 in 2 years.

VAN: We have heard two approaches here concerned with stock selection on the basis of high or low P/E's. Apparently, the stocks to stay away from are in between—they do very badly. And that's just as valuable to know as what to buy.

GEORGE: It's a horrible thing to see, because it turns out that 70 percent of what you hold is in the in-between category.

GENE: That's because when you talk about the traditional diversification, you are buying lots of stocks in in-between categories in order to get industry diversification.

VAN: If you cut that 70 percent down to 50 percent——

GEORGE: This is the penalty of a lack of activity again. We are not courageous enough to do those things. This study showed one thing— our reluctance to sell when things look all right.

NED: Well, really, in your samples both of you restructured an account completely once a year. You sold 60, 70, or 80 percent of the stocks.

GENE: That's exactly right. Lots of companies would have stayed in that top quartile throughout the whole period so you would never sell them. But plenty of others did not.

GEORGE: This proves one point, and that is that the analyst is never going to be out of business.

GENE: That's right.

KEN: Let's put that in the record. (*laughter*)

VAN: We carried this one step further in one respect. We did an analysis of what the time lag was in this earnings improvement. And we found that even after two quarters of above-average earnings improvement you still had time to buy the stock. It's easily recognizable, and you have plenty of time to act on it.

KEN: I don't think that is true in 1967.

GENE: Well, obviously not. Blue chips have gone down.

GEORGE: But, interestingly enough, stocks that appeared in the low price/earnings category in 1962 reappeared in 1967. Much higher earnings, but the low P/E stayed. I think this is a good point; you have plenty of time to buy it.

GENE: I feel that a lot more attention is paid to price/earnings ratio in terms of day-to-day investment decisions than maybe we would like even to admit. I think people have some tendency to steer way from high price/earnings ratio stocks. It certainly takes a lot less to convince an account man not to buy a high P/E stock than to buy it. And there is a tendency to equate a high price/earnings ratio with risk, and I don't feel those are valid investment criteria. I don't think there is inherently any more risk in a high price/earnings ratio than there is in a low price/earnings ratio.

KEN: Well, practically, Gene, I speak for myself—and maybe the rest of your institutions are not in this shape—I wish we had enough of these great high price/earnings ratios in our accounts to allow us to cut back on them, but it has been such a struggle to get them in over the years.

VIC: Ken, you don't mean high price/earnings ratio stocks; you mean stocks with a high growth rate in earnings that is relatively steady and predictable. There are a lot of stocks that have high price/earnings ratios that you wouldn't want. It's really the earnings and the predictability that you're talking about.

KEN: I am referring to the great growth companies that are now selling at premiums—terrific premiums over the rest of the market. The premium over the rest of the market now is bigger than it was at the end of 1961, I feel sure. Yet, this is the practical reason why I can't bring myself to sell IBM, even though I don't think we can expect much more out of it short term.

GIL: All of these are present-valuing problems in terms of the anticipated future income streams, and the existing value that reflects this stream on a capitalized basis.

GENE: If I felt that present value was a way to help to predict what was going to happen to price/earnings ratios, we would be doing a lot with it, but we've found that it isn't, so that we don't think in those terms.

GIL: Well, what I have just said is in response to Ken's remark about the relationship between, say, a P/E ratio that's high because as yet the lag factor hasn't been eliminated between the price and a decline in earnings or, in the other case, the P/E ratio is high because you have a steady dynamic rate of growth—in this case, it would seem to me that current price is an accurate present valuation of a discounted future income stream. It would be statistically inevitable. Well, let me think that over.

GUY: I think that in a great many cases some of these valuations reflect scarcity or abundance of stocks. Under certain circumstances, some institutional investors may feel that for advertising purposes they can't do without IBM or some other similar situation.

GENE: There comes a point at which you just have to say to yourself, no matter how much you like a company, you are just going to have to sell the stock if the disparity in the P/E gets so great—because of things like that.

GUY: Gene, even now I think you should make the decision that regardless of how good a stock is you don't want the stock to represent more than X percent of your total investment.

Although the topic that initiated the previous discussion was analysis of the market environment, the seminarians quickly dropped that subject and moved on to the more challenging subject of security valuation. The subject is not exhausted here but is discussed again later.

The first point there was general agreement on was the primary importance of earnings and earnings trends in security selection. Although only mentioned briefly, earnings for the immediate period ahead were stressed; there was no discussion of the necessity of considering earnings trends expected over a 3–5-year period in the future. Most of the discussion centered on the valuation of earnings, i.e., the price/earnings ratio. Several facets of this area were covered: the low versus the high price/earnings ratio stock; the large group of in-between stocks where investment decisions are much less clear-cut; the trends of price/earnings ratios in the market and in stock groups as contrasted with price/earnings ratios of individual stocks; whether high price/earnings ratios reflected high growth rates or just overvaluation; and absolute versus relative price/earnings ratios. The forecasting of price/earnings ratios is discussed further in several places. One comment regarding discounted cash flow techniques was summarily dismissed, evidencing little interest by the group in this approach.

As a general statement, forecasting earnings rather than price/earnings ratios seemed to be the easier task, but both appeared an integral part of stock selection.

GIL: Well, why don't we go on to the next issue. I think we have pretty well exhausted this one. Vic, let's return to you. You brought up the topic of security selection, right? Why don't you just review your remarks.

VIC: When you are selecting securities do you go from the economy down to industries and companies, or do you go to companies directly? Is there a method of doing industry analysis and then companies within an industry? Or do you find that this is not particularly useful; the most useful thing is to go directly to the company. The other side of that coin asks whether you find it useful for analytical purposes to aggregate companies in some fashion by saying that this group has certain characteristics, and it differs from another group which has others. And if you do believe it is useful to aggregate them, how do you do it?

NED: I would like to go back to the first one and say a kind word for industry aggregates. We did similar studies to some of those that you mentioned, and we found that of the price/earnings ratio of a given stock roughly half of the variance can be explained by the variance in price of the market as a whole. Another substantial portion of the variance can be explained by the variance in the industry P/E ratio. So if you put the two of them together, you can explain close to 75 percent of the variance of the price of the stock by the variance of the industry P/E and the market P/E.

This tells you something about the price/earnings ratio, so that you do know that if the industry's earnings are going up, and you know where the stocks in the industry are currently selling, certainly on a relative value basis, you get an idea of the sort of price/earnings multiple that might reasonably be applied to a given company. If the company is going to outperform the industry as a whole, you might expect it to have a little higher P/E than the industry.

While I am not trying to detract from this emphasis on earnings, which I agree with, I do think that taking a look at the industry tells you whether that is going to be an industry that has some popularity in the market or whether it is going to be an unpopular industry. You could have a good company in an industry that the market doesn't like, and it will sell at about the same price/earnings ratio as the rest of the stocks in the industry. And nobody wants it because it is in a bad industry, regardless of the fact that it might have completely different earnings characteristics than the rest of the companies in the industry.

GUY: You can also have a fairly marginal company in what looks like a good industry, and the stock goes up to the roof.

NED: We have seen that happen, say, in color television, where some had virtually zero profit margins five years ago, which gives them a huge potential earnings expansion. Sales go up 5 percent, profit margins go from 1 percent to 2 percent, and their earnings expansion might be outdoing Zenith, but it is not a Zenith. It may be a company with lousy management and a highly inefficient operation, but it will rise on up with the rest of the industry. I could come up with some specific names I think have poor management. The narrow profit margin is what helped them to have fast growth. Anything would have helped them.

VIC: Would you conclude, therefore, Ned, that you should buy the Zenith rather than the other stock?

NED: Not necessarily.

VIC: In other words, taking the automobile industry as an example, you can make a point that everything you want to say about Chrysler vis-à-vis General Motors is not favorable to Chrysler. But if you really want a market performance there, you get it in Chrysler, because you have had leverage working for you when things are going up.

NED: I think Vic's question is: "What quality stocks do you want to buy?—" And maybe you don't want to hold Chrysler in a conservative account, but you are willing to hold it in an aggressive account. But you should make the analysis, because each stock in an industry has some influence on the multiples of the other stocks in the industry.

VIC: Yes, I agree with that. I gather, Gil, there is no exception to the idea that you have to look at industries. How about problems of aggregation beyond the industry level? Do you do any further aggregation? Do you find it useful to look at growth stocks as a segment, to look at the utilities as a part of the regulated industries? There are any one of a number of different classifications. One firm has devised a six-fold classification. Another has one that is based on GNP classification. Those are two I can think of offhand. I have used and published articles on the cyclical and moderate-growth and high-growth classifications. There is no one answer to this, but what are the alternatives? Have you found others more useful?

NED: For diversification purposes?

VIC: No. For security selection.

NICK: Well, you really mean diversification, though.

VIC: Insofar as when you are selecting securities you have a diversification concept in mind, yes. But basically the question is: Where are the attractive areas?

NED: I think all of us probably get trapped into using one system and not changing it too often. Probably we should be using several systems simultaneously. We should be running classifications on an account four or five different ways to get a real understanding of what we've got in the account.

GENE: The problem it has created, though, is the fact that when you begin to look at, let's say, utilities maybe more than any other group you begin to look at them as a breed apart almost. And then you look at a stock which may be a little out of line with others in the group. But maybe today the market is saying we are not going to look at utilities as a separate world anymore; we are comparing them with industrials, and if we think an industrial company is going to show a better growth than a utility, why, we will pay more for it. And so you are having an impact on utility P/E's that we wouldn't have expected if we were just looking at utilities as a separate universe.

NED: It is true we are seeing more and more different classifications of stocks, and we are thinking about them, even if we don't use them ourselves. We happen to use something like this, and it is completely traditional.[3] Here's what most people used 20 years ago, and we still use it, but at the same time when we are reviewing an account there is a strong tendency for us to look at a stock as being stable slow growth, stable fast growth, medium growth, cyclical slow growth, cyclical fast growth, dead, you know. (*laughter*) We bracket the stocks we are reviewing in some sort of standard classification system, and then we look through it a second time and say, all right, do we have enough high technology stocks? Where are the budding young industries that are going to participate in Medicare or the information explosion? Are we participating in about a half-dozen attractive areas? I think portfolio managers are getting more sophisticated.

VIC: Ned, let me ask you this. When you use these various aggregates, is the fundamental thread that runs through your aggregation process the earnings trend and earnings volatility, or is it market volatility, or what?

NED: It's earnings.

VIC: It's earnings. In other words, whatever aggregative process you've used, the basis of it is earnings, or earnings trends and their volatility.

GREG: In talking about earnings, do you want to include some reference to the nonrecurring earning factor that does show every so often and distort the normal pattern? Actually, the analyst is going to come up with it, I am sure. Is it a factor to include in the consideration? This does happen when a company—and I think you see it more and more—sells off part of its business and takes a nonrecurring profit that shows up in earnings with a temporary bulge. Maybe they can spread it out over a longer period than an immediate point of time.

---

[3] See Appendix A, Exhibit I.

NED: I am talking too much. I'll shut up after this. We have reached almost an absolute conviction that the market is not paying too much attention to it at all. It pays attention to the reported earnings.

VIC: However derived.

GUY: I agree with that.

NED: It doesn't matter what the reported earnings are or how they are faked. The market doesn't care if we are right. We can be right for 20 years, and the market is still going to look at reported earnings.

VIC: The advantage, I think, of doing the analysis is that it gives you some assurance of the quality of the earnings that you're buying.

GUY: That's true.

VIC: You know, maybe the market won't look at it, but if you are getting good, solid earnings you feel a little bit better, because if they are not good, solid earnings, somewhere down the line the chickens come home to roost.

KEN: It prepares you for the possibility of a surprise.

NORM: What's going to happen when you've seen two earnings? Most of the time, as you know, beginning in 1967, the accountants are going to show you two earnings figures.

VIC: Whatever the company emphasizes——

NED: It's the biggest one. (*laughter*) It's not those figures in the back of the annual report; it's that little thing on the left of the first page in the front. (*laughter*)

NORM: But you are going to see two figures now—in *The Wall Street Journal,* in the front of the annual report, and in every other place where there is an important nonrecurring item. Beginning this year you are going to see two.

NED: Well, of course, I think this is a good trend. I am for it.

The discussion on methods of aggregating stocks evoked few new ideas. Apparently, the seminarians follow the traditional approach of aggregating by industries, with the industry groupings of the Standard and Poor's 500 Stock Average as a guide. However, several alternative classifications or groupings were suggested in order to ensure representation in dynamic areas, to point up representation in dull areas, and to ensure that a fresh look at the portfolio is taken at regular intervals. Underlying each approach was the idea that classifications are made on the basis of earnings trends and volatility rather than market performance, although it would be reasonable to expect that market prices of similar groupings would be comparable to earnings movements.

VIC: The next subject—this limited or wide selection of stocks—this is a really important policy consideration. I think all of us at one time or another have read that memorable speech by Charlie Buek. The gist was that we spend an inordinately large amount of analytical time chasing around looking for the Xerox of the future when our real area of concentration should be those 150 or 200 stocks of investment quality.[4] You can do very well in there if you do your homework. Another factor involved here, particularly in larger accounts, is the question of marketability. There might be 150 or 200 stocks where the marketability is such that you can move around if you want to, and I raise the issue here whether a proper job of a trust department should not be to devote 90 percent or more of its time to a relatively small number of stocks—quality blue chips, if you will, where you have marketability, predictability, access to management—or should you be looking for the new, the unproven companies—the ones that are going to skyrocket. How do you do this? What sort of policy approach would you use in a trust department in this area?

GUY: Does this depend partly on the kind of accounts you have? If you have a lot of accounts or funds where a very aggressive approach can be taken, I think whether you like it or not you have to spend some time looking for the Xerox of the future.

KEN: Charlie Buek would disagree with you. He would say that you then have to educate your customer to the fact that it is just as easy to get a double out of two blue chips by selling one right and buying the other right as it is to get a double out of some small, obscure company. And you could do it in multimillion-dollar pieces, rather than invest $50,000 and dry up the market.

VIC: Well, would you agree with him, Ken; is his statement true?

KEN: Yes, I think it is true. But, on the other hand, I think to freshen your list you ought not to shut your mind to any new ideas. I think just as you prune individual accounts, as we talked about it earlier, you have to keep pruning your approved list every year also. And I hope the new name that goes on is not some blue chip that you should have put on there 15 years ago and are finally putting on now. There should be two or three additions of smaller companies.

---

[4] Charles W. Buek, "A Suggested Role for Portfolio Analysts Today," *C.F.A. Readings in Financial Analysis* (Homewood, Ill.: Richard D. Irwin, Inc., 1966), p. 531. Originally an address before the New York Society of Security Analysts, March 10, 1966.

VIC: Is the bulk of the research time of trust departments and the institutional brokerage firms that service the trust departments—is the bulk of their research time in these areas? In the area of the 200 blue chips, which you keep sort of fresh, are they basically the same stocks all the time?

GENE: Not in terms of written material, no. The brokerage house analysts are much more inclined to write up a Teledyne, which they would be recommending.

KEN: The institutional research houses—aren't they concerned primarily with trust grade stocks—big companies?

GENE: That's their basic service, giving you up-dated reports.

VAN: Yes, but take your own analytical department. I think we spend less time on our top 10 holdings in our trust department, which has greater influence on the average account, than we do on the miscellaneous-type company that we think we are going to get a quadruple out of.

GENE: But you are not proud of that, are you?

VAN: I should say not.

KEN: So Charlie Buek is right?

GEORGE: I don't know. I question that. I think in a few years all of us will be looking at the same 200 companies. We are all going to be competing with one another for the same items. There will be such a standardized approach for buying and selling these items that a fellow must be able to anticipate an anticipating person ahead of himself before he makes any money. I think you have got to freshen your list with some of these new stocks. I think with the passing of time a lot of these smaller companies that make progress, that move from $50 million to $100 million in sales, and so on, are the ones that we should be able to get reasonably early and which will have a significant performance. To answer your question—I did a little study on this thing, and the accounts that did spectacularly well were those that just by luck had an occasional $10,000 or $15,000 in Polaroid, Xerox, and Litton Industries, bought a long time ago. Those are the accounts that did well, spectacularly well.

KEN: But you didn't get that for all of your trusts. Why didn't you?

GEORGE: We didn't for the simple reason that at that time most of these stocks were considered speculative vehicles, but the point I am getting at is that those few items in several dozen accounts made those accounts perform.

VAN: Yes, but George, how much time did you spend on getting rid of the ———— or ———— [two fading blue chips] or that type of stock when you should have? That is what I am getting at. I think we should be looking at new names and adding some, but I don't think we spend enough time on the old ones we already hold.

GEORGE: All I can say to you is this. You will be competing with the other fellow who has looked at the Xerox and the ———— [fading blue chip], and you all can't get in and out at the same time.

VIC: George, the difficulty there is your assumption that we will all have the same earnings estimates, and we will all be using the same valuation technique and all buying those same 200 stocks. That doesn't necessarily follow. I am distinguishing here between narrowing your universe to 200 stocks and not necessarily agreeing that if we do this we are all going to arrive at the same conclusion. We would have disagreements all over the lot.

GEORGE: I think you'd be surprised—you'd be amazed—at how often we sell and buy together. You know (*laughter*) we all do the same thing. I bet that if a vote were taken around this room of the 10 favorite purchases of each one of us, 80 percent would appear on almost every list.

GLENN: That is maybe high, but I bet there would be considerable agreement.

GIL: We haven't time for a poll, but is there a general consensus, Vic, that we might put in the record at this point?

VIC: The consensus is that more time, if you will, or the bulk of your analytical time should be spent in the high-quality, blue chip area.

GEORGE: I wouldn't question that.

VIC: George, I think, would argue—and I think he has a good point—that you should spend some of your time, although not too large a percentage of your time, looking around. I would say that from a purely administrative point of view the way you get over this hump, I've found, is you get one or, depending on the size of your department, two analysts, truly senior men, and they are your generalists. Their job is to float around and catch these oddballs as they come along. And if you know you have these analysts, you can say to the rest of your analysts, who are always looking for the flaky stock in their particular industry, "That is not your job; your job is to stick with the tried and true. We've got somebody here who will go chasing after these if necessary."

KEN: Are we also saying that what you already own hurts you or helps you much more than what you buy?

Vɪᴄ: That's exactly right.

General agreement was reached that more research time should be spent on the large holdings that comprise the bulk of investment portfolios where quality, predictability, and marketability are present. A strong plea was made, however, to periodically freshen up this list and to spend some time, possibly by use of a few senior analysts, looking at new areas. As a corollary to this idea, some large trust departments have created special situation pooled funds for stocks that cannot be used broadly in trust accounts but that can be used in accounts that can assume greater risk.

Gɪʟ: Let's go on with the topic—marketability considerations.

Vɪᴄ: Do we in the trust investment field have a marketability problem? Or is that achieved only when you are a multibillion-dollar trust department? Where do you run into marketability considerations in limiting your security selections?

Vᴀʟ: I think you get into it with the question that Ken raised when George was describing the accounts that had had this good performance, because they had small holdings of Xerox or something of this kind. If you go into this area, how do you defend yourself? If you buy a few stocks that don't have marketability, you are very limited in what you can do. How do you defend yourself from your beneficiaries who ask, "Why didn't you do that for me?" And I don't think you can.

Gᴇᴏʀɢᴇ: You can't—no, but these were done proportionately.

Vᴀʟ: I know that, but I am trying to answer Vic's question of——

Gᴇᴏʀɢᴇ: You look at an item, for example, where you take a $30,000 original investment and see that it is worth $6.5 million, it makes a little difference.

Kᴇɴ: All this emphasis on increased concentration and increased turnover means that marketability is of greater concern to us now than it has ever been.

Gɪʟ: You say it is of greater concern?

Kᴇɴ: Sure.

Kᴇɪᴛʜ: In other words, you have second-class accounts?

Gᴇɴᴇ: Yes. That's right. Also, you have to think in terms of your research capacity. The analyst has the ability to follow only a limited number of stocks. If he has to follow too many stocks, then you wind up putting poor stocks into accounts. You are not using his capacity to the best advantage. He can't follow——

Gᴇᴏʀɢᴇ: That's not always true, as in the case of Xerox. Initially, it was a small holding, but because we had to follow it, it later became one of our big stockholdings.

KEN: You got your start.

GEORGE: And this is the type of thing that you never know.

GENE: I don't mean that you say to your analyst that you can't follow all stocks. I mean that's just a consideration. You can't have hundreds or even dozens of little companies, because you will wind up spending all your time on those and there will be——

GEORGE: We have a standing rule in our operation that any small company that ever attains eminence is the responsibility of the analyst. If he has missed it, he has some accounting to do.

NORM: I agree. To you or whoever else he works for. (*laughter*)

GREG: Attaining eminence by being absorbed by a parent somewhere that wasn't a parent at the time?

GEORGE: Now something like that you can't foresee. But anything that makes progress over a period of time and is missed—I think the analyst should be held accountable.

The marketability problem was not fully discussed, either because of the proximity of the lunch hour or because it is a concern only of the largest trust departments. Nevertheless, it is a subject of growing importance as the institutional demand for stocks increases and as the quest for performance leads to greater emphasis on concentration and portfolio turnover. Moreover, the statistical data in this area are woefully inadequate, and the research has been sparse. Apparent again was the conflict between adequate coverage of the large listed companies that comprise the bulk of trust accounts and the search for the small, rapidly growing company that could make a significant contribution to performance. The issue was not resolved, and no general resolution seems likely.

VIC: Next, risk considerations. Do we set or should we set some limit of either earnings or price fluctuations, either historically or prospectively, that we won't go beyond? If a stock historically has had earnings fluctuations of a certain fashion, or if you anticipate that it will, you just won't be interested in it. It's too risky. Second, do we really make any attempt, either qualitatively or quantitatively, in a particular security to evaluate some of the risks to which it is exposed? Either a cyclical risk, a business cycle risk, or a foreign risk? For many years, we were paying the same multiple for foreign earnings as we were for domestic earnings, and now we are rethinking that and remembering the time immediately after the war when we didn't give a nickel for foreign earnings. There are any number of risks of individual companies. Should we make some specific attempt to evaluate these risks? I think risk is something that is talked about but is not often tackled.

GREG: Isn't it part of the analyst's approach to study a company and come up with the risk factors, whatever they happen to be?

VIC: Does he come up with these in a qualitative sense, or do you have a quantitative measure of risk in a stock? Or do you use the historic fluctuations of the earnings—for the last 10 years or something like that? How do you go about measuring risk?

KEN: You equate risk, don't you, with whatever negative factors there are about the company? They are different with every company. And I think that all of our analysts, in their reports that are presented for consideration as to whether we should buy or sell a stock, list the negative factors as such. Summarized right on the front page so that we can see the particular risks in this situation. It may be the high price/earnings multiple, or it may be a lousy management, or a poor industry——

VIC: So what you are really saying is that it is a qualitative risk evaluation. You don't try to work out some mathematical formula.

GLENN: You might break it down by an industry, and say that 20 percent of the sales and earnings of this company are in an industry for which we are not going to pay more than 10 times earnings——

KEN: Eastman Kodak's foreign earnings and John Deere's foreign earnings are two different things.

NICK: Would you consider a stock that had experienced a loss in the past two or three years?

KEN: If there is a good reason for it.

GENE: Oh, risk is in every stock. To me, what we try to equate risk with is our ability to come to grips with the unlikely possibilities. What are the probabilities of things happening? The analyst says, "Well this company could earn anywhere from $2 to $4 next year."

KEN: That's a risk.

GENE: Yes. That certainly is going to influence us as to whether or not we use that company versus another company where we can really zero in on what's likely to happen. This is what we tend to equate risk with, i.e., the ability to forecast earnings.

NICK: Well, now, let's pursue that just for a moment. With your technological stocks, I am quite prepared to argue that your earnings estimates are pretty shaky in themselves.

GENE: I don't agree.

NICK: Most of us simply use what that type of company tells us, and most analysts on Wall Street, on whose numbers we are relying, are doing exactly the same thing.

GEORGE: I think that is generally true.

NICK: Look at the basis on which you determine one company's earnings. How do you forecast a company's earnings for next year?

GIL: Well, this will take us too far afield for the moment.

NICK: All I am doing is questioning this great reliance on earnings when the earnings are unpredictable.

GIL: The only reason I don't want to get into that is that I would rather get a clear idea of what Gene had in mind with respect to this quantification procedure as related to risk. I think this is the direction we are now going in this discussion. As I understand it, you were developing some probability calculation. Right? With respect to at least a maximum or minimum likelihood of certain things happening. You can't get much closer than that to a number—a magnitude that specifies the risk.

GENE: Right! Let me give you an example—a fine old company that was mentioned earlier, making 0.3 percent to 0.7 percent net profit on its sales. There are so many tiny little things that can happen to that company that could either double or cut earnings in half.

VAN: But none of them happen. (*laughter*)

GENE: That's the trouble. But, for instance, reserve for pilferage is 1 percent of sales. (*laughter*) A very minor change in something like that, all of a sudden it is going to knock earnings one way or the other. The earnings will change. You have to appraise that.

NED: Gene, you were talking about earnings estimates where there might be a spread from $2 to $4 on a stock. This is pretty wide, and perhaps on some other stock the spread might be $2 to $4.50. If your analyst puts a buy price and a sell price on his stock, would he have a much wider spread on the buy and sell price of the stock with a wide earnings estimate spread, and a narrower spread where the earnings were highly predictable?

GENE: We don't use exactly that technique, and I should expand on my statement. Let's assume that the company had earned one year, $6 per share, and the next year the analyst comes up and says that they could earn from $2 to $4 per share. That tells you a pretty clear story about the company, regardless of that variance. In this case, that is a very useful earnings estimate. On the other hand, if the company had earned $3 per share one year and the analyst comes in and says they are going to earn from $2 to $4, then I don't see how we can use that earnings estimate in making an investment judgment. You just don't reduce it to a buy point and sell point in the terms of price. We ask him to make his best estimate, and we ask him to make his judgment on P/E, which we express in terms of percentage of a target. And that comes up with a price. We don't go any further than that.

GIL: OK, Ned?

NED: All right.

The discussion of risk again could hardly be called conclusive, although several ideas did emerge. A qualitative statement of risk, or the negatives involved in a stock selection, was called for, and it was suggested that this be placed in each company report. Such a procedure is not typical of most security analyses, and wider adoption of this practice may add significantly to the value of reports. The main risk discussed was not the possible price fluctuations in the stock but the inability to forecast earnings. Perhaps more analytical reports that have single figure earnings estimates should include a range within which earnings could be expected to fall, thus indicating the margin of error in the estimate. Obviously, the single estimate of earnings per share for an aerospace stock is less reliable than that for a large electric utility! Although other risk factors were alluded to—foreign earnings risk, competition, management change—they all seemed to be synthesized into the single risk of earnings forecasts.

GIL: Well, Vic, let's go into our next topic—price judgments on securities.

VIC: Under that we have two headings. Probably part of the topic can be disposed of quickly, because as I have listened to the discussion thus far today everyone seems to say that at a price they would be willing to sell a security. Stocks are not a buy and hold for eternity. But how do you make price judgments? I think that is a different problem. Here are what you might call the extremes. One is the absolute value, the intrinsic value, there is some inherent value of the stock based on its earnings; and once you determine the value, this is it. If the price is there, or below, you buy it.

The other extreme is the relative value approach, which says that regardless of where the market is you try to pick those securities which look relatively the most attractive in that market.

In between those two extremes there are all different ways of doing it. The issue here is how do you fix those prices which tell the portfolio manager, "You buy at this price, and you sell at this price." How is it done? Is there any quantitative approach?

GENE: We try to make a P/E judgment, which we express as a percentage of a target multiple.

VIC: A target multiple for the stock?

GENE: Right.

VIC: Is that multiple related to the market multiple?

GENE: Right. The analyst studies the company, giving special attention to whether it is cyclical in character and what its growth rate is; then he estimates that it should sell at a price/earnings multiple of 120 percent of whatever the S & P 425 stock multiple is. This 120 percent is the target multiple—not a target price. But we can calculate the target price, because we know the multiple of the market and our earnings estimate for the company.

We have a chart that shows the price/earnings ratio of the stock, historically, quarter by quarter, based on latest 12 months' earnings relative to the market, so that everybody can see what the past relationships have been.

NICK: Do you use an absolute P/E?

GENE: It comes out to an absolute P/E at any point in time. It's 120 percent of the P/E of the S & P 425.

NICK: It is a relative technique of arriving at it. This wouldn't protect you against a serious deflation in all P/E's.

GENE: Right. You have to attack that separately. If there is a 20 percent risk in the market P/E, and you think a stock is 20 percent above where it is going to sell relative to the market, then you have some quantification of the kind of risk you are facing in the price of that stock.

NICK: Are you determining independently what you think the market P/E should be currently?

GENE: That is sort of in the background. That is a separate thing which you have as more or less the framework for looking at all stocks.

VIC: Gene, the cyclical stocks sell at high P/E's relative to the market when their earnings are depressed, and low P/E's when earnings are above normal——

GENE: In fact, that's how we define a cyclical stock, when you get an inverse relationship like that.

We plot three factors on one chart. The relative price performance, relative earnings performance, and the relative P/E. I don't look at the P/E as the product. I look at it as one of the causes of price change.

We have found a way—it's been pretty good—of keeping the Dow P/E ratio in some perspective. The Dow is a cyclical stock; you have an inverse relationship between the trend of earnings and the trend of P/E. Over a long period of years, the Dow has tended to value peak earnings at a lower P/E than trough earnings, so that you can draw correlation lines which give you P/E ranges for the Dow. This has been helpful in terms of keeping all these relative things, these many, many variables going into one number, in some sort of perspective.

NICK: The Dow may be selling at 14 times, but you feel it should be selling at 16 times.

GENE: We are trying to deal with a range. We are not trying to predict month to month what the Dow Jones Average is going to do. We would like to be able to say with some degree of accuracy that over the next year we expect a low multiple of 14 and a high multiple of 18— something like that. Something that has some relationship to history. If the multiple is at the 18 level, that obviously is a basic factor in what you do with stocks specifically.

NED: I think basically you are saying that you have an absolute value program in that there is a trend somehow through history—I guess in an academic community you would say that there is a biological interest rate for common stocks—but that you don't just accept history blindly. You adjust it for what you anticipate in the future. That is, competing investment media on one side and the degree of risk involved, and so on. But somehow or other you establish something that you think is normal value. Then you are relating these stocks to where you think the Dow Jones natural range is. While it looks like a relative-to-the-market approach, it is really an absolute value approach.

GEORGE: The price/earnings ratio for the Dow Jones Industrials was at 24 times in 1961. Following that, you had one of the sharpest rises in earnings in the history of the United States. In making long-range forecasts, how could you have foreseen that?

GENE: It was entirely in past history. As earnings spurted, the P/E came down, and that is the way the Dow has worked for 20 years.

GEORGE: Do you mean that in terms of history you could have foreseen the P/E's at 10 and 12½ times earnings last year? The highest earnings in corporate history?

GENE: The P/E range for last year was—we were exactly on target. Exactly on target.

GEORGE: At 12½ times earnings?

GENE: Yes, sir.

GEORGE: At the cyclical peak in earnings?

GENE: Right.

GEORGE: That I've got to see.

GENE: I don't have that with me. (*laughter*)

NED: I'll give you a chart that goes back to 1927 on the counter movement of earnings and price/earnings ratios.

GENE: In the early part of 1966, using this technique, we came up with the startling fact that the Dow was going to hit 756 point something or other during 1966, and it scared us to death, I can tell you. And it was only later in the year we were rooting that that was going to be the worst that we were going to see. The Dow price range was exactly within the prediction to which this technique led us.

KEN: What are you saying now for the future so we can——

GENE: See me later. (*laughter*)

NICK: I think it's interesting that your technique is not deriving an absolute number to start with as your key number; it does not involve either the Graham and Dodd intrinsic method of analysis, nor apparently does it involve the discounted future value technique of analysis.

GENE: Well, that I agree with—the second for sure. We have just not found that to be a useful predictor of P/E ratios. And I hate to even spend this much time on P/E's, because what we are really trying to do is to get a population of the very best stocks and discriminate within the population on the basis of variance in terms of value and P/E ratios.

NICK: Could I ask a question of this group? Has anyone in this group, in trying to come to a key number that we were talking about on the Dow, used either of these what are now historical guideposts? I mean textbook approaches? You either use the Graham and Dodd intrinsic value method or——

GEORGE: Central value theory?

NICK: Yes.

GENE: That's right.

NED: I don't think anybody uses absolute approach—not in the textbook sense at all.

NICK: Well, do they use it at all?

VAN: It's fundamental analysis that we use today, I think, rather than central value theory.

GENE: To me, one of the worst traps you can get yourself into through this central value thing is to say, well, there is a *right* price/earnings ratio. It's a puritanical approach.

NICK: No, I am talking about for the average—for your Dow average.

GENE: We just aren't using this approach in terms of the Dow multiple as a general framework. We would like to have some conception of whether there is more chance of multiples going up or down. We have a range, then, of what we expect to see in the way of multiples, and we like to know where we stand today within that range.

NICK: But, you see, I am interested in your logic in getting to that point—how you arrive at the range.

GENE: At the range? OK. This is an historical analysis.

GEORGE: Again, I am a little bit confused. In the late '50's we had virtually no change between the 1955 and 1960 Dow Jones earnings. Yet, the multiple went up from 7 to 24 in 1961.

GENE: Right.

KEN: But that was an attempt at predicting the earnings gains that took place from 1962 to 1965.

VIC: No. Come on, Ken, the market wasn't then predicting the '62 to '65 earnings.

KEN: I submit this is at least a partial explanation. The rise of institutional demand and the small, new equity supply must also be considered.

VIC: I don't know. I think it was one of the great unanswered mysteries.

KEN: Unless you can give me a better reason for why it happened, why, I stick with the fact that it was predicting the rise that came later. People wanted to get aboard. They knew that this earnings plateau wouldn't last forever.

GENE: This approach has a fundamental assumption that there is an underlying increase in earning power year by year, so that with two years in a row of the same earnings, the second year you would be applying a somewhat higher multiple to the same earnings. And the third year the same earnings would rate a still higher multiple.

GEORGE: What I cannot reconcile is the accuracy you seem to imply —it doesn't make sense. During this five-year period, you had no change in earnings; price/earnings ratios were up to well over 20 times. Then, within a matter of about three months to four months the price/earnings ratio dropped catastrophically to 12½ times.

GENE: You mean during 1962?

GEORGE: Right. Then it moved ahead; earnings continued to rise; and in the face of rising earnings the P/E dropped down to 12½ multiples. The thing that bothers me is this hiatus period that I am talking about—this past six-year period when——

GENE: You see there was an underlying growth in the companies in the Dow Jones Average. It's just that it wasn't translated into earnings. But when we had a different sort of economy, and we had expansion, then it came a lot faster—the earnings came a lot faster than the underlying growth, and the multiple declined during that period of time.

GEORGE: Because your earnings and the Dow Jones multiple are almost identical——

KEN: But Gene is talking about the big, upward move.

GEORGE: Oh, yes, I am talking about those five-year periods.

KEN: The upward move was so strong the multiple couldn't possibly keep up with it from the level at which it started.

GENE: Right. So you relate the Dow multiple to earning power, and you see a very high correlation, which happened to work real well in 1966 and has worked beautifully in 1967.

VIC: The thing that emerges from this discussion is that some of the textbook ideas of how stocks are valued are not used in practice, but what seems to be used in practice is some combination of absolute and relative values. I am not quite sure that I understand the procedure, but it seems to be essentially some concept of the relationship between the multiple of the stock and the average.

NICK: With the average determined on a historical, somewhat intuitive basis?

VIC: I haven't seen that written up anywhere, I don't believe.

NED: I think you are right. There are a lot of silent people around the table, and I have an idea each of them has his own secret approach.

Let me confuse you. One of the things we use—and this may seem as crazy as anything you can find—is a theory that the return on equity—that is, earnings to book value—and the earnings yield—that is, the earnings divided by price—tend to set limits for the overall rate of return of a common stock investment. It's difficult for an average company over a period of time to have more or less return than the spread between these two. The formula we use is this.

$$\text{Return (total return in appreciation and dividends)} = \sqrt{\frac{\text{Earnings}}{\text{Book value}} \times \frac{\text{Earnings}}{\text{Price}}}$$

When you are averaging ratios, the way you do it is take the geometric mean, or square root of the product.

GENE: Can you think of a typical example?

KEN: Give us a stock.

NED: All right. Suppose you've got a company that has a return on equity of 15 percent. I assume that you generally wouldn't buy a company unless the return on equity was above average. If this were true, the price/earnings ratio might be—I don't know where it would be in today's market, but it might be 17. So 1 over 17 comes out 5.88 percent.

GENE: That's the earnings yield?

NED: That's the earnings yield. The return on this stock would be the square root of 5.88 percent times 15 percent.

$$R = 5.88\% \times 15\%$$

We maintain that the most likely overall return on this stock is the geometric mean of 15 percent and 5.88 percent, which would be the product of the two. It's going to be about 9 percent.

GENE: Which is 10½ times earnings?

NED: No. No, we are not talking about P/E ratios. We are talking about probable return. We can calculate an earnings multiple out of it, easily, because we can decide what the return on this stock should be. If it's A.T.&T., we may be willing to buy it on an 8 percent overall return basis. We know the book value. We know the earnings, and we can solve for the price.

If it's General Motors, maybe you don't want to buy it unless you get an 11 percent return. There are very few stocks we would want to buy unless we saw at least a 10 percent return.

KEN: How would a drug stock with very low book value, or maybe an advertising agency, for example? How would that work out?

NED: Well, give me a drug stock with its earnings and book value and its price, and we will see. The average drug stock is earning over 20 percent on equity.

GENE: That's right. Take Merck—25 percent on equity—selling at 30 times earnings.

NED: Earnings yield is 1/30, or 3.33 percent, and the return on equity you said was 25 percent; well, that's going to be 82¼. The square root is about 9.1 percent. So you are buying Merck on a 9.1 percent total return basis. Overall return—that's a combination of dividends and long-term capital gain at that price.

GENE: Is the logic of this that the company is reinvesting money at that rate of return, and that's what——

NED: Well, the theory behind it is that the company will pay out all earnings—or most of them—if the earnings yield is higher than the return on equity obtainable on a marginal reinvestment in additional assets. And if return on equity opportunities are higher than the earnings yield, management can reinvest to more advantage than the stockholders can, and dividends should be small.

The theory assumes that the company is using the optimum dividend payout. It is not exactly true, because for a fast-growth company payout is generally a little too high, and for a low-growth company it is generally a little too low. But it is a workable formula. We have calculated hundreds of them and then plotted them to see if returns do fall in between E/P and E/B, and they do fall just about on the geometric mean.

So we use this as a basis for one valuation system. This is not the only approach that we use. It is just one of many, but we like to think in terms of the return at which we would buy that stock. This is sort of subjective, but it is based on historical experience. In this sense, we are taking an absolute value approach, but it's in no way related to the textbook present value of all future dividend payments, and so on. It just doesn't have any relationship to that. We are saying the return on the stock is created in another way altogether. The point is really that all of us, to some extent, use some sort of relative approach and some sort of an absolute value approach. I don't think any of us would say, when the Dow Jones is selling at 50 times earnings in a peak earnings year, that we would be too happy about the market. We would feel that something was wrong. That it just wasn't going to hold up.

KEN: When you have a hunch that it's above some absolute value?

NED: Yes, that there's something wrong there.

This section on price judgments introduced several novel approaches, and again none of the traditional techniques was advocated. Underlying the thinking of most of the seminarians was the concept of some combination of absolute and relative values in making price judgments.

One of the thoughts that recurred but was not explored at length was the postwar trends in price/earnings ratios, and the fact that the movement of the ratios for prolonged periods seems to have perversely refused to reflect the trend of earnings. For example, from 1955 to 1961 corporate earnings were relatively flat, but multiples increased. Conversely, the great earnings rise from 1961 to 1966 was accompanied by declining multiples. Is this because the market is anticipating earnings several years ahead? Or is it market recognition through lower multiples of current above-trend earnings? Perhaps it is caused by shifting investor interest in different segments of the market, with the market multiple a result of changing individual security valuations. Ample room is left for further argument and research on this subject.

CHAPTER FOUR

The investment process: implementing policy

The administration of business organizations has been well covered in text-books. Quite appropriately, these textbooks emphasize that suitable authority should be given to any person who has responsibility. Various levels of decision making are permitted, but it should be perfectly clear always that a specific type of decision must be made at a specific level of management. Ultimate responsibility for what happens must fall on the top man or on a committee charged with the job of supervising a department's work. Effective decision making requires adequate sources of information and a prescribed communications system. Decisions made at the top level should normally be of a policy nature, and a system of controls and record-keeping is necessary to assure those in positions of responsibility that the policy is being carried out.

With these generalities on the nature of the administration of any business organization, the reader should view the dialogue presented in this chapter as representative of the views of those involved in the practice of personal trust investing.

In a bank, the board of directors has the ultimate responsibility for operation of the trust department. This board is permitted by law and regulation to delegate its authority to such committees and individuals in positions of authority.[1] One conditioning influence on the committee system, and the method of supervision and review of trusts, was given brief mention in the discussion. This is the organization outlined in Regulation F of the Federal Reserve System, once the governing framework for the operation of trust departments by member banks. Regulation F placed strong emphasis on

---

[1] Appendix B may be helpful in visualizing the organization of particular banks.

group judgment in arriving at investment decisions as well as in monitoring the administration of trusts. However, the present Regulation 9 has been much more liberal in giving banks flexibility in organizing their trust departments.[2] As will be seen from the discussion, much thought was devoted to the place of committees in setting policy, in reviewing performance, and in reaching recommendations.

The reader will doubtless be most confused by the abundance of committees mentioned. This is simply because titles of the various committees and their duties vary to a great degree among different trust organizations. Thus, it may be well for us to try to disentangle some of these committees for the benefit of those readers who are not familiar with trust departments or trust department terminology.

The **trust committee** is generally the senior committee concerned with trust department matters, and is frequently made up of directors and senior officers of the trust department. It has general responsibility for the operation of the trust department, and it may be responsible for decision making on specific matters such as legal problems of specific trust accounts, the acceptance of new accounts, authorizing encroachments from an account, and so on. In some banks, it may be required only to review the technical operation of the trust department once a year on behalf of the board of directors. Its duties may consist merely of reviewing the internal audit statements or the report of the National Bank Examiners, or its duties may penetrate to the smallest details of trust department activities.

A **trust acceptance committee** is set up for the purpose of accepting or rejecting new accounts.

A **trust investment committee** is one charged with investment decisions. Sometimes, these decisions are of only broad policy nature. At other times, the trust investment committee may be involved in the review of each individual account, deciding on every move that is made.

If the trust investment committee is primarily concerned with broad policy, it is often called the **trust policy committee.** Such a committee would normally receive and approve economic projections, industry and company reviews, information on the condition of the stock market, and markets for various fixed-income securities. Based on this information, it would make rather broad decisions, such as to increase or decrease percentages held in common stocks, to extend or reduce the length of bond maturities, to emphasize a particular industry or group of industries in the composition of equity portfolios, to approve lists of securities suitable for purchase or sale, to set the investment objective of each new account as it comes into the trust department, and similar matters.

The job of reviewing individual accounts is often delegated to a committee

---

2 See Appendix C.

called the **trust review committee.** Such a committee may not only be required to review each account at least once a year but also to review any account that was influenced by a policy decision or that had special problems in need of attention.

Obviously, in many organizations specific investment decisions may be delegated to a single individual or to small groups of individuals acting as subcommittees.

Another area that may be a cause of some confusion to the uninitiated reader is the group of controls traditionally found in a trust department. The increased use of computers and related data processing machinery has improved the information and controls of the modern trust department. Typically, the following information is readily available on a current basis: (1) the number of shares or amount held in any given security, along with collateral information, such as the account name and number, the tax cost basis, the name of the administrative officer, and ad valorem tax information; (2) a list of the current security holdings and cash balances in any account, with adequate descriptions; (3) a system of tickler files, showing when conversion features expire, expiration of rights, options, and warrants, changes in redemption provisions of bonds or call features of preferred stocks, and so on.

In addition, internal publications provide the latest economic forecast, reports on industries, reports on companies, market studies, statistical studies, and other tools that may be helpful in making investment decisions for a specific account.

At times, there is confusion within an organization because of the opinions expressed in such papers. The policy-making committees do not always go along with recommendations in these reports. In such cases, the members of the trust policy committee should always state the official view for purposes of taking action.

There is great variety in the terms used in the trust business to refer to certain useful lists of stocks.

A guidance list is generally a broad list of stocks considered to be of suitable quality for use in a trust department, but not necessarily attractive in price. This list may be referred to by other names, such as common stock list, approved list, or representative common stocks. Such a list generally shows such things as price, earnings, dividends, yield, price/earnings ratio, quality rating, relative attractiveness, industry classification, estimated growth rate, estimated future price/earnings ratio, and estimated earnings for a year or perhaps five years in the future.

Another group of common stock lists may have titles such as current purchase list or buy-sell list. These are action lists, which are generally produced daily or weekly, while the guidance list is the type provided more for information than for action and is needed less frequently. The same information, however, may show up on both lists. Samples of such lists are shown in Appendix A, Exhibits II, III, and IX.

Readers should have little difficulty in recognizing the type of list intended in the dialogue of this chapter when a speaker refers to the switch list, hold list, approved list, buy list, and so on. Also, it may be helpful to the reader to state that the words research staff and others are used frequently in this chapter to refer to the security analysis division as opposed to the portfolio management section. The term "investment officer" is used interchangeably with "portfolio manager." Similarly, "research officer" is used to refer to a senior security analyst or the head of the security analysis division.

KEITH: When I was asked to introduce this subject, I sat down and made up a short list of some of the tools that have been helpful to us over the years. I would like to emphasize that I'm sure we're all aware of the fact that computer techniques are going to outdate an awful lot of this stuff that we've been using. Nevertheless, perhaps this will be of some use. I set down a few ideas that I will go through. You can follow the list, and maybe it will give you ideas for later discussion.

Responsibility for investment policies rests with the senior officers in their capacities as members of the policy and/or trust review committee, subject to the approval of the board of directors. That's a basic statement, I think, with which we generally agree, but maybe not entirely.

These policies may vary widely from broad changes in bond/stock ratios, through changes in industry emphasis, to more modest changes in bond policies affecting maturities or quality of issues purchased, or perhaps geographic areas that should be emphasized or avoided. Development of all of these policy decisions in the first instance must be based on the flow of studies from the research division and the economics section to the policy-making groups for their review against the background of present policies and information on the current status of all personal trusts. Periodic material from research should include industry studies and detailed company reports that grow out of field research with the company involved. We publish general stock lists, showing tabulations of comparative data, earnings, yields, price/earnings ratios, relative performance, and so on.[3]

We have one-page summaries of all stocks regularly reviewed, con-

---

[3] See Appendix A, Exhibit IV.

taining complete financial information for 15 or 20 years, which we find is a useful tool.[4] This also protects research personnel from spending too much time with customers at the expense of their research effort. This material is readily available for the directors or the trust committee in their regular monthly review of trust department activities. The stock sheets are often distributed to the customers by administrative officers in connection with investment recommendations involving the particular issues under consideration.

Earnings forecasts must be prepared by the research staff against the background of a uniform economic forecast without forcing the analyst into too tight an economic straitjacket—an area we discussed earlier.

In addition to his short-term forecast, the economist must work with the research people in establishing a three- to five-year forecast as a base for their earnings projections, and he will receive considerable help from the security analyst, who will have assembled useful projections from the long-range planners of the companies he visits and from their trade associations. There is a lot of feedback from industry.

A major change in investment policy would be stated for the record in the minutes of the investment committee. These minutes might then be made the subject of a somewhat expanded memorandum, with illustrations if necessary, for distribution to all officers and, most particularly, to the trust administrative officers of the personal trust division and all investment personnel, both portfolio managers and the research staff. Many policy changes will not require a minute or a special memo if they brought up an investment decision taken by reason of relative price changes rather than fundamental business changes.

Many of these changes will occur increasingly in the search for above-average performance. These policy decisions will be communicated through a weekly or monthly current investment list, or buy-and-sell list, with due regard to both income and growth—perhaps separate lists. They grow out of changes in relative value between companies and industries as related to their longer-term projections, but the decision cannot rest entirely with the analysts responsible for the companies, since they work with comparatively few industries. This decision might better be a function of the officers in charge of research and portfolio management, and their assistants. Three or more people might be involved in the construction of the lists after the analysts have made their recommendations; with the analyst, however, being responsible for price limits on the individual stocks.

---

[4] See Appendix A, Exhibit V.

A regular meeting of senior research and portfolio people to review these changes should be scheduled so that there will be complete communication as to the reasons for these additions and deletions. Periodically, it will be appropriate, perhaps, to prepare sample diversification schedules, without being too hard and fast about industry percentages in view of widely varying account requirements. Such schedules might change appreciably from year to year with the ebb and flow of relative investment values among a wide assortment of industries on the current investment list; the thought being that at any given time, say, utilities might creep up on the list and steels might go down. As a result of these changes, your feeling as to what concentrations in an industry might be appropriate will change. From time to time, policy changes may dictate the setting aside of reserves for future distribution or for investment.

These reserves will necessitate the use of a series of symbols to code the purpose for which the reserve is held, in readily recognizable form. If the reserve is for future permanent investment, it must be tickled [listed on a tickler file] for review—periodically, perhaps monthly or quarterly—and listed on a master list of bond or stock reserves. This reserve list is particularly useful, we find, in considering, say, a new bond issue.

In the area of fixed-income securities, it's very useful to have the officer in charge of corporate bonds and private placements prepare a weekly or biweekly new issue list of acceptable corporates, including rumored private placements and giving comparative data, estimated prices, and his recommendations. A similar list would be prepared by the municipal bond officer. In addition, the corporate bond man would provide a useful service with a weekly corporate bond purchase list, covering outstanding issues—mostly recently sold issues, I suspect— available in the size required, which he considered attractive for use by the portfolio people.[5]

In the area of controls, a number of procedures are useful. A weekly new deposit schedule, presented to the investment committee, ensures that no newly received asset will be held for long if it is on the sell list. Similarly, a weekly open order list will reveal to the committee the instructions that have not been carried out by reason of price changes, and it may suggest an alternative course of action.

If a policy of reviewing all accounts every 90 days is observed, and

---

[5] See Appendix A, Exhibit VI and VII.

if account recommendations have not been carried out in this period, the officer in charge of the division should receive a report from the investment or administrative officer involved, and these should become part of the record by being spread in the minutes.

Admitting the difficulty of preparing valid and useful performance studies of personal trusts with widely varying and ever changing objectives, it's nevertheless a useful exercise to record each research recommendation with the analyst's initials opposite it, for future review. An easy method that we have found for following the analyst's record is to use a relative performance graph of individual stocks, and use a crayon color code. If, for example, the analyst has put a stock on the buy list and kept it there for four months, you color the line green for that four-month period; and if it's in the hold category, you color it with yellow; and if it's a switch, you put red on it; and then, subsequently, it's very easy to look back and see how good the recommendation has been—how well it's worked out—six months or a year later. Basically, we're talking about relative performance rather than absolutes, and we've found this a useful technique.[6] This summarizes the items that I started with here, and I'm sure I've hardly scratched the surface.

GIL: We're probably moving into an area where we're going to get a lot less controversy than we have had. But you may have some additional suggestions or observations to make with respect to those administrative and operative techniques that Keith has spelled out here. This, of course, you know, is just half of the general discussion. The measurement part of it will be handled by Ned, and it may be that there'll be a little more room for debate on what Ned has to offer than on Keith's contribution, but I'm sure we haven't exhausted this topic by any means. So who wants to get the ball rolling?

KEN: I believe that the fewer the members of your board of directors or other noninvestment people you are able to get away with on your committees, the better off you're going to be.

GLENN: Hear! Hear!

KEN: They are of no help. They can be a great hindrance to you and——

NED: Half of the trust departments in the country have a serious problem of having directors, attorneys, administrative officers, and economists on their committees, and in some cases they dominate the

---

[6] See Appendix A, Exhibit VIII.

committee. Seven men who know nothing about investments and only three that do!

VIC: I would modify that. The problem you are trying to solve is to prevent investment decisions from being made primarily by people with a noninvestment background.

NED: Right.

VIC: But I would say that you could certainly structure your own organization so that the investment decisions are made by the investment people. Nevertheless, I would argue—at least I've found it true in my own experience—that you can draw a good deal from some of the commercial officers of the bank and from the directors.

GUY: I agree.

VIC: The question you have is not to put in the record that you get rid of these individuals, but that you see if you can work up an organization structure that will allow them to contribute but not be the deciding factor in your investment decisions.

GLENN: In making this contribution, they don't have to serve on your trust investment committee.

VIC: Let me give you an example of how we operate. The directors' trust committee meets once a month. Their primary interest is in the earnings and the operations, and the openings and closings of accounts. At the end of the meeting, for about half an hour I report to them our thinking about the business and market environment and what our investment policy is. The invariable response is one of keen interest, and they are anxious to help. They want to know if they can contribute any special knowledge or expertise, or answer any questions. We usually have one or two questions, we get their help, and they say, "Thanks a lot; we'll see you next month; we're grateful."

Our relationship with the directors seems to be one of their being interested. They want to be kept current, but they in no way attempt to control us. They may raise the question whether we think the life insurance industry is worth investigating, or something like that, but that's as far as they go.

GLENN: But I think you have to be pretty careful here to keep the decision——

VIC: We don't go to them for decisions.

GLENN: The trust committee doesn't make decisions. They establish policy——

GEORGE: You are talking about two different types of committees —a trust committee for directors and a trust investment committee.

VIC: Wait a second. Let me finish the story. That's the directors' trust committee, and that's how the directors are involved in the trust department.

GARY: They don't review any individual accounts?

VIC: No, sir! Now we have a trust committee which has the senior officers of the bank on it, and this is entirely an administrative committee. I'm a member of the trust committee, but we don't discuss trust investments at all. The trust investment committee, of which I am chairman, is the primary investment decision-making committee in the whole organization. That meets once a month. It has on it five out of nine people who are not in the trust investment division. Their responsibility is to review an agenda submitted by the investment department, which gives our business outlook, our money market outlook, our statement of investment policy broadly applied to accounts, and our investment diversification. They also get industry reviews and reports on approved companies for inclusion on our security guidance list. That's all their monthly meeting is devoted to.

The trust committee has said that any two members of the trust investment committee constitute a quorum, which means that the four members in the trust investment department do everything else. They make the decisions, they review the portfolios, they set the price limits on securities, and have essentially the investment decision making within the department.

My own experience has been that it works out all right because we can draw on the commercial officers, the bank's economist, the members of the bank bond department. They can bring to our policy discussions and our company evaluations their background and wisdom. But they have no interest in reviewing individual accounts; they have no interest in price limits; they have no interest in investment decisions. Their only function there is what they can contribute. I think they contribute a good deal.

VAN: How about policy decisions?

VIC: Policy decisions on the recommendations are reported by the trust investment department to the trust investment committee. We discuss things like fixed/equity ratio and diversification for different kinds of accounts. I have no trouble. They go along with it.

VAN: They are part of the policy decisions?

VIC: They are part of the policy decisions. They ask questions and contribute ideas. We get some fine suggestions from the bank bond department, but the general attitude is: it's an investment decision, a trust investment matter; we don't want any part of it. You recommend it. We are for it.

If we didn't have these commercial officers around, I think we would lose something. We'd lose the expert assistance these people can give. I think the problem is to make sure that they don't get involved in deciding whether we buy General Motors at 84 or not.

GENE: Well, your directors have only a review responsibility.

VIC: We say, "Thank you for the advice. Our current policy is—" whatever it is. That's it.

GENE: This is similar to what we have. We have only a review relationship with our directors.

VIC: That's right. The directors review, the trust investment committee approves policy, but they don't get down to detailed investment or portfolio reviews.

GARY: The law requires that a trust be reviewed at least once a year. Does the law say anything about what kind of review that has to be done?

VIC: It has to be done by a trust investment committee. That's all it says.

GUY: Within 15 months of the last review.

KEITH: Under Regulation 9, you don't have to have a trust investment committee.

NED: It says you can delegate within the bank.

VIC: It says you can delegate, and it has been delegated to a subcommittee—basically it's a subcommittee of four. The members of the trust investment department.

KEN: I submit that investment decisions are best made in the atmosphere of give and take such as we've had here the last couple of days, but not by this large a group. If all of our chief executive officers were here with us, I think the record would read a lot differently. I feel they act to restrain honest difference of opinion. Yet get a young analyst in here talking to George, as we are, and I'm sure George wants him to give his honest opinions; but if the president is sitting next to George, this analyst is going to cut his throat before making some statement that might get him in hot water. He doesn't mind getting in hot water with George quite as much. (*laughter*)

GEORGE: I encourage it. As a matter of fact, you have to. Any analyst should talk back. I expect him to make a statement, and if he doesn't I'll fire him.

VIC: What kind of structures do you have, and what problems do you have with noninvestment officers or directors on your various committees that influence decisions?

VAN: We have an economist on our committee who has been a perennial bear, and I'll tell you that inhibits your investment operations plenty, because you have no capability to counteract his forecast of 12 months hence.

VIC: The only offer of sympathy I can give you there is that we have the bank economist on our committee, and you know I'm an economist too, so I can look him in the eye and fight with him.

GREG: Well, the directors are responsible for the operation of the trust department. There is no question there.

KEN: Just as they are for every other department—even the safe deposit vault.

GREG: Every other department of the bank. Now, then, the directors' trust committee, or whatever you call it—in our case, we call it the trust committee—is composed of some of the directors and senior officers of the trust department. This committee is informed of decisions already made by other committees. The trust investment committee is the operating investment committee. It consists of senior officers of the trust department, including two investment officers, and that's it. There are no outside directors or anything else—this is the operating committee.

Now, if there was a major matter of policy the chairman would discuss it with the top management of the bank before the thing would be carried through. But, normally, all actions going to the trust committee have all been done, confirmed, and reported as a matter of information. If there is any question—if they think we have done wrong—why, we have to listen.

NED: I gather that we did reach a consensus that the investment decisions should be made by professional investment men.

VIC: That I think is clear.

GEORGE: Professional people of what type?

GLENN: Analysts?

GEORGE: That's the point I was getting at. To what extent should investment people, or even portfolio managers without research skill, be weighted in investment decisions—policy decisions.

GLENN: Our directors' committee consists solely of directors and is strictly a review committee, monitoring what's going on in the trust and investment departments.

Our trust committee consists entirely of officers in the bank, two from the trust department. They are there to be informed of what's being done in the accounts they have an interest in, and they speak up if they find conflicts. But this is rare because we look closely before it goes to committee.

Our trust investment committee is composed of two trust officers, three investment officers, property management officers, and one credit officer on a revolving basis—we have the committee weighted with trust investment men who are research men.

GEORGE: Research men?

GLENN: That's right. We are listened to, and we know enough about our business—certainly know more about it than the others on the committee—so that it's rare we have any serious difference of opinion. I think that is quite similar to what Vic was talking about—that decisions are made by investment people after careful thought.

VIC: The interesting thing in our trust investment committee is that the head of the trust department, who is my boss, is a member of the committee, but I am the chairman. He is chairman of the trust committee.

GLENN: May I say one more thing on just that point? In our case, and this has been true for 18 years now, the investment department does not report to the head of the trust department.

GUY: This is true in our bank.

GLENN: And we have responsibility not only for analysis of securities but also for account management, and also for the purchase of securities and for their custody and control.

VIC: Well, whom do you report to, Glenn?

GLENN: We did report to a senior vice president, who had the trust department among other administrative responsibilities. He is still with us, and he is still head of the trust investment committee, but I no longer report to him, so I don't know who I report to. (*laughter*) I report to the president of the bank. He doesn't think the trust department is very profitable and worthy of much attention—so there we are. (*laughter*)

VIC: I am rather puzzled by having the trust investment operation separate from the trust department. It seems to me logically that it is a part of the trust department.

GLENN: Well, it is, Vic. And I would agree with you. Historically it has been. On the other hand, I think we find that the very difficulty that is of concern here is that the investment decisions might be guided by the veto of a great legal mind in the trust department. If you want to avoid that and to give scope and potential to your investment people, you don't want them to be stultified. We want our investment people to look forward to something better than to being restricted by an administrative officer.

VIC: Is that a general characteristic?

NED: How many of you do not report to the head of the trust department? (*A show of hands*) Five. And how many do report to the head of the trust department? Eight.

NEIL: I report to the head of the bank. That's the difference here.

NED: Well, this is an interesting difference in structure.

VIC: While we are on this subject of structure, let me ask another question. In the portfolio management area, do your portfolio managers specialize by type of account? Do you have men for investment advisory, personal trust, pension and profit sharing? Is pension and profit sharing usually considered a part of the portfolio function?

GUY: In our case, it's separate.

GENE: We have an employee benefit plan group, an administrative group; and investment officers are part of our portfolio——

NED: We have a branch banking system, which probably gives us special problems. We have one man assigned to each branch office for all kinds of business. But for the main office accounts, we've eight or nine administrative units, and there's a pension and profit sharing unit, and an investment advisory, so we have no mixtures in the main office.

GREG: We do this also, except in one primary area, and that is pensions. We feel that the centralized pension unit can better control all pension funds, whether they are out in a smaller town, or wherever. Other than that, we have the same pattern you have.

GUY: Do you assign all guardianships—say, for minors or incompetents—to one particular officer? (*laughter*)

VAL: Glenn, I didn't understand whether your trust investment committee, the operating committee that really does the work, is all research men, or do you have any people with portfolio responsibility? I wasn't quite clear about that.

GLENN: When I said we had three investment men, I included the chairman of the committee, who is a senior vice president of the bank with general administrative responsibilities, including the trust and the investment departments. While he obviously no longer has any portfolio responsibility, he came up through the investment department. I included myself, as head of the investment department. I have responsibility for research and portfolio management. I also included the secretary, who is a member of the committee. He is the senior man in the department, who had his training in it, and is currently responsible for portfolio management.

VAL: So it isn't strictly an analysts' committee.

GLENN: They've all been analysts.

KEN: The problem is that people like to serve on these committees. This is from directors on down. It is very easy to get volunteers to serve on your investment committee. It's not like a committee concerned with corporate trust problems—you know, trust operations—they're too busy for that.

NED: It's hard to get them off.

KEN: We have only one committee.

GREG: Is the trust investment committee, which is the operating committee, appointed by the board of directors?

KEITH: That is true in our bank.

GUY: Ours is appointed by the trust committee.

KEN: And the trust committee is appointed by the board.

GUY: That is correct. The trust committee is half outside directors, half trust and investment men.

GREG: One other thing I wanted to mention. Though it meets every morning, our trust investment committee saves time by delegating to a securities committee the discussion of all industries and securities in reaching decisions, which are reported back to the trust investment committee. Similarly, in portfolio matters the largest would go direct to the trust investment committee, but otherwise the committee will see the minutes covering the smaller portfolios that our portfolio committee has reviewed.

GUY: A great deal of our information is received and reviewed by memorandums passed around the committee. A set of recommendations is drawn up, usually after consultation with one or more of the senior officers. The memo goes around. People write their comments on it, and the majority vote is the decision. If there are lots of disagreements, they are hashed out in a second memorandum. This saves lots of committee time.

GENE: I'd like to change the subject and ask a radical question. We've spent all this time talking about committees. Do committees help your product? Do they help make investment decisions? Are they a help or a hindrance?

GIL: Now that's a good question.

NED: I will say yes. (*laughter*) I think group judgment is a very valuable asset to banks. This is one of the things we advertise as being one of the secrets of our success—our group judgment. I think applying group judgment down to too fine a detail almost invariably ends up with so many compromises that you can do no better than mediocre performance. At some point, group judgment should have laid the groundwork and then the brilliant individual takes over, and takes the action.

GENE: To me, committees basically have only veto powers. Ideas are thought up by people. Committees can only approve the ideas that the guy thought up or else veto them.

GLENN: They can monitor the quality of the job being done without making the decision. This is the discipline the committee supplies—constraints.

GUY: I think the committee has additional value—exposure of people to different kinds of problems.

KEN: That's not what Gene said. He asked if it is helpful to the decision-making function.

GENE: No, I don't think it is. In fact, a lot of what we were talking about is removing the investment committee from making decisions.

GLENN: But sometimes the committee without making decisions, through monitoring the quality of the work, can actually be a stimulus.

GENE: I think the committee has a function of communication. You let people see other areas and sit down and talk about things, which is not the decision making.

NED: I think maybe we are talking about the same thing. I think that, ultimately, you get down to the brilliant individual—that's the guy who really handles——

KEN: If he isn't fed up by trying to get something through a committee, working through someone else, or has given up on trying to get his ideas through.

NED: The committee does have certain restraints—helping a man to find his blind spots. It will help him sometimes from making a major error, but if it has too strong an influence it prevents him from doing the brilliant job he might be capable of doing.

KEN: Let me confess to you how policy is set at my institution. I hate to do this. Our policy committee meets on my call, when something has been suggested to me, and I think we ought to have a meeting because there is some change in policy indicated. And then I—there's *no* membership on this committee—I invite to that meeting those who I think will be helpful to me in reaching a decision. If I'm going to talk about common stock policy, I have a different group from that which I would have if I'm going to talk about the outlook for the economy, or bond policy, or what-have-you. If I wanted to decide by myself, I suppose I could, but I would just like these points of view.

GENE: I think you make a better decision by yourself.

KEN: It's my responsibility.

GENE: I think that is the answer to the question you asked earlier. Should you have only analysts, or should you have account guys? I think it is an individual matter—the kind of guys you've got.

In the investment world, the trader is the person responsible for placing orders for the purchase or sale of securities. He is in communication by telephone with brokers and dealers in securities, and millions of dollars worth of investments may change ownership through a brief conversation.

Banks may purchase bonds for their own portfolios or in their capacity as trustee or agent. Some banks also act as brokers or dealers in government and/or general obligation bonds of the states and their political subdivisions. Sale of securities owned by a bank to its fiduciary accounts is considered self-dealing and is not ethical. Stocks and bonds are bought by banks for their trust or agency accounts, and occasionally as an accommodation for other customers.

The trader must keep himself familiar with the most likely contacts for the purchase or sale of particular securities, and must study the quotation services for possible alternatives. He must know the commission and transfer tax rates, so that he can weigh the advantage of buying from a dealer, who owns the security and sells at a net price, or a broker, who receives a commission. He must follow current market trends and exercise his judgment in buying and selling so that his action has a minimum effect on the market price. He must be able to recommend the use of the various forms of block distribution or purchase of securities when appropriate.

Specialized dealers ordinarily handle government, state, and city and corporate securities, and when the trading function is divided among several people this is a usual line of separation.

Since stock exchange commissions are uniform for all exchange members, and bonds being distributed through a syndicate may be obtained from any of the dealers at the same price, the trader has some area of discretion in giving business to investment firms. The trader's responsibilities are discussed below.

VIC: Keith, where does the final responsibility rest for deciding the price at which the stock will be purchased? Now, the security analyst would make a recommendation—he's got limits. Does the portfolio manager have the responsibility of telling the trading department, "I want to buy this stock and this is my limit," or "buy it quickly," or "buy it slowly"? Or does that rest with the committee? You know, ultimately, the buck stops some place. Where does it stop?

KEITH: It stops at the head of the trust investment research section. He supervises the analytical staff. Presumably he's getting feedback from the senior analysts, who follow all the industries, and basically it's his decision, with some help from the head of the portfolio managers section.

Now, there's one thing about price limits. We found it to be very important if the list is only produced monthly, which is the way we've done it until recently. We've established a basic rule that the trading department can't execute an order to buy a stock at more than 5 percent above the price indicated in the program. Frequently, if you have to get a cotrustee's approval this is two weeks after you've made the recommendation. This kicks it back if the price has gone up. Similarly, if you're selling something you can't sell at more than 5 percent below the program price. This problem will lick itself when we get this list run on a daily basis, tied into the reproduction of New York Stock Exchange close quotes on magnetic tape.

Nevertheless, Vic, I think the analyst has to be responsible, in consultation with his supervisor, for establishing a limit beyond which he doesn't want to go in the stock. We have felt that the supervisor of trust investment research, though, should make a final judgment, in view of the fact that we're talking about relative values. The oil man may know all about oil stocks, but not what's going on in the nonferrous metal field in terms of relative values between the two industries. So, we don't think we should charge him with the full responsibility for establishment of the price.

NED: Keith, we probably put the bee a little bit more on the trader than you do, in that he has, say, a common stock program. The program shows cost as well as market value, so that he can see roughly what gain and loss is being taken. If there's an upward move in the stocks that he's going to purchase, and at the same time there's an upward move in the stocks he's going to sell, he can still complete the program, but there may be more capital gains tax to pay. He is supposed to determine in his own mind whether this is sufficient to justify his going back to the policy committee or the portfolio committee and saying, "Well, what do I do now?" If prices go in opposite directions, of course, he has a problem.

One of the more interesting disputes that developed in this chapter concerns the role of the portfolio manager.

In many trust organizations, the portfolio manager is also an administrative officer who has direct contact with the customer. In some organizations, the administrative officer starts off as the person acting as an executor of an estate, and he subsequently becomes the person in charge of certain trusts set up under the will of the deceased. Thus, the customer deals with the same administrative officer throughout his contact with the trust department. In other banks, an administrative officer handles estates only, and when the trusts are created the portfolio manager becomes the contact man for the customer. There is, however, a growing trend toward highly specialized portfolio managers who are extremely well versed in investments and quite sophisticated in their portfolio strategies. These men must be insulated from the customer if they are to remain effective decision makers. Portfolio managers who act both as decision makers on investment matters and contact men with the customer suffer a severe disadvantage, because their attention is diluted by the distractions of customer contact.

Where the portfolio manager and the administrative officer are separate persons, a team system is often used. The administrative officer knows the entire family in a specific account. He generally has a rather good idea of their ages, their tax brackets, their current personal wealth, sources of income, possible future inheritances, personal preferences, and a host of other details, which may have some influence on the ultimate investment decision. By using the buddy system, the administrative officer can convey to the portfolio manager the necessary background for him to make the right investment decisions for the specific account within a framework of policy laid out by the appropriate policy committee. Such an arrangement comes much closer to meeting the true objectives of the account than one that fails to provide the portfolio manager with adequate account background information.

Within the financial analysis profession there are interesting contrasts, geographically, in the attitudes toward the importance of the portfolio manager as opposed to the security analyst. It seems to be characteristic of the older and very large investment centers to place the great emphasis on the security analyst as an idea man or decision maker, and to select as portfolio managers persons who are dropouts from the security analysis division. In these cities, a portfolio manager frequently is looked on as being no more than a capable clerk, perhaps with some personality if he must meet the customer, and one who should be free from any decision-making responsibility. In such an environment, policy decisions are handed down from above, even to the degree of instructing him exactly what percentage he may have invested in each industry, and he is expected merely to parrot the party line.

When one gets farther away from New York (and other older financial centers) a different pattern seems to emerge. In a regional financial center, investment research staffs are likely to be much smaller, and are often heavily dependent on security analysts of brokerage houses and correspondent banks in New York City or other major financial centers. Thus, decision making is forced to the top of the organization. The portfolio manager is then generally a man who was previously the best security analyst.

If the reader is in doubt about the relative prestige of portfolio managers as opposed to security analysts in his own city, he will find that local attitudes are revealed rather clearly by determining who makes the biggest salary and who makes the final decisions.

This monograph provides no satisfactory answer to the debate on the relative merits of portfolio managers and security analysts. The editors would emphasize, however, that a topnotch portfolio manager must be an excellent security analyst himself and must be backed up by strong security analysts.

VIC: How about it? Do any of you leave the ultimate price discretion in the hands of the portfolio manager?

VAN: How do you do that?

KEITH: We have limited them on that. I suspect that it is a result of the available personnel and the rating of the jobs. Our portfolio managers are not really portfolio managers in the sense that you're thinking of. We have such people in our investment advisory section. Most of these people—our portfolio managers—were semitrained in research, and their talents and instincts seem to be better used on the other side than in research. Let's say they're not quite as bright. (*laughter*) They're under control all the time.

We felt it was useful to have a pretty uniform policy applied to similar type of accounts. We wanted to keep this under control. We didn't want to have two customers in similar financial circumstances and background run into each other at a cocktail party and one says, "The bank has treated me very well. They sold my ———— and bought me Xerox a couple of years ago." The other fellow says, "Gee, I have that ———— in my account and they didn't do that for me." Well, we felt that in our community it is very important that investment policies have a consistency to them. So our portfolio jobs are not as highly rated as our research jobs. We are somewhat unhappy with the fact that a lot of them are high-grade clerical jobs, really, except in the pension area. But in personal trust, which is what we are talking about, this is the way it is.

GREG: Do I get the point that the orders to buy a certain stock in a particular account emanate from the portfolio manager or not? In other words——

KEITH: He makes up the recommendation which goes through the trust committee.

GREG: He goes over the portfolio and decides which stock?

KEITH: He works with the administrative officer. The administrative officer does not exercise veto power in investments, but some circumstances surrounding the account may dictate some slightly different treatment, so the portfolio man makes up the program for the trust investment committee. Well, this committee meets every day, so there's no holdup there. The program in typed form is submitted to the committee, and let's say it is approved. Then a copy goes back to the portfolio manager, but he has no further responsibility in regard to that program. From then on, it is an administrative responsibility. The customer contact man, an administrative officer, takes over from there. If we have sole authority in an account, the administrative officer will initiate the transaction—"please do" on it—send it to the traders, and it will be done. If it requires correspondence with a cotrustee in a distant state, then that is done by the administrative officer.

VIC: Keith, do you find in some instances, however, that customers are interested in investments, and the administrative officer isn't the most effective one to talk to the customer? I find that we have some accounts where the administrative officer is the chief contact, but there are other accounts where they want to see the portfolio man—they want to see the investment man. You can't shield your portfolio managers from that kind of interruption.

KEITH: No, you can't. Not entirely. Fortunately, many of our administrative officers came up through investments. They are, of course, not unwilling to practice this trade they developed. They don't want to make any investment decisions, but they do know what our line is at the moment. They can talk it in general terms.

If it has to be more specific, they can get a research man or his assistant. We've got these in teams. There would be two or three men following an industry. Get one or another of them briefly. But we want to insulate the research staff from this kind of thing.

That's the reason we went to a one-sheet annual stock report. These are to pass out or mail out with letters, so that the administrative officer doesn't have all of his time taken up in the yes–but discussion on individual securities; he doesn't have to feed it back to research or portfolio. That was the idea for building up these short stock reports, and many of you have the same kind of thing.

Ken, you have industry sheets and company sheets, and all that kind of thing, and we have found it useful in protecting our research people.

VAN: I would like to pursue this thing on the discretion given to portfolio managers with respect to price discipline, just to see what others are doing here.

KEN: We do the same thing Keith does, only we buy stocks that go up faster. (*laughter*) We use a 10 percent limitation. Well, particularly in the kind of market we've had. When a stock goes on our buy list, the price limit is usually 10 percent. It may be a little narrower than that; it may be a little higher than that. The price limit is stated right there next to the current price, so the portfolio manager knows that this stock is likely to be on the hot list, from a price standpoint anyway, during the period that it sells between this price and——

VAN: Well, Ken, if then that stock goes 10 percent above the maximum buy price——

KEN: God help him if he buys without checking with us.

GENE: I think our traders would normally do that as a matter of course, because we don't have a system set up to do that.

GARY: Does your trader have discretion——

KEN: Our portfolio manager. Let's take a stock like Zenith. It might go all the way up to 50 with a price limit of, let's say, 57, and the portfolio manager knows that if the stock is 54 when he gets his approval back, or when he reviews an account that he thinks could use that stock, why, he would put the buy order in. If it's 56, he would buy then. He would say to the trader, "Now this has got to be bought at 57 or better——"

VAN: But 58, though, he's got to check back. That's the rule.

VIC: Ken, don't you have to let the portfolio manager, in some cases, get the limit because he's just got so much cash. In other words, he has to buy it, let's say, up to 55. If he goes up to 57, he's got an overdraft.

KEN: Or buy about 10 shares less.

GREG: That certainly has to be within his judgment, but I think your research department and the analysts who handle whatever area it is, with the approval of the appropriate committee, put X stock on the list—they also determine a buy limit. Now we have, as you all have, guidance lists. Ours is revised weekly so that we have 52 of them a year. We have a meeting once a week of the committee that passes on any changes. This includes changes in the buy limit. The discretion is still with the portfolio manager. Let's say that it is just a point over the buy limit. He can go back in just a few minutes and contact a majority of the members of the committee, and get it okayed at three or four points over the buy limit if the account is large enough, and he would like to buy it anyway.

KEN: And often the whole market has moved, Greg, so you're going to have to move the buy list up or you're out of business.

GREG: That's right.

KEN: Or pretty soon you haven't got a buy list.

VIC: In a somewhat smaller department, in my own organization, we have a guidance list which we reprice every two weeks. It can be done more often, but I work in consultation with the head of the portfolio management section who is responsible to me, and the head of the security analysts, who is responsible to me. The three of us sit down and set price limits, and if there has got to be a vote I'm afraid I carry the heaviest vote, because it is my ultimate responsibility. Then we have a meeting of the security analysts and the portfolio managers and tell them what we did. If there are any complaints or objections, we can get them on the line there, but the portfolio managers can give instructions to the traders about what their restrictions are. That seems to work out reasonably well.

VAN: But doesn't this reduce the portfolio manager to nothing more than a statistical clerk?

KEN: That's why Keith's got clerical people doing portfolio work and has his best talent working on analytical work.

VAN: Well, then, the conclusion of this group is that the type of person who should be doing this work [portfolio analysis] is a clerk.

GUY: I think it depends on the background of the people. Since ours is a much smaller bank than you have, with a number of very large accounts as well as smaller ones, a good many of our administrative officers act within limits which we have very closely established, and through use of approved lists they can make limited changes in portfolios. Anything beyond this has to be discussed with one or more members of our investment staff. And we don't ordinarily set formal price limits, but if there have been any substantial changes in price our senior research and administrative people get into some kind of discussion. We're within reasonably close distance of one another.

VIC: Van, I wouldn't say that the portfolio manager has become just a high-priced clerk, because he does have to make decisions and recommendations on fixed/equity ratios, on industry diversification, on the selection of names. The only area that I don't think he has any tremendous talent in is in setting price limits, because he is not in the analytical area; he is not that close to the analyst and frequently doesn't have that particular skill. I think he makes a contribution in terms of the recommendations he comes up with. But as to the price limits, I am a little reluctant to let him go that far unless he happens to be really one of my senior men and, well, then you listen to him.

NED: Isn't the real talent of a portfolio manager the ability to blend a group of securities? Like making a cake. He's trying to make a devil's food cake, and if it comes out pound cake he hasn't come up with the right product. I think he's got to be fairly sophisticated and pretty well experienced in investments, even though he may not be as sensitive to prices and values as a security analyst. What you've got to do is have a steady flow of the proper sort of information to him so he can find out what the right buys are, but he should understand the characteristics of those companies well enough so that he can blend that cake and have one that is edible for that account.

Portfolio analysis is getting more sophisticated with the computer doing spectral analysis and measuring covariance to see if we really have the diversification we think we have. Portfolio management is no place to have your clerks.

GREG: I would like to say another word in behalf of the portfolio manager here, so that he isn't reduced to the level of the statistician. Over a period of many years, a portfolio manager has in many instances become the prime contact with the account. The administrator becomes merely the one who sees the accounting force through—that the checks are taken care of, and so on. With a branch system such as we have, it has become an increased expense item because we will be sending one portfolio manager to one city for a series of appointments. Another one will head down to a different part of the state and will have appointments in two or three cities. Some customers come in, and some sessions are held at our branch offices in smaller communities. But this has been increasing, so we have had to build and build this portfolio management staff. But we feel in the long run it will enable us in a better way to compete with investment counselors who give that kind of personal service. And also in collateral business.

GEORGE: I think this is very important. The minimum requirement to attain competence is at least two years of research, and as a matter of fact we have two portfolio managers who are C.F.A.'s and who have moved into portfolio work after varying experience—from 8 to 12 years research experience. The reason for that is the caliber and type of person that we do business with in the pension trust area. Also, in the investment advisory area there are an increasing number of executives and other sophisticated people who have substantial funds. They bring their funds in to equal the results of a pension trust performance, and they will not talk to anyone but a competent senior person.

VAN: Well, that's the direction of the business—the portfolio side rather than the research side. Management of portfolios today has become more of a sophisticated art than the research side.

GREG: That's right.

NORM: I disagree with that.

VAN: Well, perhaps I'm being a little too strong there, but certainly the performance [mutual] funds have achieved their success through the management of portfolios rather than through strict research. The portfolio side has been the determining factor.

GENE: The record is achieved by an investment decision and not by research.

VAN: That's right.

NORM: But what happens if the decision isn't correct?

GEORGE: They don't have research!

VAN: They use other research.

GENE: Research is just a secondary tool.

NORM: It all depends on what mutual fund you're talking about. As far as the ———— Fund [a mutual fund], which is outstanding; I know they have tremendous research.

GENE: Some of the very, very successful investment counseling firms operate without any real research staff at all.

GEORGE: You will find invariably that the man who has done the job is a research-oriented portfolio analyst who knows the values of those securities.

GENE: Right. That may be, that may be.

GEORGE: That's the point I am getting at.

GENE: That's what it takes.

GLENN: I think it might be a mistake to divert your not-so-bright analysts over to an account like that. A better qualification might be that they are personable, and sometimes your analysts aren't.

GEORGE: If you are going to stay in the picture, you are going to have to move your bright research fellows into portfolio management.

GENE: And investment counseling work, too.

GEORGE: Yes, that's right. Though maybe to a lesser extent.

KEN: We don't have an administrative officer and a portfolio manager. We have only one, and he has investment background.

NED: Ken, you aren't talking about the average administrative officer that might be involved in estates or something?

KEN: Not in estates, but in personal trusts——

NED: Yes, I just don't want any of my highly skilled investment men out counting sheets and pillow cases. (*laughter*)

KEN: I thought we were talking about personal trusts. Personal trust administrative officers are investment trained.

NED: Personal trusts often come out of estates, under the will.

VAL: I lectured at the Trust School for several years on this administrative problem, and in going around, trying to prepare what I was going to say—because I was advocating exactly what you are—I found that the administrative officer comes in at the start of an estate, and as soon as the trust is established he's through, and then it's handled by an investment man, who is a trained man. And I discovered in talking to people around the country that if they ever let a beneficiary get close to an investment man they could never get him back to the administrative officer.

VIC: That's right.

VAL: They want no part of him. Which is what made me feel so strongly that this is the trend we should all be working toward.

GREG: There is a feeling in many trust departments, however, that the administrator should be legally trained.

VAL: Oh, I agree; I said as soon as you get rid of the estate——

GREG: It's the blending of the law that relates to——

KEN: We are disagreeing——

VAL: No, I'm not.

VAN: Your administrative officer could be a lawyer if he wanted to.

KEN: We only have one administrative officer. I'm saying the customer never deals with two people.

GUY: Very wise. Only one person represents the bank.

KEN: He might bring a lawyer in if he's needed, for half an hour or whatever.

GEORGE: We protect our investment people, for the simple reason if we didn't do it this way we'd have a lot of these people coming in with their personal problems, their tax problems, taking this man's time. We find it could be very costly.

KEN: They're going to do that anyway.

GEORGE: No, they won't.

KEN: Once they've been exposed to your investment man, they're going to come in with all their problems anyway.

GEORGE: To keep people alert, we have done one thing I think is rather interesting. Recently, we have expanded the so-called staff management committee by bringing in someone of increasing importance in research who attains a senior officer status. These committee meetings are as large as 12 to 15 people. It is amazing the impact this has had on the understanding of what is desired in carrying out both policy and recommendations, and it is also a good morale boost for the research man. We have found that it minimizes the communications problem considerably and makes for uniform policy. Sometimes, you get off the track, and somebody has got to say, "No, let's stop here." It doesn't happen too often. But the thing is that this is a research man. Now, we put the burden of the price on him. He's got to come across with more than a name. Once he agrees on a value and establishes a limit, if the policy committee agrees to it the burden's on him from that point on.

I've been amazed. I didn't approve of this initially. I didn't think it made any sense; I thought we had a whole roomful of maniacs, but it didn't turn out that way. It turned out that it had a significant impact all around. It made them all part of the team, and they like that.

GIL: I've been unable to detect any major disagreement with the presentation that Keith made here. Except for different emphasis on ultimate responsibility, the summary that Keith gave us seems to me to have been fairly well accepted.

NORM: I think that we certainly should have on the record that there is a difference of opinion about the portfolio manager's role. I mean this ought to be definitely in the record that the way Keith's bank does it isn't necessarily the way we feel it should be done. I think the majority is probably in the other direction, that the portfolio manager serves a much more important role.

KEN: I agree with Keith.

NORM: Are we talking about the same thing?

KEN: You're talking——

NORM: I was quite sure you agreed with me.

KEN: No, I don't.

NORM: You were saying your administrator—the man who has the contact—deserves an important role.

KEN: I said he should be an investment man——

NORM: Right.

KEN: But I think you have got to remember that every organization has only so much talent, and you've got to be very careful that a good share of that talent stays in research.

GEORGE: That's right.

KEN: The portfolio manager making the pound cake and the chocolate layer cake; he can't make either cake if all he's got to work with is mud pies, no matter how skillful he may be in blending. (*laughter*)

NORM: Just remember that Keith's portfolio manager is just a glorifield clerk. This is the point I was making.

KEITH: One reason the portfolio manager would have to be so skillful is to explain the mistakes that have been made by the research department to the customers of the bank. (*laughter*) Let's not confuse them.

Partially, this has developed by reason of, first, a shortage of people to do the portfolio job you're describing, and second, it was the structure of the community. We wanted a uniformity of policy, two different portfolio managers. One grows up through the oil industry, another through the autos—they would have their individual loves and hates for a lifetime of portfolio management, and we didn't want that.

GENE: We are all faced with limits in terms of the number of guys we've got, and obviously a strong research department is going to take a fair account manager and make him a lot better. If we could have both, I don't think any one of us would not welcome that event.

GEORGE: That is going to be the direction.

GIL: Well, one of the reasons I didn't want to get this topic out for complete discussion at the moment—and I see you've gone into it now —is that I want to see what develops later when Gary discusses the role of the portfolio manager.

NORM: But you made that statement, that we all went along with Keith——

During the session on measuring performance, the seminarians returned to the debate on portfolio managers versus security analysts. The dialogue is shown below in an abridged form.

GEORGE: One point I would like to dwell on is evaluating the performance of the two areas—the research and portfolio management areas. It's inevitable that you are going to have to do this.

GIL: In other words, you weren't satisfied with the initial discussion on that?

GEORGE: I just want a little greater discussion, because I don't think you can take away the wide difference of imagination due to the unusual account manager. There's no question about it. Either it's a daring or just a creative mind, or a more flexible mind. He'll do an outstanding job if you give him more than one choice in an industry.

KEN: Right.

GEORGE: That's not a research man's responsibility.

KEN: Should you give them six chemicals so that they can make a choice, or before it ever gets out of research should it be narrowed down to one?

GEORGE: No. The way we do it the research man always indicates his choices in the order of preference.

GENE: But you don't hold the portfolio man to it in the order of priority?

GEORGE: No, he may buy the sixth one and be right.

GENE: But Ken was saying he wouldn't give him discretion.

KEN: I wouldn't give him that leeway.

GEORGE: I would.

GUY: Has he the knowledge to decide which one? Admittedly, he will have enough different characteristics in the chemical companies— they are individual operations, definitely—but does your portfolio man know these companies sufficiently well to be able to make a reasonable decision?

KEN: Does he know them as well as the chemical analyst? If so, why isn't he a chemical analyst?

GENE: I don't see why he has to. He is dependent on the analyst for the information and the numbers and the knowledge of the companies, but that isn't the only thing that goes into making an investment decision on what all the different companies are going to earn. There are other things, too.

GLENN: He may not want a Du Pont. He may want a specialized company.

GENE: Right, depending on what else is in the account.

KEN: But you've got Chrysler and General Motors recommended in the automobile industry. You might not want to take that much risk in a Chrysler. You want the income in General Motors. These are account considerations.

VAN: But General Motors is ranked first, Ken, in the analysts' mind, as the best buy. But the portfolio fellow says, "I don't want General Motors; I want to swing with Chrysler."

GENE: But the account man has to know his accounts.

GEORGE: If most of us will think back 15 months, I'll bet most of us would have had ———, ———, ———, ———, ———, or ——— [six chemical stocks]. Only two of those survived. Now that's research—choosing among those six companies.

GENE: Yes, that's research's responsibility.

GEORGE: All right. But even if you have that down and have your estimates, and the analyst has the story, and the portfolio manager has the views of the analyst; he still may feel—for whatever reason—a bit more cautious. Maybe he knows more about chemicals. Maybe he read the newspapers and found out about an impending buildup in capacity, and he thought maybe he had better not do this. He would rather buy other smaller ones where these problems were minimal. Whatever the reason, he guessed right.

GIL: Is it *conceivable* that the analyst himself would not also have read that in the newspapers?

GEORGE: He did, but he didn't believe it.

VAN: Well, I—Ken, are you going to dictate to the portfolio manager what he has to buy?

GEORGE: You reduce him to a moronic level.

GENE: This is what we were talking about before. It is a continuation of it.

KEN: I would like to have my security analysts so highly regarded that the portfolio managers would be eager to believe them and use their recommendations. I don't think that the portfolio manager wants as much decision-making responsibility as he now has in most cases.

GEORGE: The other four chemicals would not be on that list if the chemical man didn't want them on there.

GENE: Right.

KEN: I think it is up to the chemical man to point up the attractiveness or unattractiveness of his industry, as well as selecting individual stocks.

GEORGE: A very good point again. We decided we would like to buy three steel companies last October. And all for the same reason—Armco, Bethlehem, and National. But one man liked Allegheny Ludlum.

KEN: Did he buy it?

GEORGE: Yes, he did.

KEN: Did he buy it from something he read in the papers or something he learned from your steel analyst?

GEORGE: Something he read in the newspapers.

KEN: Why didn't the steel analyst tell the other portfolio managers?

GEORGE: He did.

KEN: Why didn't they believe him?

GEORGE: They believed him. But this lad [the portfolio manager] read the newspapers a little bit deeper. He began reading about the SST program. He went a little deeper, and finally he decided this is the company I want, and he turned out to be right.

GIL: Ken would say blame it on the research department.

GUY: I think he's got a point.

KEN: I'd put him *in* the research department.

VAN: I'd keep him in the portfolio section.

GEORGE: He doesn't want to go in the research department.

VAN: I think our greatest weakness in the trust business today is in portfolio management, not in research. We've increased the capabilities in research tremendously in the last 20 years, and we've done nothing about portfolio management.

GEORGE: The reason is that we are treating them like morons.

VAN: That's right. And the opportunity in portfolio management lies from this point forward, because research has been brought up to a terrific level. It's available to all of us in a highly sophisticated form, and we don't have to have our own research departments, necessarily, to produce it any more.

KEN: We have to believe somebody's research.

VAN: Sure. Right. But we can use it as a tool in portfolio management now.

GEORGE: As a matter of fact, it's the portfolio manager and committee who are the biggest problem.

VAN: Right.

GEORGE: Don't forget the committee, because they make most of the mistakes.

GENE: The biggest shortage, and the biggest need, is for investment decision makers.

VAN: In portfolio. We've got all the research people we need, coming out of our ears.

GENE: You can build up your ability to make investment decisions by practice, by being given the responsibility. I think people can grow in account management, and they can become more skilled if you give them the responsibility to make decisions.

And if you take that away from them, then I think your whole operation suffers, because the more skill you have making investment decisions, the better off your whole operation is going to be because it will spill over. Like the guy who picked Allegheny Ludlum—next time the steel analyst makes a recommendation, well, other account men are going to be listening to this man, too.

GEORGE: If you reduce your portfolio manager to the role of mechanic, the research department will do you no good.

GENE: Right.

VAN: You see this in your own shop. There are portfolio managers who do a better job with your buy lists than you do.

KEN: I also know that there are certain analysts who are believed right down the line by the portfolio managers. For example, our airline analyst is very good in my opinion, and in the opinion of the portfolio managers.

GEORGE: He has been right?

KEN: I'm talking about choice among airlines, now, not the industry. If he says buy American Airlines, nobody looks in the paper to see whether TWA is a better buy.

VAN: I wouldn't look in the papers, either. I agree with you there. But, another account manager hears that story from the analyst on the airlines, and he says, "I just don't want only a little American Airlines; I want 10 percent of my account in airlines." And that's why he does better.

GREG: I think we've lost sight of the fact that the portfolio manager is compelled to weigh some of the account factors which may prevent him from having the greater performance rate that will occur for some other portfolio managers who have accounts where fast performance is what they're after. But, here, this portfolio manager you were talking about, because he was after a different type of performance in these accounts that had different objectives, either because of age or whatever, went for other issues—maybe excluding an entire industry from the portfolio.

GEORGE: That's an account problem.

GREG: To measure them from the standpoint of performance in securities selection is a very difficult thing, because they may be influenced, and properly so, by the account factors involved.

GENE: It may be difficult, but it's got to be done. I think under some of the systems we were talking about I don't see how you can measure the account man, because he really hasn't had very much to do with the stocks that are in a particular account.

GEORGE: Yes he has. Once he inherits the account, it's all cash, subject to the tax considerations and commissions we were talking about earlier. That's an overriding factor. Except for that, it's all cash. His account starts out fresh every day. He can sell everything and start from scratch.

GENE: Except that if he doesn't have too much to do with the decision-making system——

GEORGE: But that's the point I'm getting at. He should have. He should have. But from the buy list, that has already been determined by the analysts or the committee.

VAN: You know, all these things we've been talking about—the drive for performance, the turnover—that didn't all come out of research. That came out of portfolio management. The things that we are suggesting here today as good practices are portfolio considerations and not research considerations.

GEORGE: Research *selections* are very important. It's selection to have made the switches. You have to have the right horse or you don't win the race.

VAN: But the opportunities lie in taking advantage of the switches.

GUY: You can't win in the race unless your horse is entered.

VAN: We've had those buy-and-sell recommendations for ever and ever. Research has been supplying those buy-and-sell recommendations for 20 years, but nobody has done anything about it. We haven't had the *application* of what research said to the account!

KEN: Wouldn't believe them.

VAN: Oh, they were believed. There's just been a reluctance to make changes for fear of legal consequences—of accusations of trading the account—fear of somebody's comparing what we bought with what we sold. And laziness! But that shows you what you can do if you really want to move—if you have confidence in your research, and if your research is really good.

NORM: I have a question or two. This question of how you keep the number of securities down. I take it, Keith, that in addition to a buy list you have some kind of a list that lets the department know what your opinion is about the securities you are not buying. Is that correct?

KEITH: That's right.

NORM: How large a list is this—and how do you keep it under control?

KEITH: 171 names.

NORM: On the guidance list?

KEITH: Yes. It gradually grew, unfortunately.

NORM: You take some off.

KEITH: That's right.

GENE: I don't think that is a serious problem.

VIC: We talked about that earlier in the sense that there are about 200 major companies, and most of us feel that this is what we ought to restrict ourselves to, and that's our backyard. We ought to know that backyard real well. If you want to wander off the reservation, why, you can do it occasionally. But most of your efforts should be in the things that you are going to have in the bulk of your accounts.

GEORGE: We follow reasonably well 500 issues and remarkably well 350 issues; and by remarkably well I mean at least four field trips a year, and the other 150 at least once a year. With all the research we have done, we still have responsibility for over 2,000 items we can't get off the list—Widow Jones or Grandmother Sue who insists that this is a great company and her great grandfather owned it. It's got to stay in her trust.

GLENN: How many names on your buy list?

GEORGE: Buy list? The buy list is never more than 50 items.

GREG: For what it's worth, our current buy list as of April 24, 1967, is 42 issues.

GLENN: On the buy list?

NORM: How many are utilities?

GREG: Utilities are——

KEN: You can pass it around during coffee break. (*laughter*)

GEORGE: Of the 50 items on the buy list, 30 are industrials, but of all of them no more than a dozen are heavily favored at any one time. We need at least 12.

From the above discussion, it is easy to see why a variety of internal structures, policies, controls, and practical tools are used within different trust departments. The variations are not necessarily bad. Each trustee has to adjust its mechanical tools to fit the people who are available, regardless of what an ideal trust department **should** look like, or what a textbook on business organization propounds as being correct. The important thing is that the job must be done, that decisions must be made, that controls and communication must feed the correct information to the right people. The actual setup in any given trust department represents a combination of historical development and the strengths and weaknesses of the available personnel. The implementation system must make up for weak personnel in various areas and levels of responsibility.

The method of implementation of policy decisions is influenced heavily by the size of the organization. A close-knit group, sitting in a single room in a small trust department, has little difficulty in communicating, implementing decisions, and having a feedback of information to tell the top man whether or not the job has been done as directed.

The problems are more complex when the size of the organization is large, or when it is scattered over a substantial geographic area because of a branch system. In these cases, more formality, more rigid mechanical controls, more written communication is necessary in order to do an effective job.

An obvious influence on the internal system needed by a trust department is the type of accounts it handles. A trust department that specializes primarily in handling estates will inherit a huge number of stocks of small- to medium-size companies, plus many unsatisfactory stocks of large companies. The trust department has responsibility for these securities, and they must be reviewed at least once a year. It is not unusual for a trust department to have holdings of 1,000 to 2,000 common stocks, many local and inactively traded issues. A good deal of effort must be devoted to constantly weeding out the undesirable holdings among these smaller companies, replacing them with larger and more desirable names from the current purchase list. (The process is somewhat frustrating, since every time one clears out that last holding of a slightly undesirable local stock, it shows up again in the next estate.) The problem seems to be that a $1 billion trust department generally has about as many names to cover as a $10 billion trust department.

Another factor is the average size of the accounts. A billion-dollar trust department with 100 accounts would be structured quite differently from one with 5,000 accounts. Such a disparity in the number of accounts for a given size of trust department as represented by the seminarians undoubtedly influenced their views on the best ways to administer accounts.

CHAPTER FIVE

Portfolio
management

Although many other chapters have needed bridging paragraphs, this section on portfolio management flowed smoothly from one topic to the next without too many excursions into side topics not particularly related to the subject. Several questions required additional information, which has been inserted in the appropriate places to preserve the flow of ideas.

The discussion ranged over many subjects, including diversification, risk considerations, bond management, and tax considerations.

On the subject of objectives, no one advocated stating objectives of an account in specific terms because of the danger that for some particular time period they might not be realized. However, all the seminarians seemed to be well aware of what might be achieved in the market. They favored performance and meeting the account's objectives, rather than the safety of doing a mere routine job.

On the fixed/equity ratio topic, two interesting points were raised. The first covered a concept of a reserve: i.e., should market judgments on security prices be made, and stocks sold, and the proceeds held in short-term investments awaiting more favorable market opportunities? Although there was some question whether this procedure could be construed as permanent investment of funds, which may be looked on as speculation on stock price movements, general agreement was reached that if investment judgment required such action it should be done. The second point, which stirred spirited debate, was whether bonds should be used at all in many accounts. One seminarian advocated substituting utility stocks for bonds in accounts expected to be in existence for many years. This idea brought up questions of both legality and investment prudence. Nevertheless, the group endorsed higher equity ratios than might be expected by traditional trust thinking.

On the subjects of risk and diversification, the question of number of names in an account was well covered, with little support for use of many names and a broad representation in all industry areas at all times. Concentration and selectivity were much more in style.

The section on bonds was particularly interesting. Bond management was staunchly advocated, and an extensive discussion of management procedures, especially tax-exempts and the use of ratings, should provide many helpful hints to other portfolio managers. The discussion ranged over spacing of maturities, downgrading quality, playing yield-spreads, and developing strategy on use of convertibles. Estate taxes must be considered, and a by-way is explored when the subject of policy with respect to a liquidating trust is raised. The twin questions of quality and ratings is joined with observations on the appropriateness of local nonrated issues. For the most part, bond ratings get a better reception than did ratings on common stocks. At the same time, bond **trading** involves ticklish legal questions with respect to possible loss of remainderman's claims to principal.

Finally, tax considerations were reviewed, and suggestions were made to overcome the often encountered situation, "We have a profit, so we can't sell."

VIC: We are now turning to the broad area of portfolio considerations. The first group of thoughts is on statement of objectives. Should objectives be stated in general terms or in specific terms? Let me ask it another way—does anyone state objectives in specific terms?

KEN: No.

GENE: No.

NICK: Vic, I think your main idea is that any account basically falls into one of three categories. This approach is interesting.

VIC: Yes. We state our account objectives in three categories. One is the conservative, income-oriented account—the widow and orphans type; the second type of account is the businessman's risk, where we are seeking both moderate income and moderate appreciation; and the third is the performance-oriented account. Most accounts fall into one of those three categories. But we don't attempt to take each account as it comes along and say this account is going to try to achieve a 10 percent return, or an 8 percent return, or some minimum return, nor do we try to say that in this account in any given year we can afford to have the value drop by 15 percent or 20 percent. We don't try to be specific. Does anybody do that? Or do we all do it pretty much in general terms?

KEITH: If a beneficiary learned of these specific targets, we would be digging our own graves if we mentioned specific figures in trust accounts.

KEN: I would quarrel with your three classifications. I think you have a growth-oriented account, and I think you have the business-man's account. He thinks he wants both income and growth, but what he really wants is growth. The third category, the widow, has to have income, but she wants growth too. (*laughter*)

GENE: Not only wants growth, but she should have it.

VIC: The modification you are making, Ken, is what I am talking about. How do *we* look at it? You are talking about how the customer looks at it. (*laughter*)

KEN: Well, he is paying the fee.

VIC: This raises an interesting side issue here. When you set the objectives of an account, do you set them by what you think the cus-tomer needs or by what he says he wants?

GEORGE: You should tell him what he should do. (*general agree-ment*)

GIL: Apparently, there is a great measure of consensus on this.

VIC: Let's take it to the next point—the fixed-income/equity ratio —and see how much of a consensus we get here. How high an equity ratio do you set in accounts? Not more than 65 percent in equities for widows and orphans, and in a businessman's risk account 80 percent, and in a performance account 90 percent?

GUY: I'd be willing to go 100 percent in performance accounts.

KEN: Why aren't utility common stocks just as good as bonds? Why don't you go 65 percent in industrial companies and put the other 35 percent in utilities? I'm just trying to be the devil's advocate.

GEORGE: Utilities are almost as bad as industrials.

KEN: I'm talking about safety. The reason you buy bonds is for income. A survey over the 25-year life of a bond would show that the utility stock would do a lot better than the bond.

GEORGE: Except for short periods.

KEN: Yes, but I said over the life of the bond. If you are going to buy lone corporates—I'm not arguing about short-term fixed-income securities—but the idea of buying a long-term corporate bond——

GEORGE: I think you have to look at it carefully. In a year like last year you would be awfully hard put to say you shouldn't buy govern-ment bonds, or even today.

GENE: We have certainly proved that if you come to a situation where you had to liquidate those bonds, it can be just as disastrous, or more disastrous, than stocks. I mean last summer, 1966.

GEORGE: Well, that's right, but that was an unusual period. I think you'd get 5¼ to 5½ or better yields in very high-quality bonds.

VIC: Let's assume investment logic is on your side, Ken. Would you use those utilities as a trustee? Would it be a prudent thing to do?

KEN: The only reason it wouldn't is because it has never been done.

VIC: That's my point.

KEN: We do it for ourselves, individually, around this table. As trustees, we might wait until somebody else breaks the path.

GEORGE: I think you would have an awful time in court, proving you're prudent. I don't see any reason why you couldn't do as well for a widow and orphan, remarkably well, being two thirds exposed in good-quality common stocks and the rest in bonds. I think with proper selection you could do as well as many or most do with 80 and 90 percent in stocks.

GENE: That's right.

KEN: I made a study to try to disprove that point, because I was hoping to say that not only the individual issues you own are important but also how much you own in the way of stocks is important. I took the ——— Fund [a high-performance mutual fund] as against the Dow Jones Average. A combination of 53 percent in ——— Fund and 47 percent in bonds over the last 10 years would have done as well as 100 percent in the Dow. That remarkable ——— Fund has shown selectivity.

GUY: Isn't it true that they are buying stocks we wouldn't ordinarily buy in trusts?

GENE: You were saying that if you equated a portfolio of the Dow Jones Average with one of the ——— Fund and bonds you could go down to almost a 50–50 mix before your performance would equal the Dow.

KEN: Yes. I was investing 50 percent in the ——— Fund and 50 percent in S & P high grade bonds, as against 100 percent in the Dow Jones Industrials.

VIC: Well, I gather then that this, too, is a departure. Certainly, if you look at some of the statistics the average common stockholding of trust departments is nothing like 65 percent; yet, we talk around here as if 65 percent would be acceptable in the most conservative account, and we might go up to 100 percent.

NED: I think the statistics we get are all wet, though. They include accounts restricted to legals, escrow accounts, construction funds, the state highway department, and so on. If you looked at the total assets in our trust department, you'd think we loved bonds. But if you looked at personal trusts only, excluding accounts restricted to legal investments, we are probably 75 percent to 80 percent equities.

VIC: I would still make the point, Ned, that to get a group of trust investment men to agree, as we apparently do, that you would go as high as 65 percent in equities in your most conservative account is something of a departure from what I thought was traditional trust thinking.

KEN: The percentage has grown with the market.

VIC: Yes, it has grown tremendously, and this is the change.

KEN: I would like to take a poll of all of our customers who own corporate bonds, not municipals, and ask them why they think we own long corporate bonds in their account. I would be interested in the answers we get back.

VIC: They'd probably tell you, "Because you put them there."

KEN: Yes. Because we thought they were safe. Or because it's customary.

VIC: What are the reasons we use bonds?

KEN: Well, I don't know, myself. (*laughter*)

GEORGE: We're all raising our stockholdings.

VAN: I hope we keep raising the percentages.

VIC: Ken, would you argue, essentially because of a conviction that cyclical fluctuations will be moderate, and because the long-term trend of prices, the general price level, and the stock price level is upward, that over a longer period of time you should really be 100 percent in commons?

KEN: This would have been desirable over most periods of stock market history.

GREG: Well, then, the rest of the time you should have been in bonds.

KEN: For purposes of reserves, or illness, or an elderly person, or death taxes, but not from an investment viewpoint. I can't think of anything worse than a 30-year straight corporate bond as an investment in the atmosphere that we have in this country—and not just since the war.

GENE: Well, yes, for longer than that.

GEORGE: Can you say that, considering the high yields in the past six months?

KEITH: If you have no power of invasion in the trust and you require a certain income, and the income on bonds is twice what it is on stocks——

KEN: Then you have to do it, but I'm talking about an overall return standpoint—your investment standpoint. I don't think 6 percent tied up for 30 years is attractive compared with Xerox.

GEORGE: A certain fixed minimum income is very attractive.

KEN: Oh, but 3 percent inflation a year cuts you down to 3 percent net in today's market.

GEORGE: And at this particular level of the market, it could be very safe for several years.

NED: You might have a very nice capital gain two years from now.

GARY: The studies of the securities markets at the University of Chicago show that over their complete period, taking every stock on the stock exchange, the average return on common stocks was the equivalent of 9 percent, at random. That includes compounding dividends.

GEORGE: What was the return for the first 15 years? On the first 10 years?

KEN: Why don't you just put 5 percent of your money in Xerox and 95 percent in corporate bonds? You'll look terrific against the averages.

GEORGE: That we think in terms of a less cyclical economy is good and probably valid. But you know, we have gone through 20 some odd years of rising stock prices in this country, and rising dividends every year, and yet one of the most sober lessons I have ever learned was that of 1937–38, when earnings dropped 50 percent and dividends 54 percent. We could be wrong on the economy.

Nothing is more sobering to a customer than to have General Motors dividend go down from $4 to $1.

KEN: But you got the General Motors in your 60 percent of aggressive stocks. The most successful profit sharing trust I ever worked on was a fund that was about 60 percent on average; they used to swing a lot so they would vary it. But say 60 percent in aggressive common stocks and 40 percent in A.T.&T.-type passive stocks. That was their bond account—no income worries right through the depression.

GEORGE: That's true, and that's all right for a pension fund. For an individual, even though we may and do appropriately reduce stocks if they are too large, we don't know what is going to happen. These people scare very easily. And I think to have a defensive position by using the type of bonds you're able to get today is a very good position. They make sense for reasonable preservation of capital.

VAN: The record on common stocks is so conclusive going back to 1900, measuring every period of time you want to——

GEORGE: You take any 10 year cycle from 1926 to 1940, and you look sick in common stocks.

VAN: But you are buying a 30-year bond or a 20-year bond, and if you have an account you are investing in for 20 years, then I agree with Ken, you should have every cent in common stocks.

GEORGE: The rates you are now getting in high grade bonds due in 20 years you haven't been able to get in 45 years.

KEN: You should have had these rates the whole time, because any lesser rate would have been a real gyp, with what bonds have done for you—that is, loss of purchasing power.

GUY: Going back to the question of decreased cyclicality, do you think this will be true of corporate earnings as well as corporate sales because of more rigid labor and other costs?

GEORGE: No.

GUY: This is what worries me.

NED: Here's another point, and this is the stability of dividends. We have had such a beautiful trend in dividends over the last couple of decades that we have blind faith in them. You look at corporate liquidity as it stands today. There's practically no cash on the balance sheet, and what's there is not free cash; it's compensating balances for lines of credit, so it isn't available to start with. And you wonder a little bit about downturn in earnings and what it might do to dividends. It might do a great deal more to dividends than to earnings.

GARY: I think that what is in favor of Ken's position is the demand and supply figures on common stocks. Take a look at the amount of new common stocks coming to market each year. As I recall, in the last few years it ran a little bit less than $2 billion. You take a look at the SEC data on the net purchases of common stock. Pension fund purchases alone, purchases minus sales, are greater than the amount of new common stock in the market. Then you take a look at what your endowments are doing, what your trustees are doing, what mutual funds are doing, and they are increasing the percentage in common stocks in their accounts.

VIC: And you find that individuals have been selling them on balance since 1957.

The recorded part of the seminar did not pursue this very interesting question of supply of new common stocks coming to the market and the demand of institutional investors for an increasing share of the available stocks. During one of the evening sessions, this point was discussed in greater detail, and perhaps in a more realistic light.

The first point expressed was that the apparent shortage of stocks may be more a state of mind than an actuality. This subjective point of view reveals itself if the reader will assume that he believes common stocks are dirt cheap at today's prices. If this is his assumption, he must believe that the supply of stocks is substantially in excess of the demand, and therefore that there is a **shortage of buyers** rather than a shortage in the supply of stocks available.

Similarly, the assumption that stocks are overpriced reflects a point of view that stocks are in short supply and that the excessive number of buyers has resulted in demand far in excess of supply.

A second, and perhaps more fundamental point of view, is that the net new offering of stocks does not represent the true addition to the supply of available stocks. The plowback of earnings by corporations creates additional values, because presumably the retained earnings will be reinvested and provide additional profits, which will justify higher market prices for the stocks. If American corporations had decided, say, in 1966 to pay out all their earnings as dividends, and to sell an amount of common stock equal to the $27 billion they actually retained, the total net issue of corporate stocks would have been $29 billion instead of $2 billion. When this $29 billion is related to the net demands for common stocks by institutional investors, the supply–demand equation comes a great deal closer to being in balance. As far as the corporate balance sheet is concerned, there is no difference between the **earning assets** that would result from retention of $27 billion in undistributed profits, or from the combination of paying out an extra $27 billion in dividends, and simultaneously selling $27 billion in additional stocks.

Another way of looking at this same question is to view the supply of common stocks as being some fundamental multiple of earnings. Since earnings should rise at perhaps 5 percent a year, the effective supply of stock is also rising at 5 percent a year. A 5 percent increase of earnings of $48 billion is a $2.4 billion increase. If these earnings are worth a multiple of 15 times, the supply of stocks has increased by $36 billion, a figure that is also somewhat comparable to the net investment of institutions in common stocks.

There was also some debate on the validity of statistics, indicating that the individual is a net seller of common stocks. The following points were made.

If a man had invested $100,000 in common stocks some years ago, and market prices had risen to a point where his holdings were worth $200,000, the sale of $10,000 of his common stockholdings still left him with an increased position $90,000 above his original $100,000 investment.

Another point was that some of the statistics had been derived from round-lot sales, but without any adjustment for odd-lot purchases. Many odd-lot purchases are of stocks that are subsequently split and sold as round lots. A third point about the individual as a common stock owner is that the sale of common stock and subsequent purchase of a mutual fund merely transfers the decision making from an amateur to the professional, but does not take the individual investor out of the stock market at all.

While the above points were not a part of the formal seminar, they do reflect on one facet of the topic under discussion, that is, the apparently persistent upward trend in common stock prices during the postwar years.

GUY: I am sure that most of us have read Sidney Homer's recent speech. The gist of it is that the price of stocks overall is going to be set at that point which will persuade individuals to sell to institutions a diminishing supply of stocks at a constantly higher price.

VIC: Let me ask a question. Would that 65 percent or whatever percentage you have as your equity percentage—would you get there and stay there, or would you have some discount from that under certain conditions, and if so what would they be?

GEORGE: Shouldn't that vary with the account objectives?

VIC: No, George, I'm not talking about varying the maximum equity position as account objectives change. Let's say that in your widow and orphans account you would go up to 65 percent. Would you be at 65 percent all the time for the next five years, or at some time would you be 55 percent and the other 10 percent would be some kind of reserve——

GEORGE: If she's going to be, say, 65 or 70 years old in 5 years, and she has certain health problems, I think I would go down to 50 percent.

GUY: I agree with you.

VIC: That's a change in account objectives. I'm talking about investment policy considerations for conservative accounts, assuming no change in the account objectives.

GLENN: Are you asking whether we would change percentages in different, varying market environments?

VIC: Yes. Would you drop from 65 percent to 55 percent or 50 percent?

GENE: What if you were 65 percent in stocks in October, 1966? Would you have been scaling down all the way through January, February, and March, taking profits all the way through to keep it at this maximum 65 percent, or would you say: "The market is pretty strong. There's a lot of buying in stocks. We will just let this go until we think the market gets too high, and then we might cut back to 50 percent——"

GUY: We cut back in our accounts below $50,000 in the summer and fall last year partly because the bond market was going down. It was important in accounts at that time.

KEN: It's important to decide whether you are cutting back to reinvest permanently in bonds or whether you are taking a reserve out of the market that you hope to put back in the market.

VIC: If you do that, aren't you speculating? Isn't this against trust law? (*laughter*) This is a critical point. You are making a short-term market judgment if you use the reserve concept.

GENE: You are not really, because you are faced with stocks that you think are overpriced, so you sell those stocks. And you then say, "Am I going to reinvest in other stocks now? Well, maybe not."

VIC: You are making a market judgment.

KEN: Can't you make market judgments?

GEORGE: You are making an investment judgment.

KEN: What you said is ridiculous.

VIC: The point I am making here is, as I understand it, there's a court case that says you are not supposed to do this.

GEORGE: What is this court case?

NED: *Wells Fargo* v. *Talbot.*[1]

GLENN: Let's not get confused on that particular case. That's not the situation.

NED: Well, that question was argued.

GLENN: In that case, there were three brothers, and two of them approved a cutback in common stocks; in fact, one of them had instigated it contrary to the policy of the Wells Fargo Bank at that time. The third brother never answered the letter approving the cutback. With a kind of hindsight later on, the court said, "Look, you did something contrary to your policy and, therefore, you are going to have to make good." I don't think we should conclude that the court said they should not make market judgments. If Wells Fargo had made the same market judgment with all accounts, or with a group of accounts at that time, then this would have been a prudent thing to do in their eyes and would have been accepted by the court.

NED: Yes, but the judge did rule that to sell stocks for the purpose of buying stocks back at a lower price later on was a speculative act.

---

[1] *Wells Fargo* v. *Talbot,* 141 Cal. App. 2nd 309; 296 P2d 848 (1956).

GLENN: Quite possibly the attorney for this particular brother may have raised this point, but it is my understanding that the court hung its decision primarily on the fact that Wells Fargo did something that was contrary to its own judgment.

VIC: I don't say this disapprovingly. I agree that this is exercising investment judgment, and this is what we are supposed to do, even though it might be misinterpreted as some form of speculation, which a trustee shouldn't do. I think it's important——

KEN: But it's all right to sell long—how do you ever get money back in the market? You don't. You ride the ratio up to 80 percent, cut back to 50 percent; when the market takes you to 80 percent, cut back to 50 percent, and so forth. This is the history of the trust business, and this is why we have people come in who look back 10 years and say, "You sold out that IBM and put it into corporate bonds, and you never bought the IBM back." You are constantly cutting, aren't you? It's the only thing you can do. You never build up stocks.

VIC: Ken, we said we wouldn't do this. We would permit stocks——

VAN: If your economic policy is one that raises questions on the economy and you have stock prices at 25 times earnings, I think you are under every obligation to sell stocks.

KEN: Then, how do you get the money back in stocks?

VAN: Follow your economic policy, and you will buy them back. You buy them back with the bond money.

KEN: It's not all right to sell short-term bonds. You've got to buy 30-year bonds and take that risk. If I buy short bonds, I am hoping to put that money back in the market at some time. That's all right to do?

VIC: Yes.

KEN: That's not a reserve to buy stock?

GLENN: Yes, it is.

KEN: But I thought that was wrong.

VIC: Ken, let me explain my point. On the investment viewpoint you are correct. The only point I am making——

KEN: If I'm going to get sued, I don't want to do it.

VIC: That's the point. The thing I am trying to point out here is the difference between what I think is prudent investment judgment where I would agree with your position, and what is not approved by legal precedent.

KEN: That's the only way you can vary your percentages.

GLENN: Vic, you used the language "market judgment," which

may have thrown us off a little bit. I think if you had said, "Should we use judgment on the economy or judgment on the values of stocks we might buy——"

VIC: OK.

GLENN: Then I think we have agreement——

VIC: What you are telling me, then, is that I can do it; I just have to be careful how I phrase what I did.

GLENN: A trust investment man should make some judgments on the economy, and they should be reflected in the stockholdings of accounts.

VIC: Of course.

GLENN: But you think it might be illegal to do that?

VIC: I am raising that question. I would try to find some way to make it legal, because it makes investment sense.

GLENN: We should have minutes here and make it legal. (*laughter*)

GEORGE: This comes under our definition of investment judgment.

NICK: Would you clarify for me the difference between speculation as we attempted to define it earlier and what we are talking about right now? What's the difference?

GEORGE: Investment judgment is investment value. Your judgment is that equity prices are high in terms of earnings and dividend prospects as you see it. That's judgment——

VAN: Based on thorough analysis.

NICK: What's the difference? How have we defined speculation?

KEN: That we didn't have the knowledge to take the action that we took.

GUY: Aren't you, in effect, reducing—at least when you are selling stocks—reducing the stock market risk in that period? You recognize that you still have a long-term problem, and in order to take advantage of the long-term depreciation of the dollar and the growth of earnings and so on—they indicate common stock investment. It is desirable to be in a position to do so at the minimum interim risk to the account.

VAL: I agree with you, Ken, that if you think prices are high under the conditions you laid out, and if you don't acquire a little reserve, you don't have any money to buy when you want to buy. This is my argument. What I get thrown at me is, "Well, you always have something you don't like in an account that you can sell to buy the stock you like when the time comes." This is the argument I find very hard to answer.

KEN: Let me say that also from a practical standpoint—and I've found this to be true time after time—you get an awful lot of credit with your customer for having made a slight move at the right time. You've got a $1 million account and you sell 100 shares of General Motors; everything else goes bang! Down! You hold everything else. And he'll say, "I remember when you sold stocks." (*laughter*) So they make you put that $10,000 back in at the bottom. Your timing last year was perfect! You may have carried the rest of the account down and back up again.

GENE: Let's call it a strategic reserve, which might be a very logical thing for an account man to have in his account, some cash to take advantage of an opportunity as it comes along. Is that making a market judgment? The kind of thing that you said was proscribed?

GLENN: You are certainly not under any obligation to ride them up and ride them down again. If you don't set up a cash reserve, aren't you going to do just that?

VIC: But if you have the cash reserve, are you "permanently investing funds"? (*laughter*)

KEN: Another case. As the market keeps going up, the effect of your reserve is smaller and smaller. The account is so happy because the rest of the account is going up; the drag of reserve isn't bad at all. The market is going down, you are delighted to have it to use. You can almost make a case for always having some reserve.

VIC: All I am saying is that for years I felt the same way you do until I got into the trust business and found out that this was frowned on, and it has upset me more than any other single thing that's happened.

KEN: It's frowned upon because it takes a lot of work. When you've got a lot of reserves, you've got a lot of extra work to do.

NED: Is everyone agreed that the best way to invest money is to make shifts when your judgment tells you to?

GLENN: This is the prudent thing to do.

GEORGE: I think there is one point I might bring out here, because it's fairly interesting. In order to prove the validity of raising reserves —we face this problem very seriously—I had a member of the staff take the 50 major industries we had investments in and measure the cyclical performance in the periods from 1953 to 1957, 1957 to 1962, and 1962 to 1966. As an illustration, the aerospace stocks were number 1 in the first cycle, and in the next cycle number 50. From 1 to 50. First to last. And the next cycle it was up to 4. Business machines, office equipment, were among the first 10 in the first 2 cycles; in the last cycle, until recently, they are about midpoint. As a matter of fact, it was amazing to see how these groups differed from the midpoint in each one of these cycles. The international oils, for example, were 13 in the first cycle; the very next cycle number 47. You just show this to people and it's amazing. You believe in switching and you hope to sell this idea. We showed this to our customers, and three came back and said, "You are not doing enough switching. We had no idea this took place." I think it's a very easy point to prove. I don't think you'd have any trouble with that at all.

GIL: The only unsatisfactory thing about this, from my point of view, is that apparently this issue is really a dispute over a matter of fact which crept in here and is still not resolved as far as I can see.

GENE: We are all clear as to the best way to proceed.

GIL: The basic element here is in terms of what the legal constraint is with respect to the reserve element. That has not, it seems to me, been clarified one way or another.

NED: We were discussing a case—*Wells Fargo* v. *Talbot*—which involved a trustee who at the request of a beneficiary reduced the percentage in common stocks from 78 percent to 22 percent of the account. The beneficiary had argued that the market was too high, and that the trustee could reinvest in common stocks later on at a lower price. The trustee acquiesced to the beneficiary, although it was not making a cutback in other trust accounts at that time. In the case, which I now have in front of me, on page 665, the trial judge, the Honorable Raymond Scott, is quoted as saying, "In our opinion the decision to buy such an unbalanced amount of municipals, in the hope that in the future they could be sold and the proceeds of the sales, or the proceeds of redemption, could be used to buy back the common stock sold was contrary to the requirement of permanency, as set forth in said section, and constitutes speculation which is frowned upon by said section." Thus, the bank lost its case because (1) it had not exercised its independent judgment in making the sale; (2) the transaction was speculative; (3) the transaction was imprudent. This is not an ideal case to point up the attitude of courts toward trustees who are changing the percentages invested in stocks and bonds, simply because a larger question was whether or not the trustee had exercised independent judgment. However, this case is one in which such a change is clearly ruled as *speculative*.

I certainly want to say that I disagree vigorously with anyone who says that changing the percentages of fixed income securities and equities of an account, with the expectation of changing them again later on, is necessarily speculative. It is unfortunate that the law is based on precedent, and this, and other similar cases, can be used in the future to inhibit the use of investment judgment in the continuous management of funds.

I'm afraid that this particular judge, in his desire to punish a bank for not using its discretion, may inhibit all future banks in the use of their best investment judgment as to the proper equity/fixed-income ratio for an account.

VAL: Ken, the answer to your question is—the published record. The written record of your bank should never show that you sold to raise a reserve. This is your answer. You never say that it was for that purpose.

KEN: Of course not. Besides those two-year governments look very attractive. (*laughter*)

GIL: All right, Vic, go ahead—why don't we move along?

VIC: Well, the next general area is this matter of diversification. Earlier we talked about broad and narrow selections. The considerations here were should you change your diversification pattern in industries from time to time, and should you attempt to cover more than one possible outcome in the economy or the market, or should you concentrate on what you think is the most probable? Do you try to hedge in your diversification? Or do you concentrate just as you concentrate in the number of securities you buy?

GENE: I think you would analyze securities by relative industry analysis; that you pick stocks, and then see what your industry diversification is after you have made the stock selection; that you don't ever motivate a stock selection on the basis of heavy representation in this industry or that industry. You only do it if you feel that ——

VIC: Gene, you are arguing that you get your diversification pattern on the basis of your company stock analysis, that is, from the ground up. We can do it that way, but I say that in addition to that we can do it another way by coming down from your economic analysis and attempting to determine those attractive areas of the economy under your economic assumptions.

KEN: I think Gene's point is that we shouldn't say we've got to have 7 percent in chemicals as a minimum—and 12 percent as a maximum —so if we don't like chemicals we will put only 7 percent of the money in chemicals. A lot of people used to do that.

VIC: I know, but I gather that nobody would defend that here. How about the problem of account size?

VAN: The bigger, the better; the bigger, the better. (*laughter*)

VIC: Some of us are not so fortunate. We have little ones. (*laughter*) My general observation has been that the smaller accounts have a tendency to be more concentrated than large accounts.

GENE: Right. You mean fewer names.

VIC: Fewer names and larger percentages in industries and companies.

GLENN: Different holdings, perhaps.

NICK: In fact, the comptroller's manual specifically allows it. It says that accounts under $50,000 might have greater concentration than accounts over $50,000.

NED: They should all be in the common trust fund.

GUY: Sure hope so!

NED: The answer is the common trust fund, but if you can't get in it for one reason or another, then I think you typically buy maybe four stocks that are highly diversified companies. You don't get very good results, as a rule.

NICK: But isn't this illogical?

NED: It's inconsistent, yes. It's illogical.

NICK: We all agree that it is logically inconsistent.

NED: To do what?

NICK: To buy fewer stocks in a smaller account.

NED: And stocks that you don't want, at that!

GIL: Well, what you're saying is you can't do anything about it. Right?

NED: No, I say we are wedded too much to the ideal that we've got to buy either 50 or 100 shares in a small account. And why can't we buy 12 or 15 stocks when we can go to the third market and buy for an eighth of a point commission, and get it cheaper than we could buy a round lot on the New York Stock Exchange? I don't know.

VAN: Because you have to collect the dividends, you have record-keeping.

NED: That's not a good investment reason, but that's a good reason not to take the account.

VIC: That's right.

KEN: And that's why we have common trust funds, too.

NED: A common trust fund is the obvious answer if you can get into it.

GENE: I'd like to make a little bit of a case for not carrying this trend toward fewer names too far. I think you ought to say we are going to pick out the top 10 percent, say, of 500 stocks. I think you ought to give yourself enough chances to be right. You ought to own the stocks you think rate at the top. You ought not try to discriminate to the point where you are picking out the 5 out of 50 that do relatively poorly. You should own 40 or 50 stocks in a good-size account.

NICK: Well, here is one of those things again, where you let it evolve. If you have a market that's highly selective, you may come up with 25 names.

GENE: We are following 500 to 600 companies, and I think we ought to say we are going to own the best 10 percent of the companies we're following. Those will change, but it will always be the top 10 percent.

KEN: If you let it evolve, you will have an awful lot of stocks in your account—your biggest account, because your account manager knows that all of a sudden you like the ABC Company and he says, "I'll have a little of that," and he will have 50 names in there before you can bat your eye, I think.

GENE: This is the best reason that I can think of for limiting the number of names he has to decide on.

NICK: I'm not talking about that side of it. I'm talking about the side of how few names you have.

GENE: That shouldn't go too far——

KEN: I disagree. I'm saying that if you let it run where it will you will have an awful lot of names.

GENE: No, I mean you should say how many stocks should be in the account, but don't say 10 stocks. I think you ought to be in the 40 to 60 range.

GEORGE: In how big an account?

GENE: In a good-size account.

GEORGE: What's a good-size account?

KEN: $5 to $10 million.

GEORGE: Oh, yes. I think that is true. You have to.

GUY: I think 30 names would be the outside, probably in an account of that size.

GENE: Top side or bottom side?

GUY: Top side.

GENE: We try to say this. Assume you feel you have a certain success ratio, let's say, in making decisions. It's good enough so that you feel you are more than earning your keep. You ought to give yourself a fair shake at having that same success ratio year after year. It's like taking a great ball player, Willie Mays or somebody who bats .350 every year. If you send him up to bat twice in the course of a year, the chances are that he might bat zero that year. You have got to give him enough times at bat, and if you do he will come close to his proven ability.

VIC: We have covered the diversification area; concentration in individual issues we have discussed. On this general concept of security valuation, the first couple of points are statements rather than controversial issues. I don't imagine there will be any disagreement here. You will be looking at what you've got as well as what you add. The securities combined in a portfolio are different, particularly with respect to risk in an individual security. Turning to the risk-return measurement, I think we defined what return is, and I doubt that there will be much difficulty, so that I think we might get into some sort of discussion on risk in a portfolio. What is it, and how can you measure it? Can you quantify it?

GIL: For the portfolio as a whole?

VIC: Yes. Do we ever, when we are looking at a portfolio, try to figure out what is the risk exposure in it, and do we do it by the seat of the pants, or have we got some measure of it?

GLENN: To a degree, we try to do this. We may say to ourselves if we are going to be venturesome and acquire some borderline stocks in terms of marketability or multiples we don't want to have more than 10 percent or 20 percent or some such amount of that kind of issue in an account. So to that extent we try to quantify. And that would vary with the objectives and the beneficiaries of the trust.

VIC: Do you ever try to quantify it in the sense of relatives and say this account is riskier than some other account?

GENE: I don't see the benefit, actually. It would be good, I suppose, to make sure that you are optimizing the return or the potential, but you are dealing with such a difficult concept.

NED: Well, there are two or three things you *can* measure. And there are some fairly simple ways of measuring the volatility of a portfolio relative to some standard—Standard and Poor's 500 or whatever it might be. And the volatility of the portfolio does tell you something about the market risk in case the market is going to go down. Generally, the volatility of the portfolio is not too far from the volatility of the earnings of the individual companies held. If you took a weighted average of dollars invested in various stocks multiplied by their earnings volatility, using standard deviation, you can get a figure that's not too far from the volatility you might anticipate for the market value of the whole portfolio.

There's another little risk area that I think is interesting, and that is what some people call quality of return. Dividends are a fairly stable form of return. Interest is a highly stable form of return. Capital gains are a highly volatile form of return. So if you are getting a return of 10 percent on a portfolio, and 1 percent was dividends, and 9 percent was from capital gains or appreciation, you would have to say that the quality of that return was not especially good, that it was something that could disappear in a hurry and fluctuate widely from year to year. If it were turned around the other way, and you were getting 9 percent in dividends, interest, and rent, with 1 percent in market action, then I think you could probably say the quality of return was pretty good.

GLENN: Which account is the more speculative?

NED: I think it could be either one, but it's going to depend on a lot of things. I'm talking about income. The quality of return does have something to do with what portion of it comes from income and what portion comes from capital gains.

GENE: Even in a bond, of course, you will have some capital loss, too. If you measure the return in bonds, the bond portion has been showing no return. It has been showing a loss year after year, and yet the only return that you ever thought you would get was cash, so you'd give a pretty high rating to the amount of cash you're going to get under that concept, and yet it was rated a very unrisky investment.

GLENN: Vic, before you pass on to the next point may I ask a question? I am asking this to find out whether anybody else has the same approach or whether anybody else thinks it is of any value. We formally assign a percentage of a model account to each industry. We do this periodically, and we write it up. The oil analyst speaks up, and he says I think we ought to have 10 percent in oils, and everybody shouts him down; or maybe we let the 10 percent ride, and we wind up with 160 percent in stocks, and he loses out later on, but we try to formalize this. The account men use this, and they know they should have 15 percent in office equipment and may be zero in insurance stocks or something. Does anybody else do anything like this, or am I just talking about the same thing everybody else does anyway——

NED: We tried to set up nine target accounts, and ended up with tables of securities for each of these nine types and examples for each one. We tried to keep the examples up to date, but the system wasn't entirely satisfactory, because we often would find an account that was halfway between two of the target accounts.

Sometimes, the best thing was to get two or three portfolio managers together, looking at a problem account and imagining it was all cash with the identical investment objective. So they would make a target account for this particular account and see if it was practical to start working in that direction, depending on tax costs, losses and gains, and that sort of thing. We were making improvements each time we tried.

Now, I think this is something the portfolio managers do more and more on an informal basis, writing down names and percentages they would like to have in an account.

I think this target concept is worth thinking about.

VIC: We attempt to have our common trust fund—the equity side —as close as we possibly can to our current diversification.

GLENN: And then that becomes——

VIC: And that's the model account, if you will.

GLENN: Do you do this by approaching it from the industry standpoint? You decide that you don't want more than 6 percent in utilities, and you might want zero in another industry.

VIC: You might want zero. That's right.

VAN: We run this model account, too, but we find it a little unsatisfactory in terms of attempting to achieve performance. In other words, you are making a model account for the average account. The objectives in personal trust accounts, I think, are different from pension and profit sharing accounts.

GENE: Yes.

GLENN: So you have several model accounts.

VAN: And that begins to be a burden——

VIC: Glenn, just to clarify that, our model account, as I said, is the common trust fund. I mentioned before we have three types of accounts. The common stock side of the common trust fund is performance-oriented, and then in the smaller accounts we vary the percentages that we put in the fixed-income and in the common stock sides.

GLENN: We might have a range. We might say 6 to 10 percent in utilities, and we might say 10 to 20 percent in office equipment, and then you adapt to the aggressiveness of the account.

KEN: Why don't you do the same thing in your small individual accounts rather than buy widow- and orphan-type stocks? Why don't you buy the aggressive stocks there and vary it with the bond portion? Isn't that what's in your common fund—small accounts?

VIC: Yes.

VAN: He is talking about his common fund, which is a performance fund as far as his stocks are concerned.

KEN: This is interesting to me because most of our small accounts are in our common fund.

VIC: So are ours.

KEN: And the small accounts by and large need high income and freedom from high risk. Yet, you use the common trust fund.

GENE: And make it a performance-oriented account.

KEN: You will make it a performance-oriented account on the one hand. On the other hand, you think you should take a very conservative approach in individual investments as far as stocks are concerned.

GENE: I don't think that is consistent.

VIC: Touché.

GLENN: I don't know. Going back to this matter of setting up reserves and reducing the portion of common stocks, depending on our judgment of the economy and the attractiveness of stocks, does anybody in doing this formalize it, or does the trust investment committee prepare a memorandum in which they give the pros and cons and come up with the answer—they think there should be 10 percent below our maximums?

VIC: Yes.

GLENN: So do we. I didn't know whether anybody else——

GUY: We do it only in a very few accounts.

NICK: Let's get another question in on this before it's left. That's this problem of how do you invest your funds when you have new money in an account. You don't have 100 percent cash. You don't buy 35 stocks; you buy one, or you buy two.

VAN: You can always sell some that you have. You've got cash all the time.

GENE: You are buying stocks when you hold them. That's the way I would like to look at it.

GEORGE: That's the point I was getting at when I said the reason for not getting good performance is the fact that we don't treat accounts as cash—the bulk of the portfolio. You check where performance is bad, and invariably you find it is a great company with a great name, but it just got nowhere.

KEN: Your portfolio is always cash.

VIC: You mean you always have cash *after taxes*.

KEN: *After taxes*. That's good.

NED: All of this, I think, reminds me a little bit of what we said about turnover. We expected to have some turnover in good performing accounts, and from what we are saying here, substantially more turnover is in order to get the sort of performance we want.

GEORGE: In order to remove obstacles to portfolio managers in a situation like that, we have a designation called cash equivalent, so they can never say they don't have any spunk in an account.

VIC: I think that the next section on managing a bond portfolio really has two parts. Others may occur to you, but the basic question is: "Do you manage a bond portfolio?" The old theory used to be you bought bonds and held them to maturity; you spaced out your maturities, and that pretty well took care of the bond problem. But I have a feeling there's a growing belief that bond portfolios should be managed as aggressively as stocks, whether it's an all-bond portfolio or as a bond portion of a mixed portfolio. So the two questions I had were, one, should it be managed; two, what are the pros and cons of spreading out of maturities, or concentrating the maturities, or making other changes? How do you go about it? Is there anyone here who doesn't believe you should manage a bond portfolio?

GIL: We can record the answer as *no*.

VIC: Yes, everybody manages bonds.

NICK: But how do you manage accounts? Should you space maturities and average the yield over a period of time, which, as I understand, is the traditional approach?

GREG: I think you space the maturities in a normal pattern if you have an account that's large enough. Now if your account is not large enough to do it with, you know a $100,000 fund wouldn't go very far. I think getting the best income from the bonds would be the better policy, especially if you were in a reasonably high interest rate period——

KEITH: Along with that, Greg, if you get into a period of rapidly changing interest rates such as we had last year, it makes it possible to do a little advance refunding——

GUY: This I agree with thoroughly.

KEITH: Sell maturities coming up in '67, '68, '69, '70, and extend maturities. I don't know where you cut it off. The dollar discount on the shorter maturities is very slight, even if the yield differential is great. Then you move your maturities out at 6 percent on AA corporates——

GREG: With noncall features.

KEITH: With strong noncall features, and so on, which I think we've all been doing in the last year or so.

GUY: Well, it's also true that there are times when the spread between governments and corporates gets to be quite narrow. This gives an opportunity to shift, say, from corporates to governments at a small sacrifice of income. A plus for treasuries and agencies is that most are noncallable for a long period of time. For several years, we made new purchases entirely in Treasury bonds. Today, when we have quite a wide spread, you can reverse this switch, and we've done that to some degree.

VIC: How far down in the quality rating would you go, and, second, would you play this spread between, let's say, the AAA and BAA ratings? If that gets to be too wide, would you downgrade quality, still keeping it fairly good quality, but try to play that yield differential when the spreads are unusually wide?

GUY: Vic, I think this depends partly on quality and partly on whether you can spare people to give time to lower-quality bonds. Most of our accounts are 75 percent or more in stocks, and our feeling has been that if you have that amount of exposure you ought to make pretty sure of the quality of your bonds.

VIC: Would anybody here buy below BAA?

KEITH: Sure.

GLENN: In the convertibles, certainly, but not in straight debentures or mortgage bonds.

GENE: In personal trust accounts?

KEITH: Vic, it occurs to me that when there are reactions in the stock market and you have fairly good bond prices you may very well be moving from AA bonds, for instance, to BAA convertibles. If you bought the converts without significant premiums for the conversion privilege at a time when your equity ratio was perhaps a little below standard by reason of stock market action, this would give you a little added equity play at a time when your customers are nervous about the market, and probably not in a hurry to sell bonds and buy stocks.

GLENN: This is true for me, too. There is a growing tendency on the part of trustees, instead of buying bonds and holding them to maturity, to realize profits or losses by offsetting them with profits or losses in the stock portion of the portfolio. We now treat the whole portfolio as an investment medium rather than deal with the bonds and stocks separately. And this to me is sound portfolio management.

VIC: I suppose we should mention that some accounts have fixed obligations to be paid in the future so that you might try to get maturities around that time.

GUY: Well, other account considerations also come into bond portfolio management. If you have funds that belong to an elderly person, you know there will be a tax problem at the person's death, and you know that liquidity is a consideration. You can certainly keep this in mind in buying discount Treasuries, which can be used at par to pay estate taxes, or at least in setting up your maturity schedules so that you are not going to be left with a lot of long-term bonds when it could be very disadvantageous.

GREG: I think this is particularly true if you have low coupon issues as we have had for quite a period of years. We are now in a period of good interest rates. This minimizes the problem of timing liquidation, because you are pretty well assured of the ability to sell them later on, not only at par but even at premiums. Thus, we may obtain 8 percent or 9 percent for quality paper.

VIC: Here's a question. Suppose you have a liquidating trust that is going to be exhausted in the next two or three years. Should all that be in fixed-income securities?

GUY: Yes, I would say so. What is it being liquidated for? Just to be paid out to a beneficiary?

VIC: Well, say the instrument fixes the size of the payment—so much every month—and you are encroaching principal and are going to exhaust it in a couple of years.

GUY: Oh, a wasting trust?

GREG: Yes, you're down to $10,000 or $20,000 or some small sum.

VIC: Suppose we have several of these accounts; a couple are liquidating over a 2- or 3-year period, some are over 5 to 10 years. The question is: How much equity should you allow to remain in a trust like this? When it gets down to 2 or 3 years, should it all go into bonds; if it is a 10-year trust, what should we do?

GENE: Is this one where you've sold bonds and have stocks in the account?

VIC: Yes. Should it all be switched into fixed obligations?

GENE: And pay capital gains taxes and so forth?

VIC: Well, suppose taxes are minor.

GENE: I think we would let it go in stocks, actually.

VIC: For how long?

GENE: Well, until the payments were made.

GREG: Depending on your view of the whole economic scene, I would think you're right in your position of holding some in equities and some in bonds. At least until you come closer to the time of distribution—perhaps three years ahead of time.

KEN: Sounds like speculation to me. Sell stocks and buy bonds. (*laughter*)

GUY: If this came to us all in cash, and it was a two- or three-year distribution period, I think unquestionably we'd put it all in bonds. If it was 5 or 6 years, I think we'd put about 20–25 percent in stocks. If it came all in stocks, we might build up a one- or two-year distribution reserve in bonds, and beyond that we'd keep the stocks.

NED: Let me throw out something called the Rule of Seven. I don't know where the expression came from, but it is one that several trust men from different parts of the country have mentioned from time to time. Basically, it boils down to this. During the last 67 years, there have been only 5 years in which the portfolio manager could not have bought common stocks at the high of the year without an opportunity during the subsequent 7 years to get out at a profit. Three of these five years were 1929, 1930, and 1931. If past history is any guide, it would appear that common stocks would offer an opportunity to get out even or better within 7 years, roughly 11 times out of 12. I throw that out as a possible guide for the trust that will last substantially beyond seven years. Past history indicates that you could put money that would not be needed until the seventh year in stocks and the chances would be pretty good that you would have an opportunity somewhere along the line to sell those at a profit.

VAL: I think this is something that should be included in this record.

VIC: If we're talking about individual trusts, we're probably talking about tax-exempt bonds.

VAL: Well, you wouldn't be buying corporate bonds for an individual trust of any size at all.

GREG: Probably not.

GEORGE: Except convertibles, possibly.

GLENN: Well, now, in a depleting trust aren't we setting up reserves to take care of the beneficiary for a reasonable period of time, normally one to two years, in order to avoid the necessity of selling stocks during a sharp break in the market, under adverse circumstances?

GARY: Also, if the remaindermen are anticipating a fixed-dollar amount that they've been accustomed to in the years previous, you might justify your bonds.

VIC: Of course, in a year like last year that theory got bent a little bit.

GIL: Nick, you wanted to ask a question?

NICK: Yes, two questions. One on ratings before we leave the subject of quality. About municipals first—should you buy unrated municipals?

GLENN: Yes.

GUY: If you know the community, sure.

NICK: With respect to corporates, if you own the common stock wouldn't you be willing to own a B rated corporate bond of the same company?

GLENN: No.

GENE: No.

NICK: Why?

GENE: One of the reasons for buying bonds is to hold a relatively riskless investment as part of the blend of securities. We take our risks in the common stocks and hold reserves or produce fixed income in the bond section. The basis of judgment is the *portfolio as a whole.*

KEN: You might buy a speculative common stock that you thought would triple or quadruple if the company didn't go broke. (*laughter*)

NICK: I've always thought it rather illogical to use a stock and then not be willing to buy the senior issue.

GENE: That's not automatic as far as we're concerned. We don't want to take risks on the bond side while we're taking risks on the stock side.

GEORGE: Bonds should be relatively riskless.

GLENN: The stock side is where you get paid off.

KEN: Let's get one thing on the table right now on this personal trust thing. Many personal trusts are being established today for tax reasons. They are really agency accounts. You generally have co-trustees with them; but the investment wanted in those trusts is not a personal trust investment. The trusts are set up for other reasons.

GLENN: Ten-year trusts, for example.

KEITH: Synthetic agency accounts.

KEN: That's right.

NED: They take the form of a trust solely for tax considerations.

NICK: The other question is this: Would you play the yield curves in a bond portfolio? Would you shorten if you felt interest rates were going up? Would you lengthen the portfolio if you felt they were high?

NEIL: Definitely. You had that opportunity last year.

KEITH: Yes.

VIC: One final question on municipals: Do you find in the municipal portfolios, either in personal trusts or municipal common trust funds, that a very substantial portion usually winds up in municipals in your own state or your own region? For example, our municipal bond fund has 50 percent of its issues in our own state. The reason for that is, of course, the bond department knows our municipals better than it knows a lot of those in other parts of the country. Is this considered improper diversification?

NED: We're exclusively in our own state bonds because we have an income tax and an intangible tax on out-of-state bonds, and it costs about 35 basis points in yield to buy an out-of-state bond.

GARY: We have the same sort of thing in our state, too.

KEITH: Ned, in a smaller trust where tax exemption is, nevertheless, a factor, would you go out and buy individual municipal issues to get diversification outside your common trust fund in that account?

NED: If possible, we would stay in the tax-exempt common trust fund.

KEITH: You're not concerned about geographic or economic diversification in that area?

NED: No. We think you invest your money in the best area and that's what——

KEITH: I just remembered the Standard Accident portfolio in the early thirties which suffered by reason of the fact that it was concentrated in Oklahoma and Florida bonds.

VIC: Aside from the consideration of state taxation, which I think is the rationale behind Ned's approach, supposing you don't have this tax consideration. Our directors have asked me if I consider having half the municipal bond fund in our own state's bonds inadequate diversification. Since we did it, we told them no, but I would like your reactions.

GUY: Vic, I think you're right partly because you have a very large state and partly because the tax consideration is very important. Now, in our own tax-exempts and our own bond accounts, we do put a fairly large amount in other states. In the first place, the tax penalty is only 12 percent, and the tax is, after all, deductible from the federal tax base, so this works out to a fairly small penalty in large accounts. And second, we have a rule that we will not have more than a certain percentage of any in-state bond issues in our own trusts simply because it not only ruins marketability but would cause a great deal of political embarrassment under certain circumstances.

KEN: Well, of course, your state is smaller so that you don't have the diversification that a state such as California or Texas would have within the state limits.

GUY: This is entirely true. On the other hand, we have virtual state backing for all of our school district bonds.

GREG: But even within my state, where there is a very broad selection of municipals, we still will go outside the state for a fair proportion of the total municipals in a common trust fund.

KEN: Because you always have?

GREG: We have been believers of the trust form of diversification there. Once in a while my state has its credit questioned. (*laughter*)

VIC: Greg, in your judgment, would you say that 50 percent in one large state is not inappropriate if it's a widely diversified business state?

GREG: I don't think 50 percent in your home state, if it is large, is out of order.

GEORGE: I think it is worthwhile here to say a word particularly for the smaller organizations about how we believe agency rating should be used as evaluations for a bond. This is very important for smaller organizations.

GIL: Let's give a little time to that, George, before we leave this entirely.

GUY: I think they are of some help partly because ratings have a bearing on the marketability of the bonds if you should ever want to sell them. Also, they are at least a backup of your own bond analyst's judgment. A lower rating gives you some basis for deciding, perhaps, that certain bonds are suitable only in very large and more diversified accounts. This is particularly true of municipals. We would buy A rated bonds in some accounts and not in others. I think ratings are a fairly useful check, particularly because a great many times the spread between higher and lower rated bonds is pretty narrow. Often, you're not paying very much premium for such additional quality as the extra rating would give you.

GREG: You're talking of municipal bonds?

NED: I don't believe anyone would accept them blindly.

GEORGE: And particularly corporates, but actually on all ratings unless you have a rating system of your own. But that would imply a reasonably large staff.

GREG: We stay pretty much in A and better.

GEORGE: I didn't mean from the standpoint of what we would buy. But how do we believe these ratings should be classified? Viewed as gospel?

KEN: I think a small department does treat them as gospel.

GEORGE: That's right.

NED: I would say that that is not a bad thing for a small trust department to do.

GEORGE: Well, if all of you felt that way I think we should probably so indicate, because it would be extremely helpful to really know what we thought.

KEN: I would rather say that while they're not perfect they can be helpful. I don't want to give them an unqualified blessing, because I don't think they deserve it.

GLENN: I think you ought to preface that by saying that unlike stock ratings, bond ratings can be helpful. (*laughter*)

GEORGE: The point I was getting at is that there should be a statement on the stock ratings and on the bond ratings. I think we ought to go on record on stock ratings. Stock ratings are meaningless.

KEITH: It's a little distressing, George, after having established your position on a bond credit to have its rating reduced because of continuous financing, and then the marketability and the price collapse.

GREG: You have to be a little careful of not having any indications that you're delegating part of your responsibility to someone else. Now, a rating is fine, but I think no matter how small a trust department you are it's well to gather a few additional facts concerning the area, particularly if it's a small name of some kind. We have a whole schedule of figures and ratios we calculate in every case. Take a little town in the southern part of my state. We'll show the size of the area, the population of the area, the basis of assessment, total debt, the full value ratio, and a few other things besides the rating. I think the rating is a useful thing, but at the same time if any question arises you ought to supplement it with additional data to strengthen your record.

KEITH: Greg, is it ever clear in your minutes or discussion on what the parameters are around which these figures are used? In other words, what's the limit of debt ratio per capita that you'll buy?

GREG: It's just judgment, I think. This is one of these nebulous things. We don't draw specific limits.

GUY: Well, we do pretty much the same thing.

GLENN: I believe it was established that we all buy nonrated issues in our own areas. I wouldn't like to see our recognition of the ratings in any way detract from the prudence of buying nonrated bonds where we're familiar with the background of the municipalities.

KEITH: One problem has come up in Michigan as a result of a decision in which one of the local trust institutions was surcharged for having sold at a discount Victory 2½'s bought at par and reinvesting in municipals at par. They were surcharged for the loss they took on those particular bonds. There's a feeling in Michigan that if you're trading bonds in a personal trust account, municipals or corporates, for valid market reasons you should buy another bond at the same or greater discount so the remainderman doesn't lose principal. For example, if you bought a Franklin County, Ohio, 1 percent bond due in 1965, in 1945, and you wanted to sell it 10 years later, and it was selling at 85, you wouldn't buy a 3 percent bond selling at par. You buy another bond at 85. The *Dodge* case has put this restraint on the trust people in Michigan. How do you feel about this problem?

NEIL: I think it's generally accepted, and I don't know what we can do about it.

KEN: I just can't feel that sorry for the poor old remainderman when I think of what he's got in the way of common stocks. You could say the same thing if you bought a common stock at a 4 percent yield basis. Should you sell it and buy something else on a 4 percent basis?

KEITH: If you have a program that involves both the sale of a bond at a loss and the sale of some stocks at a profit, with reinvestment in other bonds and stocks, legal decisions won't let you net out the profit and loss, you see. Maybe the overall sale program results in a profit, but the bonds have to stand on their own.

GLENN: I think that's becoming archaic if you consider——

KEITH: Well, this decision wasn't all that old, Glenn; the Michigan case was only about four or five years ago.

KEN: The fellow that made it was all that old! (*laughter*)

KEITH: It was a convenient way to get around some basic problems.

GLENN: Well, I'll grant that there are questions in offsetting losses against profits in the stock account. Imprudent investment can't be made prudent because you thought the stock prudent when it went up. On the other hand, it doesn't seem to me in a bond account that you should necessarily be held to replacing principal through the purchase of other discount bonds.

The following discussion brings together further remarks on management of the bond account.

NED: One area that I thought we might give some more attention to is the question of managing the bond sector of personal trust accounts. I had the feeling that while we agreed that you should make some changes, there wasn't much expression on what sort of changes you should make or just how aggressive you should be.

We have, in effect, said that in common stocks if you see a way to improve an account you should immediately make a decision and go ahead. But when we talked about bonds, we said, "Yes, it is all right to make a change on bonds, it's all right to own short bonds," but we didn't discuss the degree of aggressiveness. I think this may be because the bonds in a personal trust account are not so marketable or so easily traded, and the benefits are not quite so large as in common stocks. In a small account, you can't do much if you have $5,000 of this and $5,000 of that; you get slaughtered by commissions in trading an odd lot of bonds. In a large personal account, I think there are opportunities to actively manage the bond holdings, and I think we should touch more on that.

In a large trust account that has big enough blocks to trade economically, shouldn't we make shifts from industrials to utilities if the spread is wider that we anticipate will continue—shifts from corporates to governments, shifts from municipals to governments, shifts that take into account the movements in the bond market that we expect?

If you think the market is going up, you go to low-coupon bonds and long maturities. If you think it is going down, you go to high-coupon bonds and short maturities.

When we have boom conditions, you would shift up to AAA bonds, because generally the spread between AAA's and A's or BAA's has narrowed because everyone is optimistic, and business is good. On the other hand, when business is lousy you sell your AAA's and drop back to the BAA bonds, because the spread has moved out to 100 basis points and that is wider than historically it should be.

We realize that this has the usual problems of the conflict of interest between the remainderman and the income beneficiaries, and we have to be very careful that we balance those out, either over the years or in other transactions carried out in the account at the same time. We don't want to take income from the income beneficiary and create a capital gain with it for the remainderman, or vice versa. We favor neither one nor the other. Assuming that we don't have this problem, should we be doing these things, and should we do them actively?

GENE: Speaking just for our own organization, I think we should be doing more of this, and very frankly, the reason we are not doing this is the manpower question. Is it as productive to deploy our limited manpower in this versus stock selections?

NED: I agree. Stock movements are more important to the account in the final results than the things you could do with the bonds.

GENE: We should all be doing it as much as we have the capacity to do it.

NED: In other words, this is a good trust investment principle.

NICK: I would go one step further than that and say that while trading is a questionable investment strategy as it concerns stocks it is a prudent investment strategy when we talk about bonds. Trading bonds seems to me like trading 9 cents for 10 cents when you can make the trade.

VIC: I think one of the problems in this area is that most portfolio managers are common stock-oriented, and we pick them for that reason. One of the ways we have tried to work this out is to make one of the members of the committee that reviews our portfolios essentially a bond man. His responsibility in portfolio reviews is to look at the bonds to see how they can be improved. It is very rare that the portfolio manager comes up with recommendations for the bond section, but we usually pick up the opportunities at the committee reviews and at least have a feeling that we are doing something.

KEN: We have specialized men—one does municipals and one does corporates and private placements—and it's up to the account manager to get advice. If he has a hunch in the back of his mind that something could be improved in the bond section of the account, he takes it to the specialist. He doesn't have to have any great knowledge of what to do. He just says, "I've got all their low coupons," or "I've got this or that."

VIC: Do these specialized bond men keep the portfolio managers informed on things they should be looking for?

KEN: Yes, new offerings. And, of course, our bond policy at the time, and what to look for. They appear at our weekly trust committee meetings, and take about five minutes at the beginning to bring those in attendance up to date.

GENE: Isn't one answer to this trying to get more of the bond part of an account into our pooled bond funds, either municipal or corporate?

VIC: Yes, very definitely.

GENE: Then you know you are working to the advantage of the account.

GLENN: On our pooled funds we have no reluctance to send the list to a broker or a bond dealer in whom we have confidence. Then he puts it on file. If he sees a sinking fund working or something of the sort, it is to his profit and our benefit to tell us about it. We are not going to let him pick our pockets, but on the other hand if he has some suggestions we certainly are willing to listen.

NED: Do most of you have forms for bond-swap comparisons, which show swaps on a cash basis and a yield-to-maturity basis? Perhaps you want to extend maturity, but you have a loss, and you want to be sure you make up your loss before the call date and that sort of thing. Do any of you have forms of that sort? We do.

KEITH: Our bond specialist has such a file worked up and uses it regularly.

In this area, Ned, I don't think the discussion would be complete if we didn't touch on one psychological problem in bond trading. You have a revocable living trust, which, in effect, is a testamentary disposition, and you have a $500,000 account, with $200,000 in municipals and $300,000 in stocks. Your customer comes in to see you one day— he doesn't look very well. The new business people can talk about writing wills—they are for the indefinite future; but this situation calls for action *today*. You recommend a switch from these 3½ municipals selling at par, to the extent that he has an estate tax liability, into long-term discount U.S. Treasuries selling at 85. These can be used at 100 in payment of estate taxes. This is a decision we find very difficult for our portfolio men to present to the customer.

This is a revocable living trust—the glorified agency account you talked about. He has the power to revoke, add, subtract. It becomes irrevocable on death, and then it becomes a testamentary disposition and subject to estate tax. You can compute the 15 points you may pick up if he's got a forecast from his doctor that his time is running out within a year or so. You probably have a duty to do some shifting to take advantage of this. It is very difficult. You might give him a stroke right there. (*laughter*)

NED: We had home runs on two accounts—one died within six weeks and another died within three months.

GLENN: My mother-in-law died within a week. (*laughter*)

VAL: It works the other way, too.

GENE: That's right.

GUY: This is standard procedure in our guardianships for old and failing people. I can remember one instance of a very wealthy man, whose guardians went out and borrowed to buy discount Treasuries on margin. They did right well as a result.

KEITH: That builds up the gross estate, and the executor gets a fee based on it. (*laughter*)

GUY: We were not executors as a matter of fact. We were in somewhat of an advisory capacity.

NED: I have told my wife, if I am on my deathbed, to call up the bond department and buy X dollars worth of these discount Treasuries and overdraw my account.

GREG: These are factors in portfolio management of revocable trusts where you can save substantial amounts for the estate or remaindermen, as the case may be, by being alert. Sometimes, you don't have to talk to the people; you can silently appraise that their days are limited.

VIC: I have a question of a different nature. What percent of your total fixed assets would you permit to be in nonmarketable investments: notes, mortgages, and so forth? How far would you go—a quarter, a half, three quarters?

KEITH: Isn't there a statement in the regulations on common trust funds that unless 40 percent of the fund is in obligations for which marketability is readily established you cannot accept new money for the fund? You cannot invest new money in your common trust fund. Let's say the maximum you could have in nonmarketable, closely held private placements, for example, might be 60 percent or something like that. Working down from that, we in our common trust fund have established 35 percent as a good working ground rule, because under those conditions we have plenty of flexibility if two or three good private placements come along. We know then we're within the rules. So we basically stick with about a third.

GREG: This is in the generally long-term accounts?

KEITH: Yes.

KEN: I think that's the only place for them—the common fund.

VIC: I think we would all agree with that. Now I have another question that concerns tax considerations. I would guess that most of us think not only of gain in the sale but also of reinvestment of the proceeds, and I would assume you would want to have after you paid your tax a better investment opportunity, in your judgment, in the stock you switched into than you expected to have in the one that you sold. I know one bank, in particular, that looks at it on a sell-and-buy-back basis for the particular stock rather than the alternative investment. Are you willing to take a loss if you believe that a more advantageous use of this capital can be made somewhere else?

KEITH: The investment reason should prevail, I would say.

GUY: I think this is right.

KEN: But first you say, "I'd like to get out of Union Carbide and into Avon Products," and then you look at the tax, and that influences you as to just how much you'd like to get out of Union Carbide——

KEITH: You make a guess about how many years or months it will take you to get the tax back——

KEN: The computer in your mind says that getting out of Carbide at 55 is not the same thing as getting out of it at net 40.

VIC: I've encountered some people whose attitude is that if the stock has a gain you don't sell it. Or, alternatively, if it has a loss you wait until you get back to the purchase price.

GUY: If there's a good investment reason for selling the stock, sell it.

KEN: Well, I think that's a good point to raise, Vic. A lot of us in the past have looked at accounts and—the account manager—the first thing he says to you is, "Oh, the cost here is so low, I don't think we can do anything."

VIC: That's exactly the kind of account I'm talking about.

KEITH: But because the beneficiary is 87 years old and a vegetable in a hospital, you live with it.

GUY: This is what happens.

VIC: Yes, but if the beneficiary is a widow age 50, you have a new ball game.

GARY: That's different.

KEN: Well, it's been very comforting to have the account man say that, and then you can say, "Sure, we don't *have* to——" (*laughter*) And that's happened too often.

KEITH: That happens all the time, and it should in some cases.

VIC: But I gather that our position here is that this should *not* be done generally.

GEORGE: Unless there are overriding personal investment considerations.

GENE: One of the difficulties in appraising a switch when you're paying a tax is this. Let's say you have a stock at very little cost. You think it may be somewhat high. It's very difficult to really estimate the decline you may experience. This is a complication that makes it impossible to arrive at any mathematical way to go about the switch decision.

VIC: Yes, there was an article in the *Journal of Finance* in 1961, as I remember, which had a very neat table explaining just how to go about this.[2] The only trouble is that you have to get your analysts to give you a very reliable estimate of the growth rate, or the anticipated depreciation, both in the stock you're going to sell and the one you're going to replace it with. I think we realize there are some hazards in doing this particular thing, although the mathematics are very neat.

---

[2] Charles C. Holt and John P. Shelton, "The Implications of the Capital Gains Tax for Investment Decisions," *Journal of Finance,* Vol. XVI, No. 4 (December, 1961), pp. 559–80.

CHAPTER SIX

Portfolio
management
(continued)

The successful performance of a trustee can be no better than the quality of investment information available to him and the ability of the organization to exercise judgment in putting this information to use. Trust administration is a local community service, performed in many instances by the neighborhood bank. Suggestions for improving the quality of trust services by small banks received considerable discussion during this session.

It should be remembered that every trust, agency, or estate is a separate entity for administrative, legal, and accounting purposes. A trust is an extremely flexible legal instrument, which may contain many restrictions or may permit a wide area of discretion in carrying out the objectives of the trustor. For example, a trust may be made revocable or irrevocable; it may provide for the addition or withdrawal of assets in certain circumstances; and income may either be distributed to beneficiaries or added to the principal. The trustee may be given full investment authority, or may have to obtain the direction or approval of others. Assets placed in the trust may include mortgages, real estate, or unfamiliar securities as well as quality investments. The instrument may direct the sale of certain holdings or, on the other hand, restrict their disposal. Such provisions complicate the work of both analysts and portfolio managers.

Trustees take for granted certain principles that are implied in the remarks at the seminar. One of these is that a trustee cannot delegate to someone else those duties he may reasonably be expected to perform himself.

Advice and information may be obtained from other sources, but once a trust is accepted the institution must assume full responsibility for its actions.

A second principle requires that the assets of each trust be segregated, with definite indication of their ownership. Laws and regulations have generally been relaxed so that banks may operate common funds in which individual trusts may obtain participations. These funds provide diversification and facilitate the management of small- and medium-sized trusts. An effort is being made to permit banks to offer similar services to agency account customers—a development that would place banks in direct competition with mutual funds.

A third principle is that a trustee must be impartial in dealing with a number of trusts. This explains the need for setting up some equitable policy in buying and selling securities when all accounts cannot be taken care of in one transaction.

A trustee must also treat fairly all the beneficiaries of each trust. Conflicting interests may arise when two people in greatly differing tax brackets share the income from one trust. Tax-free income may be desirable for one beneficiary but not the other. A frequent occasion of differing requirements is when the income is distributed to one person, and the principal is eventually received by another.

This is the atmosphere in which the portfolio officer must operate.

GARY: I have given you some exhibits which should give you a little perspective as to who the portfolio manager is in most of our banks.[1] I have some more recent data to add to Exhibit I. At the end of 1965, there were 3,785 banks with trust powers; of these, 3,503 were actually exercising them—about the same as you see here for 1962. About half of these banks are state banks, and half are national banks.

A few years ago, I wrote to the office of the Comptroller of the Currency; I wrote to the FDIC; I wrote to each of the 12 Federal Reserve banks; I wrote to the ABA, trying to get data on the trust departments of national and state banks. The paucity of statistics was perfectly appalling! Furthermore, what data there was had a complete lack of uniformity. Assets are carried at market, book value, or some arbitrary unit value. Trust department figures may include agency accounts, escrow accounts, pension accounts. Such a compilation is virtually worthless.

---

[1] See Appendix D.

To me, it has always seemed incongruous that the prospective customer of our trust departments has no place to go for statistics regarding the trust department of bank X. He doesn't know whether that trust department is the fastest growing in the city or the slowest growing. He doesn't know where to look for the dollar value of the assets that trust department holds. There's no place in the country where you can look for that except in the bank itself, and maybe it doesn't know. The prospective customer does not know whether the bank has a few large accounts or a large number of small accounts. He has no easy way to get data on the quality of investment performance that bank has had in the past. So in a real sense your potential trust investment customer is buying a pig in a poke. In this day and age, when investment men are insisting on more and more information on the corporations they invest in, it seems to me inconsistent that the trust departments that are billion-dollar businesses don't divulge statistics on their own operations. I think if we can get the regulations changed so we can do some trust advertising, get some publicity, compare results, then it will be a different story.

My second point is that trust department assets are much more concentrated than are the assets of commercial banks as a whole. In the figures on national banks, Exhibit II, you see that 26 banks, each with trust assets over $500 million, account for more than 60 percent of total trust assets, but 70 percent of the trust departments have assets of less than $10 million.

The third point is that trust assets are also concentrated geographically—Exhibit III. You'll notice that New York, Pennsylvania, Illinois, and California account for more than half the trust assets of all the national banks, and there are six states with total trust assets of less than $50 million. These data are at the end of 1965.

I think we can draw the conclusion that the typical portfolio. manager is working in a small department, getting a small salary. He does the trust new business; he does the trust tax work; he is the trust department pension specialist, the administrator, the research department, and the portfolio manager. There are a lot of these fellows who, I think, need help. With the interindustry competition we face from mutual funds, investment counsel firms, insurance companies, pension funds, and so on, we need to figure out some way to help not only the people in our big banks but also these myriad portfolio managers in the little banks who are investing less than 14 percent in common stocks. Nearly all the banks represented at this seminar have trust assets over $1 billion, but we should look also at the problems of the smaller banks.

I think the portfolio manager should be a well-trained, broad-gauged man with an investment background, because our customers are becoming more sophisticated and they demand more sophisticated portfolio managers. From the small sample I've seen, I've been appalled by the lack of training in a lot of the men. In New York State, there was a trust investment school held a couple of years ago, with over a hundred men in attendance. They were relatively senior people, mostly portfolio managers, and many liberal arts graduates. They wouldn't know what is meant by standard deviation. They hadn't had a course in money and banking, investments, marketing, accounting. They had learned by doing in some bank.

Let me give you an interesting example. A fellow called me up and asked if he could come over and talk about bonds, and I said, "Sure." He came for the sole purpose of trying to sell municipal bonds to a university endowment fund. I explained to him that we weren't interested in tax-free bonds, since charitable organizations pay no income taxes. As he left my office, he shook his head and said, "You learn something every day, don't you."

I think our educational facilities in the banking business are excellent, not only on the American Institute of Banking level but also the specialized schools, the trust schools, three-year schools like Rutgers or Seattle, or the state schools. New York has a whole gang of trust schools—one on administration, one on pension funds, one on investments, one on public relations, and whatever else you can think of. I also think our C.F.A. program is doing a lot of good.

From what I see, the training and experience of portfolio managers is improving. There's more emphasis on hiring people from colleges of business administration, but there still isn't any formal training program, as such, in many of the banks. The portfolio manager usually learns by doing it. Investment counsel trainees are often required to spend six months or so in the investment research department, which I think is probably a good idea.

As to supervision and control, my reaction is to give the man his head. Let him do the job and be responsible for it, because he has several things backing him up. In the first place he's got the research department, which is providing him with a buy list of securities, probably broken down into trust quality and investment counsel quality, and a more aggressive list. Second, you have the trust investment committee reviewing the accounts. Third, your computers are now getting on stream so that they can do a big job in reviewing these accounts.

At our bank, we have made a review of all the stocks we own in the trust department. We have broken them down by industry groups. We go through them and say, "How come we still own these stocks? Here's one we haven't liked for months. Why is it still here?" As far as latitude is concerned, the customer can only pick a good trustee and give him full discretion to do the best job he can.

My next point is that I think account objectives are very important. If there is anything basic in investing, it is that every investment account should be tailor-made to suit its particular objectives. You have to get full information in order to do a good job in running an investment portfolio. You have to know, for example, what the man's family situation is, what his tax status is, what his philanthropic intentions are, whatever income he has, what his investment goals are. Even the job of estate planning—going over that situation with the bank's estate planning officer—I think would be helpful. Then you should work out your objectives on a highly personalized basis in the light of the information that has been secured.

As far as frequency of reviews is concerned, in theory they are done constantly. The investment department follows daily the individual industries and common stocks. At the other end of the spectrum, they have to be reviewed by law at least once a year. In practice, they are probably reviewed quarterly, and sometimes more often. Here, the computer may help us.

When the review comes up, there is going to be a change in common stock selection. It seems to me that a written memo from the research department is in order, and a meeting with the trust men to tell them how urgent it is. A selling job is necessary to get this story over.

The normal type of review, which everybody has, usually consists of a list of your assets broken down by classifications and industries, indicated annual income, percentage yield on cost and market value, and so on. Supplementing this, you can often have a five-year growth rate and a stability index of the fluctuations in the account to indicate risk. Again, accounts have to be tailor-made to fit the objective. I've talked too long, and now I'll throw it open to discussion.

GIL: O.K. Thanks, Gary. Well, Gary has given us a fast run through on some of the problems in portfolio management and construction, which means we can go back into much of our earlier discussion. Who wants to direct a particular question to Gary?

VIC: Gary, I think you made an excellent point about the number of small banks that have trust powers, but I am wondering if the reputation of the trust industry is not flavored by the fact that these small banks exercise their powers in a very ineffective way.

GARY: I think it reflects on all of us.

VIC: Really, is there anything a large trust department can properly do to help small ones? In Texas where they have unit banking and more banks than they have jackrabbits, they all exercise trust powers.[2] Usually, it's a one-man show. He does it as a part-time operation, and just isn't a trust officer. What do you do with people like that? They come in and say, "Can you help me?" Well, what do you want to do?

NED: Help them out of business! (*laughter*)

GARY: That's a good question. There was a brilliant and scintillating talk on this topic at one of the ABA meetings two years ago called "How Small Trust Departments Can Get Investment Advice." I listened to every word of it, and I gave the talk. (*laughter*) I have checked around the country to see what banks did in getting investment help for their trust departments through correspondent banks. For the country as a whole, there are very few large banks that give this help. Ken, your bank happens to be one of those that makes a point of giving investment advice to banks with correspondent balances.

It is customary for a bank to pay for services from its correspondent bank by maintaining a demand deposit of some size. Since interest is not paid on demand deposits or a noninterest bearing time deposit, all the earnings on the balance accrue to the correspondent bank. Services may include custody of securities, data processing, operating and financial advice, and information and recommendations for the trust department, as well as services to other departments.

Purchases and sales of securities in trusts are made through normal investment channels. In many instances, there are no significant benefits to be gained by choosing a particular broker or dealer. Assuming there is no significant difference in price, the trustee may allot business according to considerations such as the following:

---

[2] Certain states, notably Texas and Illinois, do not permit banks to have branches. In others, branching is restricted to contiguous areas, and a few permit statewide operation.

1. The wishes of the beneficiaries of the trust.
2. Ability to make the best market or to provide scarce merchandise.
3. Investment research assistance. This may include:
   a) Factual information.
   b) Reports of interviews with company managements.
   c) In-depth studies of industries and companies.
   d) Economic forecasts.
   e) Visits and presentations by analysts, and so on.
4. Special assistance on sales or purchases.
5. New trust business introduced by the broker.
   Larger banks frequently keep detailed records to aid in giving business in accordance with the value of services rendered.

GARY: I'm trying to set up a family trust in a bank in a small western state. I can't find, for the life of me, what bank would do a good job on a large trust. An attorney there told me about the biggest trust department, and this trust would make it twice as big. I don't think, Vic, that you can help them out of business. They went in business probably with the idea of prestige, of having a full-service bank, or hoping it would grow and make money eventually. The constructive thing is to help them do a better job and not be invested less than 14 percent in common stocks.

VIC: I can give you an example of one of our small local bankers who came in to us the other day about a man who wanted to establish a trust and set it up in this small bank. The banker said, "I can't manage this portfolio, but the trust has some real estate and a few other things we can take care of, and we know the family situation well." We used to do an investment advisory job on the account, so we said, "Yes, we will set it up as an investment advisory account and charge the standard fee." I think he's going to take it.

NED: We've got 17 banks that we work with in varying degrees. In some cases, we set up all their trust department accounts as agency accounts in our own trust department. We run them on our forms and so on, except we imprint the name of that bank in place of our bank. We take three quarters of the fee, and they get one quarter, and their man acts merely as an administrative officer.

GARY: He doesn't delegate authority, does he, Ned?

NED: No, they've got their own trust investment committee, and if they want to go on their own recommendations they can. But the chances are they won't. We don't know what they do in every case. I suppose we'd have to check back to see whether they follow every recommendation. We haven't done this. There may be a cotrustee involved, so we haven't investigated.

GUY: You have custody of the assets?

NED: Yes.

GARY: A branch trust department.

NED: Well, it is. It's an extension of our own trust department. And it is actually a way to get additional business for your trust department.

What Ken does is an entirely different thing. He sells complete investment counseling service to banks. That's about what it boils down to.

VAL: But not to small banks.

KEN: To afford the deposit is the problem. It has to be $100,000 for 1 service, $200,000 for the——

GENE: You have hundreds of banks with this service?

KEN: Yes, about 300.

GUY: Some advisory organizations are available. One in Philadelphia has an advisory service that covers Pennsylvania, New Jersey, and some of the other states. They have a lot of people with bank experience. This is one type of service small banks can use.

VAL: One thing you run into, I think, is if you get a real small bank you won't find anybody in the bank that knows what to do with what you tell them. This is even worse, because they hold out to their customers that they are equipped with all this information, and they would have been better off not to have had any. Don't you find that, Ken?

KEN: Yes, indeed.

GENE: There is nobody in the country who couldn't get more information than he could possibly use. No matter what size bank and what size trust department you are dealing with, the brokers are equipped to give you tons of material.

GARY: How is it from a quality point of view? Most of these small banks are talking to the wire houses [brokers who specialize in retailing to individual customers] and not with people whose research is of institutional caliber.

VIC: On the other hand, a banker from a nearby city came in last week, and he had never heard of———[a famous research house that services only institutions]. And he had about a six-man trust department. Where had he been? Most of these people never heard of institutional research material.

GARY: The head of research in one of the New York City banks hadn't heard of ——— a couple of years ago. (*laughter*)

GEORGE: The reason small banks don't hear about ———— is that the minimum commission requirement is $2,400. That's a lot of money for a small bank.

I think the important thing you might be able to do to help these organizations is to indicate some reputable services that can be purchased reasonably and are objective in their information.

GREG: Isn't the C.F.A. program or the Financial Analysts Federation the real answer down the road? In a small bank, one of the officers or prospective officers could take the time to attend security analysts' meetings in the nearest city, and take the necessary classes, and so on.

The point is that the C.F.A. program should try to improve the educational process in these smaller communities.

GUY: Greg, don't you think the situation will cure itself in time? Many of these smaller banks are going to go out of existence or be taken over. I have an idea that banks like this aren't an economic business. They lack management succession, and suddenly the local stockholders discover they can sell out to a metropolitan bank at more than they imagined their stock would ever be worth. So this problem will clear up in the course of 20 to 25 years.

NEIL: It's developing right now. You know they're merging them off left and right.

VAN: They're not making much progress in Illinois, though. (*laughter*)

The seminarians next mentioned that common trust funds might be made available to small- or medium-sized banks in a given geographical area. This is now done in New York State and could be worthy of more extensive application.

During the discussion on aid to smaller trust departments, which, in essence, is a problem of communication, the seminarians raised the issue of internal communications. Many of the concepts referred to in this dialogue were discussed in earlier sessions but in a slightly different context. At this point, the seminarians reconsider their earlier treatment of these ideas as part of the overall problem of communication.

The target account, discussed earlier, is suggested as one means of furthering communication among the various departments. Recommended buy-sell lists, progress reports on particular situations, and meetings with portfolio managers, also considered previously, are suggested as other means of improving communications.

As the size of a trust institution increases and its personnel become more specialized, some degree of coordination and communication among these groups becomes increasingly important. A continuing flow of information and recommendations from the analysts to the portfolio managers is necessary. And a uniform policy by which all account investment managers deal with similar situations must be established.

GENE: I think this target concept is worth thinking about. I think here we are talking about a question of communication between the research department, the account men, and the supervisor of the investment department. There are really a number of different ways of improving communication—hypothetical account, target account— this is one way; there are lots of different ways.

NED: What are some of the others, Gene? Give us examples of some you use. We need help here.

GENE: Well, for example, a research department portfolio, where the research men are really the decision makers; a real or hypothetical list of stocks they like for different types of accounts; or more direct communication between the research guys and the account men.

KEN: We schedule a weekly meeting between the account men and the analysts in our trust and investment counsel departments. Before the meeting, an agenda is established—the things the analysts want to get over to the account people, and questions the account men have for the analysts. It works pretty well. It is very informal and lasts about an hour.

GARY: Would the oil industry, for example, be reviewed that way?

KEN: It wouldn't be a formal industry review. One analyst might say oil stocks look attractive now for these reasons; here are the three or four stocks we like and a tabulation showing why, or here's a brief report on some new development. But if the oils were doing poorly, the account man could ask, "Why does Royal Dutch look cheap? Are its earnings on schedule?" The customers want to know, and we've got to tell them. When the oil analyst has had a couple of days to at least prepare for what's going to be asked, he's really loaded for bear.

GENE: We have a meeting once a week of all our account men. Once a quarter, at least, each analyst talks about all the companies he has on our large representative list. He brings everybody up to date in terms of what's going on in the company, and shows the position of the stock with relative market charts. This lasts an hour and a half and may cover more than one industry. We disseminate policy information and report the findings of our investment committee. Ideas, of course, are raised at a meeting like this.

KEN: When new names appear on our sell- or buy-, or source-of-funds- [optional sale] lists, we explain them as a matter of course at our meeting. We don't write them up.

NORM: We have a meeting once a week, but we write up what each analyst has to say about a particular company.

GENE: One other thing we do is publish a weekly newsletter. The analyst has a chance there again to communicate something that has happened if he wants to.

KEN: We publish a weekly letter of recent management contacts —a summary of the field trips made during the past week, and whether or not there is active buying or selling in the stocks. We use this internally, and we are beginning to send it to our correspondent banks.

VAN: We do that, but I think the oral presentation is much more effective. Our letters are for internal distribution.

NED: Whenever we have a buy or sell recommendation on a stock, we write an 8- to 12-line typewritten paragraph, explaining why we think this stock should be bought or sold. This is sent not only to the portfolio managers but also to all the administrative officers. We have a problem of a branch system. An account manager across the state can't get to our meetings, but he has a paragraph he can put in his letter to customers.

KEN: He will make a lot more switches if you give him that paragraph.

GEORGE: Communications are very important. We have two committees aside from the guidance committee mentioned. We have a research committee. All the analysts, the group heads and their assistants, appear at specified intervals. In half an hour, the industry analyst gives his views on all our major investments, all the information in his area. He has ratings, earnings estimates, and his opinions summarized on one sheet of paper, and the size of the holding on another. We discuss these and then question him. If there is anything he has missed, he is asked why. If anything new results from this meeting, it is brought before a larger committee. The analyst recommends a course of action in a written memorandum, not more than two or three pages long.

Along with this, if he has not done so, he makes a field check. In this check, he covers 15 salient points in no more than 3 pages, which he reports objectively. Then he has a paragraph of no more than a fourth of a page in which he gives his evaluation. The members of the committee study it ahead of time, and discuss it with the analyst and. his organization. After the questions from any one of these dozen committee members are resolved, the analyst revises the evaluation memorandum into a short paragraph that can be used to the extent needed for personal contact.

GENE: George, these 15 salient points—that's a pretty much standard format that the analyst must report on, just to make sure he has checked on all these things?

GEORGE: Yes. He has to have an earnings impression for the current year, and three to five years out; capital expenditures, budgets, competition, costs, labor relations—everything on which a question may arise warrants analysis.

His responsibility is to go out and get information on what the company is doing, thinking about doing, how it's going to do it, and what are its strengths and weaknesses. He might check with customers, or dealers, or distributors. Or look into their computer operations. Actually, the synthesis comes down to the analyst's opinion. And the analyst is judged on that evaluation.

GENE: Do you judge the committee?

GEORGE: That is an interesting point. The committee looks good. We've got a reasonable batting average, but I can tell you right here and in no uncertain terms that, by and large, the analysts are much more correct than the committee. It's the truth.

The important point is that the analyst's evaluation is heard, even though he may be outvoted. This is a valuable means of communication, because most members of the committee are portfolio managers, and they are required to relay this information to their own groups. If further explanation is warranted, it is their responsibility to bring in the research man. There is no excuse for not having a thorough understanding about what course of action was recommended.

NICK: We have talked about the onerous things in the regulations that we don't like. One of the things I suspect the medium-size departments don't like, but I think should do, is this regulation concerning industry reviews at least annually. It's not enough to analyze a company or look at an account. You must see the assets in your department within the framework of their particular industry. It seems to me this is pertinent to our discussion of trust investment policy.

GLENN: We would all agree with that.

GEORGE: We do this all the time, and the more important the industry, the more often we write it up.

GENE: The major writing jobs of our senior analysts are our industry studies. We will delegate a company to a junior man, but we want the analyst to be focusing on the industry, and he really spells out what you should do about the companies through his industry experience.

KEN: We initially write up only the industry; then afterward only those companies we are interested in buying or selling. You include any comments you want to make in the body of the industry study. Special emphasis would be the only place you'd write a report of any length.

VAN: We substitute somebody else's report that we think reflects on——

GUY: We've sent to our committee a broker's report with comments, or maybe comparisons with other companies in the margins, and it works out very well.

The seminar at this point shifted from a discussion of communication techniques to the use of computers.

Larger trust departments have long used punched card tabulating and accounting equipment for record-keeping and classification of investments. As more advanced equipment with greater information-handling capacity has become available, estimates of income, market valuations, yields, and tax costs have been added to current statements.

More recent developments in the use of computers were discussed at some length by the seminarians. All recognized the tremendous capabilities now available in processing information, relieving the analysts of onerous calculations, and coming up with answers heretofore prohibitively expensive.

In addition to security analysis, computers have possibilities in the development of economic studies and in portfolio selection. A new generation of college graduates, familiar with sophisticated mathematical concepts and computer applications, may be needed to go further in these directions.

Every institution represented at the seminar recognizes that computers have added a new dimension to the investment process and that their practical application to decision making is only beginning.

VIC: Gary indicated that he has made relatively little use of computers, but I suspect there is going to be more and more use made in the future. You can use them for information storage and retrieval, and for measuring performance. You can use them, I've been told, for portfolio management, but I've never seen a program yet that I'm satisfied with. What has been your experience? Does everyone confidently feel that they have gotten the full return on their investment as expected?

GENE: We have.

GARY: We haven't used the computer enough. We use it for pricing, and we get industry runoffs and that sort of thing. As far as performance is concerned, we measure our common funds, and check all stocks, but not otherwise.

GENE: I find usually when people say, "Are you using the computer?" they really mean, are you using some of these mathematical techniques. The fact is that the computer is the only way you can use the technique on a large scale, but the concept is the technique—it isn't the machine. We have done a lot of experimenting with the techniques, and really, to experiment you don't need to use much machine time. And they've been very helpful to us. Some of these things obviously are going to have a big impact.

GIL: Model building, and that sort of thing?

GENE: We have really not gotten into economic model building or estimating earnings through models, but in terms of dealing with information, sifting through it, and trying to put it in meaningful form.

GUY: Do you use Compustat, for instance?

GENE: Yes.

GUY: To make comparisons and update information. This is a good example of computer usage that doesn't involve anything too esoteric, but gives your analysts information they otherwise could never get together.

GENE: That's right.

NED: I think we can probably do a lot of rather simple things very efficiently on computers. In connection with portfolio analysis, there's a lot we really haven't gotten around to. This is partly because some of the other things we like to play around with are more glamorous, or they're day-to-day things so necessary they come before anything else—things like preparing investment reviews and so on.

We were discussing the way you could break down your common stocks by industries, degree of technology, cyclicality, or other criteria. I think this is going to be a great aid to the portfolio manager over the years in that we may have a large group of criteria that we may be able to use to analyze a portfolio.

For instance, one of them may be a company's method of distribution. You might run an account and find you have 12 stocks you thought were highly diversified, but they all distribute through drugstores. So maybe they aren't so highly diversified as you thought. This is just screening applied to portfolio analysis.

Similarly, you can apply some of these measures of downside risk to the dividends of the individual stocks, and a weighted average for the whole account. Figure what's the worst that could happen if all these companies were hit by a depression and cut their dividends all at once. How low could income go? How low could the total market value go?

Another thing is, what is the total expected return on the account? We show income and yield on market value for the whole common stockholdings, but with a computer you could apply an expected overall return for each stock, or put in a target price for each stock and see what the target says for the whole account. I think the potentials are quite large and limited only by our imagination. They will be developed step by step as we become familiar with what the computer can do and learn what's practical and reasonably inexpensive, and what's impractical and too expensive.

GEORGE: I believe the future lies in its use as a research tool rather than as a portfolio management tool.

GLENN: I would agree with George. The ability of a man to scan a wide range of information rapidly and thoroughly—while it's going to be important as a portfolio tool, I am hoping and looking forward to it's being exceedingly important to research.

NED: Well, this is its glamorous area—far more glamorous than the portfolio applications, unless some of this Markowitz and Sharpe stuff gets simplified enough so we can understand it. They're so glamorous that we don't know what they're talking about.

NICK: I think *they* don't know what they're talking about. (*laughter*)

GENE: Has anybody used Markowitz with any degree of success?

VAN: We used it and experimented with it and rejected it entirely.

NED: I think the Sharpe model and the Clarkson models are so much simpler.[3] There are lots of new algorithms and other simplified approaches, and they turned out to be better than Markowitz because they just ignore the covariance, for one very simple reason. They have done a bunch of studies, and the studies show that a good portfolio analyst will select stocks with relatively low covariance and do almost as good a job as a computer would anyway, so why spend the money? (*laughter*) So I am for Sharpe and Clarkson.

GLENN: As a small operation, we have kept a file on these studies

---

[3] See Appendix E.

for two or three years without implementing. Finally, the first of the year we decided we could no longer keep it in a drawer. We had to get acquainted with the state of the art and start using it either directly or through correspondents. To me, our conclusion was timely.

VIC: When you take that direction, what kind of people do you look to to implement it? Do you take one of your analysts, older, or younger, or do you go out and get a computer man?

GLENN: We've done it two or three ways. We have been advised against getting a computer man or a mathematician as such. People with some experience believe that it isn't such a difficult art, and a good financial man can become as expert as necessary for our purpose.

I would think that the graduates we will be getting from the business schools and universities will be better in mathematics, and some will know something about using computers. Through evolutions, we will pick up knowledge from their academic training, but meanwhile we have decided to stay with our analysts and acquaint them with the use of computers.

VIC: Have any of you had any success in working with professors in local schools of business or universities?

VAN: We have two on our payroll. They've both been extremely helpful. We've got four people in a research computer operation, and we've developed what we think are some very interesting research projects with their assistance.

GLENN: We've employed a university research institute in conjunction with another bank to make a study of the state of the art and to give our people some training. Find out various techniques. I don't know what is going to come out of it.

GEORGE: Is this for research evaluation or——

GLENN: Yes, and hopefully we will get some capability of developing performance comparisons.

GEORGE: Is this thing used in the modeling stage?

VAN: We are in the process.

GENE: George, do you do models?

GEORGE: We are struggling with it.

KEN: We do model economic work. We use the so-called Wharton Model and we modify it. In other words, we work closely with the Wharton School, and the model is modified in-house.

VAN: With your own input?

KEN: Yes. It works out very well. But that's on the economic side. That isn't investment analysis.

GEORGE: I think we are going to have to rely very much on the analyst. Everything I've done so far on computers has been knocked in the head by a wrong estimate. (*laughter*)

KEN: This sounds corny and trite, but these common stocks are living things, and how in the heck you can use a computer on them and get them to hold still, I don't know.

GENE: You have to deal within a dynamic framework.

KEN: For fixed-income analysis, for a bank's own portfolio, for the economy, the utilities, the computer has obvious applications.

GEORGE: The romance in utilities is gone. Too many people will come up with the same numbers, and you will wind up with bond yields in utility stocks.

VIC: Well, on the point that George is making. That's only correct if you are using the same time horizon and valuation procedure. You're looking at utilities relative to other alternatives, so the demand for them in one organization is different from another. You evaluate the potential the same, but the supply and demand for the stock in the market will be different because we will be looking at them differently for different purposes.

GEORGE: That's right.

KEN: The big money is made or lost in surprises, pleasant or unpleasant, and there are no surprises in utilities.

GLENN: I know you contemplate making computer service available to your correspondent banks. What's going to happen to Gary's small trust departments in the process with this computer technology?

KEN: You mean if they can't keep up with it?

GLENN: Does it lend itself to use by your smaller correspondents?

KEN: I think so. It's just another report that we could just as well put on by hand if we had thousands of man-hours.

GENE: That's right. I think as we learn to use computers we will be of particular help to small organizations. This is their big application—helping to deal with this vast amount of information that you're not making the best use of because it's just swamping you.

GEORGE: What we've found extremely helpful is the relief from tedium it has given the analyst.

KEN: On the other hand, the analyst has to put that input in every month or whatever, and this is another kind of tedium.

VAN: It's a discipline. That is important.

KEN: But he doesn't like it.

GEORGE: But he makes reasonably good estimates. We've got one young kid who seems to be lucky.

VAN: Don't put that word in the record. (*laughter*)

The discussion now moved from computer stock selection to the question of establishing priorities of securities in various accounts.

Discussion of the priority to be given the common trust funds in a general sales recommendation may be explained by differing points of view. One speaker looks on the common fund as a consolidation of numerous trusts, most too small to be invested in individual securities and in need of a higher degree of conservatism than the average account. Another view is that the common funds should receive a price close to the average received by all trusts under the supervision of the bank. A third approach is that first priority should be given to particular individually invested trusts.

Arguments can be raised in support of each of these lines of reasoning. Here is a good illustration of the choices faced by a trustee in making a distinction among his accounts.

VIC: I'd like to bring up the problem of the priorities given to accounts. Suppose you decide to sell a stock—you want out and you want out quick. How do you assign priorities? Who goes first?

GLENN: Do you try to do it account by account? I suppose undoubtedly you are going to do your common trust funds first.

VIC: No, what we try to do, and you may have a size of holding problem that we don't, is to get a computer run very quickly on every account that holds the stock. And where you're sold, you just bundle the whole thing together and go. You get hold of the cotrustees as fast as you can with your recommendation.

GLENN: Is there any other way?

VIC: I'm asking—I don't know. I had the problem, and this is the decision I made. I didn't ask anybody else how to do it.

GUY: We have taken our common trusts first, and next all the accounts under, say $50,000, that can afford to take the least risk. Then we take the remainder of our sole power accounts and, finally, go after our cotrustees.

KEN: If you are establishing priorities you don't take your funds first, then the big accounts, then the little accounts, then the old lady who won't know any better if she gets the top eighth. Boy, that's not justifiable.

VIC: It seems to me that with the block trading facilities that are available these days you can bundle your common trust funds and everything else in a package and go.

NED: I say first come, first served. In the first two days you get a good-sized block, and you try to block-trade that. Meanwhile, more stuff begins to come in, and when it accumulates into a block you try to move it.

KEN: The only rule we have is that our own funds—our own bank pension and profit sharing fund—come last.

GLENN: To compound the difficulty, what do you do on a new issue or a convertible bond issue that you want to buy and you get only a fraction of what you need? How do you allocate it?

GEORGE: You spread it as wide as you can, and you don't touch a share of it in your own bank's profit sharing or pension accounts. And put it out in smallest possible denominations as far as you can.

VIC: George, you know what happens in a case like that.

GEORGE: I know what happens—no one is ever satisfied with what his account received.

VIC: We inherited a rather large pension fund from another bank, which shall remain nameless, and their bond account was the damnedest mess I've ever seen. They had $10,000 blocks, they had $100,000 blocks. The account was a big collection of miscellaneous little bits.

GLENN: What did you do?

VIC: Took six months to clean it up.

GEORGE: We don't do that in such a case. We wait a reasonable period to get more. If we can't build up the size of the holding, we get out.

In fact, what brought this out was one very important account we had. One time he said we avoided a good issue solely because we couldn't get enough to spread around. He said, "Listen, if I can make $10, I want to make it any way I can." He's absolutely right.

VIC: Let me ask a question along this same line. Supposing you put together a block you're going to sell, and you've got varying amounts in 15 or 20 trusts. You find today you can sell a third, and maybe tomorrow half of what's left, and it's spread out over four or five days at varying prices. Do you have to allocate throughout the trusts for every single day? You begin to get into an accounting problem.

GLENN: We take all the smaller accounts and get them out first, and maybe a portion of the common trust fund. Maybe a tenth of the common trust fund holding goes out with all the small accounts, and then you work off the rest, dollar averaging the larger accounts because of lack of marketability. But the smaller accounts are entitled to go out first.

The reader will see that ethical questions can easily arise here.

*   *   *

Dollar averaging is the technique of buying a security in fixed dollar amounts over a period of time. The resulting average cost per share will be less than the average price per share.

The term "dollar averaging" also is used generically to describe any process of regularly spaced purchases or sales. This line of action assumes that future prices are not highly predictable and that it is better to receive an average price than to try to outguess the market. Beyond spreading the transactions in time, other refinements may be introduced, such as those involving an equal number of shares in each transaction. The basic principle is that of spreading out purchases or sales.

The following discussion outlines the use of dollar averaging in a number of situations, such as buying or selling highly valued growth stocks, or reducing investment concentrations.

NICK: Our discussion would certainly be incomplete if we didn't discuss, at least briefly, the traditional cornerstone of trust investment policy, namely, dollar cost averaging and incremental selling. Do you try to scale out your sales, do you try to dollar cost average your purchases? What is your thought?

NED: Nick, explain how you mean that. You mean in an account where you are plowing back most of the income—you pay out $5,000 a year and you are getting $25,000 in, so you dollar average with the excess income each year? Or are you talking about taking a small position in a stock at today's price and try to average the market for the next two to three years? Or you get an additional contribution to the account—do you invest it immediately or do you invest it on a dollar cost average?

NICK: Right.

VIC: I don't know how others do it, but I would certainly be influenced by my price judgment of the market and the stock I'm buying, and the same is true in selling. If something is wrong with the company, if something has affected the earnings and you want to sell it, you had better sell at once. But we are frequently faced with a situation in which there is nothing wrong with earnings—it's a fine old company, and the earnings are chugging along and everything is great. Your real question then becomes a matter of price judgment.

NED: Is this a concentration you are talking about? You just want to reduce your holdings?

VIC: Well, it could be a concentration and you would want to reduce your holding, or it could be an average-size commitment but you are concerned about the price vulnerability.

GENE: You've a better use for the funds.

VIC: Yes, that's right.

GENE: This influences how you handle the holding. If you like other things better, obviously I think you would be more inclined to sell out at once and then buy the other stock.

VIC: But frequently it is a marginal decision. In a situation like that, my general approach is to sell a portion—maybe a quarter or a third. If it continues to move up, sell some more. As far as purchases are concerned, if you have no firm convictions about the market you may want to average your funds in. Generally speaking, I would say to use your best judgment on particular stocks at a particular point in time.

KEITH: We have an actual interesting case right now. A man died and left his net estate in trust for his widow and daughter. Nobody knew he had made much money, but he had been a very successful investor. He had two good stocks that had performed brilliantly, and they happened to be our favorites—Polaroid and Xerox. We were called in as agent for the executor, and we are going to be agent for the trustees, who are some attorneys. The widow and the daughter will need income. Here we have 80 percent of the assets, after meeting estate expenses, in Xerox and Polaroid. They don't provide reasonable income. The will didn't contemplate living off the principal; the yields on these stocks are almost zero. How do you make the investment decision to diversify and do the best job you can, since nobody knows whether Polaroid is going to sell at 400 a year from now or not?

Our recommendation in this case was to sell 10 percent of the holding periodically, stretch it out over a reasonable period of a year to a year and a half, try to average out at a good price, retaining a residual of 10 percent in each, or something like that. Maybe we'll leave a little more. We're in the selling process right now at the urging of the executors and trustees. We were urged to sell immediately. Fortunately, up to now it has been a very good thing to have taken time, because they have moved up very sharply. I am convinced that 10 years from now we will wish we had not sold it.

KEN: Can you invade principal?

KEITH: Modest amounts. The language of the will is the kind where you invade for emergencies, not for living purposes; if you buy a house or something, but you don't invade for living expenses. The problem is very tricky here, because of the particular assets, and we all recognize them as having been great estate builders up to now. And, of course, we had no bond position. We would like to capitalize on these stocks a long time to the best extent we can. In this case, Nick, we are dollar averaging out over a period of a year about 75 percent of our holding in these stocks.

GREG: I think it makes sense. This is a problem we run into quite a bit in these cases when you have to build a better income position. You perform major surgery when you upset the whole pattern of the account, but this is minor surgery—a chipping-off process, the exercise of judgment that should prevail at any given time anyway.

GUY: Well, Nick, I can give you a similar situation. We became sole trustee of an estate which consisted entirely of the common stock of a small company in the dental supply business. We were directed to hold the stock as long as we considered it a sound investment. After a few years, it merged with a company half again as large as it was. Then, we concluded that the investment had changed in character sufficiently so that the language of the will no longer applied to the security we originally had. We made a beginning by selling about 10 percent of the stock, putting the proceeds into fixed-income securities. We sold another 10 percent a year or so later. We are now selling off small amounts and putting half into our fixed-income fund and half in our common stock fund. This cuts income only slightly. We'll probably go on till we get this one stock down to some reasonable proportion. That's very leisurely dollar averaging.

NICK: I assume most people would use averaging more in selling than in buying. If you got a substantial contribution to an account and thought the market was right, you would invest the money immediately.

GARY: We don't always stagger the purchases, but bear in mind Vic's point, which I think was a good one. Your opinion of the market determines how quickly you are going to buy. You might put in 75 percent immediately and 25 percent over the next three months. Or if you weren't so enthusiastic about the market, you might drag it out longer. Your pension fund cash flow makes it a harder problem.

VIC: To put it another way, Nick, suppose you've got $1 million or $2 million in cash today in this market; my judgment would be to scale it in over the next six months rather than put it all to work immediately.

KEITH: That would be true of dollar averaging into the market. But I don't think it's a practical point of view in a personal trust account if you are talking about dollar averaging in a single security. If we start dollar averaging in a stock, the price may go up, and it goes from our buy list into our hold list, or eventually for price reasons into our switch list; then you must buy another stock and wind up with a lot of little holdings. So in personal trust accounts, we do not dollar average as we do in a pension fund. In pension funds, we can buy every month. If we suddenly don't like a name, we switch and buy something else before we build up our holding.

VIC: Well, Keith, let me make sure I understand your point. Taking my example of X million dollars in today's market, would you put all the money in the buy list today?

KEITH: No.

VAL: I think what Keith is talking about is something I have observed quite often. When people are a little bit skittish, they will buy, say, half. If they are right in their selection, and the stock goes up 30 percent, it is awfully hard to get a portfolio manager to carry through because it seems too high.

KEN: It will average up, but it will also average down, which is more often than not compounding a mistake you have already made. I think averaging up is great, because you already have success, you've got a profit in your overall holding right away.

VIC: But it's hard to do psychologically.

GENE: The best statement of aggressive investment philosophy that I have ever heard is: *"If you own a stock and are not half-inclined to average up in it, you ought to sell it."*

KEN: I think that's right.

GENE: I think it is. I think that's a very basic way to look at stocks. And I am inclined to buy more today than I have been to sell.

KEN: When I look at a pension fund, for example, I always begin by looking at the 5 or 10 largest profit items to see if I want to add to those —in other words, the 5 or 10 biggest successes in the account. Why wouldn't I want to add to one of those?

GREG: What if you missed your timing on Xerox and you bought some a little high, and it came off 10 percent?

KEN: I'm not saying you should never average down. You are certainly not a criminal to average down. In cases when you have a stock that's on your buy list and you're satisfied with it, sure——

GENE: I agree.

KEN: As long as it came down from strictly market factors.

An interesting aspect of this chapter is the implication that an individual security merely plays a special part (such as protecting against a particular adversity) in the effort of a total portfolio to achieve the objective of the account. This is contrary to the legal attitude that each individual investment must stand on its own and must be judged on its own success or failure. There is quite a contradiction between the legal insistence on diversification of securities in a trust account, which implies that some of them may not work out well, and the demand that each security stand on its own.

Regardless of the contradiction, the modern concept of diversification requires that stocks with low covariance be used, so that the overall action of the portfolio becomes fairly predictable, despite the poor predictability of any single security. This question was discussed at length by the seminarians during mealtime and off-hours, and there was no indication of support for the view that each individual security in a portfolio should stand on its own. Thus, in this matter there is a clear divergence between the legal point of view and the actual practice of trust investing.

This attitude toward the part played by an individual security in the total performance of a portfolio has further implications of a legal nature. The law has consistently opposed unproductive assets as being harmful to the income beneficiaries. While the seminarians clearly supported the view that fair treatment must be given both to income beneficiaries and to remaindermen, the total portfolio approach would certainly permit the use of certain common stocks that paid small or no dividends as long as they contributed toward the desired overall objectives of the account. IBM currently yields less than 1 percent. Even if it paid no dividend at all, the seminarians would feel that at the right price the stock represented an excellent vehicle for protection against inflation, in terms of both future income and future market value of the portfolio. To the income beneficiary, it could not possibly matter whether the income he received came from two stocks that yielded 1 percent and 5 percent, or from two other stocks that yielded 3 percent each. He would still get the same overall return, but the first combination might fit the overall account objective much better than the second pair of stocks.

NICK: I have one more quick question. We have the legal problem of unproductive investments—that is, where the yield is less than 1 percent. I believe that is the way the present regulation reads?

GUY: I think this depends entirely on account considerations.

NED: Well, you know, a lot of the things we have said have indicated that we look at *permanent investments as not one security but a blend of securities in a continuously managed portfolio.* And I think this is what the people around this table really mean when they say permanent investment.

GENE: Right.

NED: These are continuously managed, and we look at the portfolio as a whole. If your overall return has met your income requirements, it doesn't matter whether you have IBM yielding barely half of 1 percent.

GENE: Well, I think what all of us have been thinking about, too, is the total return from a stock, and it really is a shame that so few trust instruments are written that give you the chance to use that concept in making investment decisions.

KEITH: Ned, we accept your point of view, but I think if the beneficiary of a trust comes in to you and says, "You have held Capital Cities Broadcasting, and it has performed beautifully, but it pays no dividend, and now have sold a portion of it. I think I am entitled to income on that investment." Perhaps you legally owe it to him. This is a life tenant versus remainderman interest. We may not call it to anyone's attention, but if they bring it to our attention I think we are stuck with it.

GENE: Did you have to sell it?

KEITH: No, we didn't necessarily have to sell, but if we have sold it there has to be an allotment of the principal to the life tenant.

NICK: Well, Keith, I recently had such an example and was criticized by the trust examiner, who takes the position that each investment has to stand on its own merit. The overall return of the portfolio is immaterial. I owned a stock that paid no dividend, and I was criticized for holding an unproductive investment. I think the portfolio as a whole should be judged, and I think our law is archaic in this regard.

KEITH: Perhaps we should get the law changed. We're faced with Nick's problem. We've all had it.

GLENN: I think this may be true if it's a zero dividend.

KEITH: Well, that's my point; it was a zero dividend.

GLENN: I think it's an outmoded concept, and the proper approach is to look at the return on the entire account. I agree with Ned.

NED: You mentioned this particular case. Maybe in that account you had Standard Oil of New Jersey, producing 5 percent. All right, we tell the customer that we have a zero-yielding stock and also a 5 percent-yielding stock. If we sell some of this zero-yielding growth stock and put it in an income-producing stock, then to get the proper balance in the portfolio we have to sell our Jersey and put it in Eastman Kodak. We are going to have to reduce the income somewhere to get the characteristics the whole portfolio needs.

NICK: In this regard, I think the law is obsolete.

KEITH: I do, too. I think we all agree. It's a symphony. You are playing all parts. The harmony, the melody, and it's all part of the whole.

One of the difficulties faced by analysts and portfolio managers in a trust institution is that they do not have complete control of the assets under their management. Received in estates, trusts, and agencies are investments that the bank would not buy and that are unfamiliar to its staff. Sale of these assets may be prevented by the terms of the will or agreement, by lack of market, by unwillingness of cotrustees, or by substantial capital gains taxes.

A trustee attempts to offer a service adapted to the individual needs of its customers, but efficient operation of a group of investment accounts requires that holdings be concentrated in a reasonable number of well-supervised issues. Otherwise, the energies of valuable people are not being used to the best advantage of the bank and the majority of its trust customers.

Before accepting an item of trust business, many banks require the elimination of items they are unwilling to follow, or may require that these securities remain under outside supervision.

GIL: Nick has a question for you, George.

NICK: This is the problem of giving opinions on or holding securities you do not follow.

KEN: That's a problem? Sell them—where you can.

NICK: Yes. A customer calls up, or a cotrustee, or you inherit. You are supposed to give opinions on it thereafter, aren't you? We are so sanctimonious in saying that we follow these things so intensively; yet, we glibly give opinions on 2,000 companies. You name it, and we'll give an opinion.

KEN: We don't do that.

GEORGE: You're right. We are very honest. We tell these people that we follow it because we must look at it and check it sometimes. But we tell them we cannot offer an opinion because it is not a name we know well. We go on record as not being able to follow it, but there is nothing we can do if they insist on our holding it.

VAN: But do you charge them for that holding?

GEORGE: In a trust, we have to. In an agency account, we throw it out. We do not charge. We have a broad classification called "no service items," and they are all there and we do not charge.

Only once during the session was there a discussion of the information utilized by analysts in reaching their decisions, and this had to do with only two sources—the management forum as contrasted with the personal interview. It seems worthwhile to list the material studied by analysts.

1. Annual and interim reports of companies in original form or as digested in investment manuals or on computer tape.
2. News articles, management releases, and articles in general, as well as business and trade publications.
3. Economic statistics published by government and private agencies, particularly those relating to monetary conditions, prices, production, and other material of value in forecasting earnings.
4. Prospectuses and other material filed with the Securities and Exchange Commission or other government agencies available to investors.
5. Information and publications from banks, brokers, and investment services, which may be factual or may carry investment opinions.
6. Management presentations at meetings of analysts' societies.
7. Forums for institutional investors held by dealers or corporations.
8. Analysts' interviews with company management. In the last several years, these interviews have become an important source of detailed information. Investment houses oriented toward institutional business, and the institutions themselves, send analysts to visit management. These meetings raise questions about whether the corporation is being impartial in informing its shareholders and also take up much time of senior officers. It is the tendency of some companies to relegate the reception of analysts to the public relations department.

The seminarians strongly recommend that before interviewing a company management an analyst should make a thorough study of the company and its industry, ask intelligent questions, and be more than a mere reporter. They believe also that senior investment officers of major institutions are entitled to a reasonable amount of time from top management

KEITH: George, I think the SEC has been asking the question whether our analysts should come back from their company calls with information that isn't available in other places. How do you fellows handle this new system that the companies are talking of—calling a weekly meeting of analysts, like Union Carbide on Thursday morning, and that's where you get your information.

GEORGE: We hold little or no Carbide stock.

KEN: Does IBM disclose so well to you that you feel——

GEORGE: IBM gives us all the information we reasonably need to make an evaluation. They're not going to tell us any secrets. We don't want any trade secrets. But we do want to get a reasonable amount of information that helps us to make an intelligent evaluation.

One of the differences that is important between us and most other organizations—we publish absolutely nothing, nothing at all. The customer will either take us on the record or give us up. In this squib I mentioned that goes out for communication to the customer there is nothing that isn't published. But the evaluation does go to the portfolio managers, and the evaluation should always be conditioned to the rating assigned by the committee. If there is any change, it goes to the committee before it is circulated.

We just feel that with our confidential relationships with our clients, and with large holdings, we rate an individual meeting without anybody else. Why should information obtained through the skill and knowledge of our analyst be available to others? It doesn't make sense.

GENE: Yes, but you said his skill and knowledge isn't based on confidential information. It's his interpretation of what he learns.

GEORGE: Why should everyone else benefit from our analyst's questions? You should be entitled to get your information alone.

VAN: Well, why should you get more information than we do?

GEORGE: We probably don't. But I do want our senior man exposed to at least one member of senior management once or twice a year, or we sell our holdings. That's all I'm saying.

KEN: George, what's the solution to this from the company's standpoint? What are they going to do to keep their policy-making officials from spending a quarter to half their time talking to a security analyst?

GEORGE: We require no more than half an hour. We can do it at lunch. Generally, it's one of their top four or five people. We visit three or four times a year if we have major holdings, otherwise once or twice.

KEN: There should be an assistant somebody-or-other down the line to screen the analyst, and if he is a really knowledgeable analyst top management should be made available.

GEORGE: That's right.

KEN: That would soon cure us of sending juniors, and we would either send a senior or get our information from some investment banking house, for example, whom we knew sent a senior analyst.

GEORGE: I think that as professionals we are entitled to an audience with the senior management for a reasonable period of time, and not with third-line management and public relations people in the company. That's all I'm trying to say. How else can we judge management?

VAL: The analyst's responsibility is to do his homework, and no analyst who isn't prepared should be allowed in the door.

GEORGE: You are absolutely right, because this is the thing you hear most from the company officials. Many analysts that come to see them haven't done their homework. To waste management's time I think is a crime. Absolutely.

KEN: That's why I like my idea of a public relations fellow screening the analysts. After talking for a few minutes he may decide, "This fellow has no depth, I'll keep him."

CHAPTER SEVEN

Measuring
performance

This chapter spends very little time on the various mathematical approaches that have been proposed for the measurement of rates of return. These are to be found in abundance in the literature of investing, particularly in a series of articles over the past year or so in the **Financial Analysts Journal.**

Performance, however, is not merely a matter of interest to the professional investor. Corporations are interested in the rate of return on their pension and profit sharing funds, universities are clearly in a state of turmoil in their search for additional sources of revenues, individuals expect their accounts with the local broker to match the performance of the go-go funds, and more performance measurement services are being offered by brokerage houses, actuaries, and others. The Financial Executives Institute has been among the first to study methods of measuring investment performance. At the same time, NABAC, recently renamed the Bank Administration Institute, is in the midst of a major project to establish a common system of performance measurement for bank trust departments. For a variety of reasons, bank trust departments have shown interest in developing practical methods of measuring investment performance, either to beat the customer to the punch, or for purposes of improving their internal organizations.

It is very easy to calculate performance once one has defined exactly what performance **is.** Calculation of yields is a matter of simple arithmetic. Compounded rates of return over various periods of time are really not much more complicated, and the complexities are merely proportionate to the degree of accuracy desired.

What is really more important is the determination of just what is to be measured. And once it is measured, against what yardstick should it be placed for purposes of comparison?

The problem is made even worse when one considers that accomplishment alone may be merely an historical artifact. That someone has climbed to the top of the hill is interesting but not impressive. That he has done so under withering fire from a superior enemy force makes him a hero. Similarly, in investing, the measurement of investment return is without significance unless one is aware of the risks that were taken, or the market conditions that existed during the period of that accomplishment. Good results in a difficult market are to be praised. Good results in an excellent market may not be very satisfactory. That someone has won a fortune at Monte Carlo or perhaps in a thin stock whose trading volume has exceeded its capitalization by three times in the past year merely indicates that statistical probabilities do not forbid a gambler to be successful once in a while.

This chapter on performance gives little satisfaction to those who want a precise definition of risk. Risk is clearly a function of human satisfactions and the probabilities that an investment strategy will fail to achieve the objectives of an account. No effort to treat such matters mathematically has been made in this monograph, although there is a glimmer of hope from the academic community in their studies of "decision making under conditions of uncertainty."

During the discussion, the seminarians returned to earlier subjects involving the decision-making roles of the securities analyst and the portfolio manager. Some discussion of investment strategies also was offered. These matters are not totally unrelated to the question of measuring performance. For the purpose of tidiness, much of this material was shifted to other chapters, which leaves this chapter with a good deal more fragmentation than would suit our sense of neatness. Readers who would like to have a rather complete bibliography of the subject of measuring performance should welcome the bibliography of Dr. Shannon Pratt included in the May-June, 1968 issue of the **Financial Analysts Journal.**

GIL: Let's turn to Ned now for this section on performance measurement.

NED: Well, this has been a touchy subject among people in trust departments, for several reasons. I think the reason I have been interested in measuring performance has been that so many of our pension and profit sharing funds have demanded that we show them how well we are performing in comparison with something or other.

This has spread rather rapidly, with brokerage houses offering services to corporations, for either a cash fee or commissions, to measure the performance of their pension funds. They offer to tell what was good, bad, or indifferent, about the account performance compared with similar accounts, and so on.

Even in trusts we find that a person will come to us and say, "How did my account perform in comparison with ———— Fund for the last six weeks?" So we are beginning to feel pressures from the outside, and I think there is a natural tendency for us to resist those pressures a little bit. But I would like to speak to the other side of that position very strongly, because I think we have more to gain by measuring our performance than we realize. I think that methods can be developed to permit us to judge our own internal organizations and decide where we are strong and where we are weak. We can determine whether or not our problem is with the *selection of stocks,* which we might blame on the security analyst; whether it is the *blending of those securities into a portfolio,* which we might blame on the portfolio manager; or whether it is *policy decisions*—decisions made by a trust investment committee. Those policy decisions would obviously include *timing* decisions. And the *efficiency with which the portfolio manager applies policy* to his accounts. All these are things we can measure for ourselves. And this will give us a much better management control of our organization than we could possibly get in any other fashion.

We should be thinking about the measurement of performance strictly from the viewpoint of what it will do for us and not worry about whether some account might not have matched ———— Fund in the last X months.

Having said that, let's move on to a couple of specific areas. One, there are various systems of measuring the return on portfolios. I don't think we ought to go into them right now, except to mention that there is one system that is highly precise—the Fisher System,[1] which is now being worked on by NABAC. It's not going to be presented to banks so quickly as most of us hoped. The last I heard there appears to be a delay. However, the NABAC system would be amenable to almost any computer system any of us would have. It will not be available for 9 to 12 months.

The principal chapters in the proposed NABAC publication are on the subjects of return, risk, classification of pension funds, classifications of pension fund assets, and valuation of assets. In the chapter on return, the draft emphasizes that a system of measuring rates of return must avoid

---

[1] Lawrence Fisher, "An Algorithm for Timing Exact Rates of Return," *Journal of Business* Supplement, January, 1966, pp. 111–18.

the yield to maturity approach, often referred to as the internal or average rate of return. The difficulty with this type of return is that it is dollar weighted, and is therefore heavily affected by the timing of contributions and withdrawals. The NABAC text recommends the time weighted rate of return, which is the rate of return that would be necessary for a single dollar to accumulate the final value of that dollar at the end of the period to be measured. While actuaries must use the dollar weighted approach, an accurate report card must be time weighted. The chapter on risk notes that rates of return are higher if risks are taken. It is important, however, that the risk strategy be adopted from the start and that performance be maximized thereafter. Historical studies have revealed that the variability of rates of return throughout time correlate well with rates of return. Thus, achievement of high rates of return will generally be accompanied by considerable variability of rates of return over short time segments.

In the chapter on classification of pension funds, it is emphasized that pension funds should be measured against similar funds, with consideration to the age of the fund, the size, the source of decision making, the willingness to accept risks, and so on.

Finally, it is pointed out that the performance of the total portfolio is the most important thing. At the same time, performance of individual segments should not be neglected. It is suggested that securities be divided into four classifications for purposes of comparison: (1) common stocks and warrants, (2) convertible bonds and convertible preferreds, (3) fixed-income securities, and (4) politically directed investments.

Another chapter dealing with the valuation of pension fund assets provides considerable technical detail on the proper procedures for the evaluation of private placements, oil royalties, sale-and-leasebacks, other nonmarketable securities, and other special problems related to valuation.

At the same time, we have other systems that are approximations. Norman Wood[2] has done a good deal of work in that area. Dr. Peter Dietz[3] at Northwestern University has a system that is also an approximation. There are many others. Which one of these we might decide to use I think is immaterial if the accuracy of the system will tell us the return within plus or minus five basis points. I don't think there is any point in getting up to the 15th decimal place if it is going to cost $20,000 more a year to do it. But if we can come within five basis points, then I think both the Dietz and Wood systems are amenable to the degree of accuracy we're interested in.

In my opinion, the study should be done on the basis of quarterly

---

[2] R. Norman Wood, "Measuring the Investment Yield of Pension Funds" (Alexander & Alexander, Inc., November, 1964) (privately distributed).

[3] Peter O. Dietz, "Pension Funds: Measuring Investment Performance" (New York: The Free Press, Inc., 1966).

performance over a period of about five years. I say quarterly because your investment reviews are generally prepared quarterly on the type of accounts you would want to make a performance study, and I say five years for several reasons. One, if you measure the performance of an account going back 20 years you are talking about a lot of former personnel who are dead, who are retired, who are no longer with your organization, and who operated under a completely different organizational structure and different concepts of investing, and so on. If you move down to five years, you probably get pretty much the same people and the same ideas that you have today, so this will give you more of an idea of the current performance situation. If you reduce it to any less than five years, your sample becomes so small in the total number of quarters that you really haven't got a statistically valid sample to work with. And 5 years is only 20 quarters. If you have a sample of 20 items, that is a fairly small universe and about as small as I think you can stand. So I happen to come up with five years done by quarters.

Now, some of you may price your accounts monthly, and perhaps you can take a shorter span and get good results in measurement and gain knowledge from it. I think it is a very debatable subject, and this is not a very definitive answer by any means. This is just my opinion.

Well, now, where do you get your basic material? I think you adjust your accounting system and your investment review system so that it will automatically throw off the raw data the machine is going to process further in the calculation of performance. On your account ledger, you throw off income by categories—that is, whether it came from equities, convertibles, or other fixed-income securities, or whatever breakdown you want to use. You would have to identify your capital gains and losses realized, by category, the additions and withdrawals, the principal and income received, and depending on the system you are going to use, the actual dates of transactions. The ideal system would require you to date the exact transaction, because you need to calculate it from the day the money was put into, say, common stocks, on out to the final date of the measurement period. In the Dietz and Wood systems, you assume the money was invested in the middle of the period, so you don't have to have the exact dates for their systems.

From the investment reviews, you can get the market values and book values by categories at the beginning and end of each period, and the principal and income cash balances of both dates.

So those are the raw inputs you would feed into your system.

My question is now, what do you measure? Well, first I think you measure *policy and timing decisions* as applied to the account. And this means changes. For instance, changes in the equity/fixed-income ratio. These changes can come about in several ways. One, they come about by changes in market prices, and this would be an involuntary change. Two, they come about by deliberate decisions made by the investment committee. Three, they come about by the availability, unplanned by the department, of money for investment. That is, someone decides to put another $100,000 into the account. So we have to take into account when money flows into the account and what effect that might have had on the equity/fixed-income ratio.

One of the things I think should be measured always is the volatility of the equities. In my opinion, one of the most sophisticated tools that will be used in the future by portfolio managers is not merely the equity percentages but the volatility of those equities. For example—an exaggerated case but—suppose you were able to pick a group of stocks that would move twice as fast as the market as a whole, either up or down. Then you would be able to match the performance of the market by using only half as many dollars as you would by buying the market itself. This is a tool with tremendous flexibility. If you have a limitation on the amount of common stocks you can hold, or if you are forced by a cotrustee to cut back common stocks, you can offset that very easily by reinvesting in stocks that have higher volatility than the ones you sold. So you would be able to get the same market action out of the account and actually have more dollars in fixed-income securities. A few people are doing work on volatility, primarily the hedge funds, but I don't think it is something being studied by most trust institutions. I think it should be studied.

As I mentioned, the security analysts' selections are something that should be studied with considerable care. In the process of making volatility studies, you generally create a linear regression or characteristic line on each portfolio and on your buy list, and it will have a positive or negative bias. And you may find that you've got good results because you had high volatility in a rising market or low volatility in a declining market; yet, at the same time, you might have a bad selection of securities in terms of whether those securities had a positive or negative bias. How much time do we have to spend on this? I would like to draw you this picture to show you what I am talking about.[4]

---

[4] A more detailed and perhaps clearer exposition of this approach may be found in Jack L. Treynor, "How to Rate Management of Investment Funds," *Harvard Business Review,* January–February, 1965; and Frank E. Block, "Risk and Performance," *Financial Analysts Journal,* March–April, 1966.

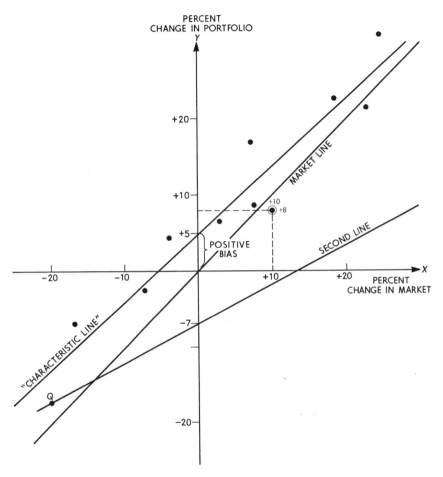

If you were to plot an all-stock account, or your buy list as a port-folio, the *Y* axis is the percent change in the market value of the port-folio, and the *X* axis is the percent change in the market. If you had 20 quarters, you would plot each quarter to reflect the percentage change in the portfolio and the market. This point right here (*pointing at the circled dot in the illustration*) would say that in this period the market went up 10 percent and the account went up eight percent. Then, you could run a least squares line on the 20 points, or just draw a line in by eyeball. You would have a characteristic line of the common stock portfolio that went something like that (*drawing a line through the points*).

The volatility of the line is the slope of the line—that is, the vertical distance divided by the horizontal distance. In this particular case, it appears that the volatility is a little less than the market, because if you held the market, your line would go up at a 45 degree angle.

So here is an account that in the past has had more stability than the market, but in most of the time periods it has outperformed the market. That is, in nearly every case we see that the dots I have drawn here fall above the market, except that dot and that dot (*indicating two points that fall below the market line*). So we were taking a little bit lower risk because we have lower volatility; yet, we have gotten good performance out of the portfolio.

But this Y intercept, where the characteristic line crosses the Y axis, is a highly significant figure in that it represents a positive or negative bias; in this case, it must be plus 5 percent. In effect, you can express this in an equation of Y_c, or the characteristic action of the portfolio in any period, is equal to M times X, where M would be the slope of the line, or the volatility, plus a constant positive bias here of 5 percent. X is the change in the market.

In this case $[Y_c = MX + 5\%]$ we've got less volatility than the market—make it 0.9—so 0.9 is our volatility. This is going to be slower than the market, but every period we are going to have a plus 5 percent positive bias working for us.

Well, this is something that tells us an interesting thing. The portfolio manager put these securities together and created something that is more stable than, say, the Dow Jones Averages. But he used securities that had a positive bias of percent relative to the market. If we came up with a line that fell somewhere near that [second line], that would be a negative 7 percent, and we would say, "Why, we've got a lousy bunch of security analysts." But in a certain type of market, we might have outperformed the market as a whole, because if we went into a period where stocks were going sharply down our points might have fallen around here [point Q] where we would have outperformed the market itself, but the security analysts sure did a lousy job. We were just lucky because we had stability and the slope of this line was very low.

Of course, the characteristic lines of portfolios have infinite possibilities. If you were a hedge fund, you could take a small short position in some stocks that have a negative bias, to offset a larger long position. You would want the shorted stocks to be highly volatile but with a strong negative bias. Of course, you would adjust the balance, depending on market conditions—whether you thought the market was going up or down. But you would want higher volatility in the short position because it involved fewer dollars. You would certainly want a negative bias to it. But this bias part is one way you measure security analysts, and the slope [or volatility] used at different times in the market cycle tells you something about your portfolio analysts. Well, this is just one approach to the problem.

Of course, in actually using volatility as an investment tool one must develop techniques to measure *future* volatility of stocks, and this is based on an analysis of past volatility characteristics. We've made some studies that showed volatility of an individual stock changes from one time to another. Volatility increases while a stock is popular. I guess you would call that the fad characteristic. What it really means is that the stock is thin in relation to the volume of trading in it.

We also found that volatility was related to the volatility of earnings, which is a characteristic of quality. Past volatility of an individual security doesn't always give a very good clue to what the future will be, unless things in the market for that stock haven't changed. As long as all the market conditions are the same, and the market attitude toward the stock is the same, the volatility won't change much.

Volatility of portfolios seems to demand some sort of spectral analysis of the portfolio, since two highly volatile stocks can offset each other by going in opposite directions. This means that the highly selective portfolio can be a good deal more volatile than a broadly diversified one. If you diversify too broadly, volatility is going to be "one" simply because you are going to do exactly whatever the market does. One thing you can be sure of: if the trading volume of the stock is rising substantially without any increase in the floating supply of stock, the volatility of that stock is going way up.

I guess I've wandered off into portfolio management a little bit, but I wanted to mention this approach as having a potential in this business of measuring performance. It can explain a lot of things about why an account is acting in a particular way.

I also think that Keith's suggestion of coloring the lines on a relative performance chart for the individual companies on the buy list is a good indication of how your security analyst's recommendations have worked out and how good your committee is in selecting or rejecting what the security analyst recommends. Of course, if your security analyst is in a lousy industry the committee won't pick any of his stocks, and he'll just have to be judged on the basis of his prediction of which stocks in the industry would perform best and which would be worst.

I'll be glad to answer any questions before we kick off a general discussion, and I'd like to hear what some of the rest of you are doing in your own shops.

VIC: Suppose you get a wide dispersion of dots so that, really, the line is not representative of the portfolio because over the time span you've examined, the portfolio has changed so much that you can't generalize the value.

NED: Yes, that's possible. The *standard deviation* away from this line will tell you how much of a true characteristic line it is.

VIC: OK.

NED: If all the dots are pretty close to the line, then you can say this is very clearly the characteristic; there is great certainty that this characteristic is valid for this portfolio. However, on any date you can estimate the volatility of a portfolio if you have estimates of the volatility of each stock and the *covariance* of the stocks [the tendency of the stocks to move in the same direction].

GEORGE: Ned, to what extent are you giving the security analyst credit that may be due the portfolio manager?

NED: Well, it's true the security analysts come up with a lot of stocks. Maybe they come up with 50. The portfolio manager takes 25. He may have taken the best 25.

GEORGE: I just wondered how you evaluate the performance of the two in a portfolio.

KEITH: Could you apply all 50?

NED: You could plot all 50 buy-list stocks and give yourself a line on the security analysis division. A good manager would beat his buy list and a bad manager wouldn't do so well, assuming that they both took the same amount of risk. I have to admit that we haven't gotten very far in determining how much risk a portfolio manager took, except by taking some sort of weighted average volatility measure of his portfolio and seeing whether it was high when the market was rising or low when the market was falling. We need a lot of help on this question, and we can't seem to come to any agreement on the best way to handle it. I know it doesn't do any good to measure performance unless you know how much risk was taken to get that performance. And, of course, you've got to use other methods, too. Take a look at the performance of the individual security analyst——

The speaker suggests weighted volatility as a possible measure of the risk in a portfolio. The commonly accepted measure of risk in the academic world is the **variability of the rate of return.** This concept is more easily handled mathematically, since the figures used are commonly historical ones rather than estimates of the future. In any event, those who consider the risk factor to be of importance may want to explore the literature for possibilities in this area.

GEORGE: I thought he said portfolio performance.

NED: This is a portfolio, but you can try to tell how much of the performance was due to a blending of securities and how much would probably be bias——

GEORGE: The blending is the portfolio man's responsibility, not the research man's.

NED: That's right.

GEORGE: That's what I'm getting at—how you evaluate the relative performance of the two. That's very important. Ned, should you evaluate the performance of the two separately? This should be the portfolio manager's responsibility. The research man's performance should be valued differently.

NED: Well, I just say that the positive and negative bias here tells you something about your security analysis selection.

GEORGE: It tells you about the securities you own—what you're using.

NED: What you're using. Yes, that's right.

GEORGE: Not in trust, but in our investment advisory work we just took six random accounts and took a three-year showing to see what happened in the accounts. Volatility and relative performance, and using the market as 100 percent, they had a variation of 60 percent. The portfolio men used the same list, only one fellow bought Chrysler instead of General Motors; one fellow bought Xerox instead of Addressograph Multigraph. This is the portfolio manager's judgment.

KEN: And a little bit of luck.

GEORGE: No, now wait a minute. (*laughter*) That's one of the elements that works in the portfolio manager's favor.

NED: Well, one thing you could do if you wanted to look at security analysis alone is take all 50 of your stocks on the buy list. Plot the list to see whether you had a positive or negative bias.

GEORGE: Actually, I think we should have two—one for the portfolio men to measure performance and one for the research department.

VAN: How about Ned's chemical analyst who did such a fine job of predicting the chemical stocks? They were all attractive sales.

GEORGE: It wasn't his fault. It was the committee's.

VAN: We are measuring his performance on that buy list. And he was left out, and he was 100 percent right, and he doesn't get any credit for it.

GEORGE: That's why I say we should value the analyst's performance separately from the portfolio manager's.

GENE: Why don't you measure the security analyst's performance though—how effective he is at getting things done? How much good is an analyst if he is great but nothing ever happens? Then he is no good to you, really.

GEORGE: He's only measured in terms of the recommendations he specifically makes.

GENE: Right. And what if nobody ever acts on those recommendations? The recommendations are great——

GEORGE: You change committees!

VAN: After all, you've got to recognize his talent. The committee is at fault. If the fellow has 10 straight winners and they turn him down, I put the blame on the committee, not on the analyst.

GENE: You know that there are analysts who are good but who just don't have the ability to communicate.

GARY: Next time he would be wrong. (*laughter*)

VAN: I'm not going to judge the analyst on a buy list that's determined by someone else.

GEORGE: No. That's the point I was getting at. It should be on the basis of his own individual recommendations.

NED: Let me go on and finish one or two points, and then we will go to a complete general discussion. What do we want to measure— one, the *return* concept, or two, *meeting account objectives?* And just how do you do this—particularly meeting account objectives? One fellow gave me an answer one time to the question: "What do you call good performance?" He said, "Happy customers." I thought that was a lousy answer—until I thought about it a while. Get away from the mathematics and just think of the holding of wealth as having the purpose of providing human satisfactions. If these people are getting satisfaction, maybe this fellow was right.

The next thing is *standards of comparison.* I think you've got to select your own, whether you want to select target accounts and have this account beat the target accounts, or beat the buy list, or whether you want to take the indexes—a bond index, a convertible index, a market index of stocks—and combine them in certain proportions and say, "All right, we want our accounts to beat those," or do we just want to meet specific return objectives? These are things we should think about.

Another point that's extremely important is to review the outside influences on the account—cotrustees, for example, or just a casual remark that the customer made, "I hope you won't buy any grocery chains; they sell *beer* now, you know." I've had that several times—in fact, ———— [a religious organization]. They wouldn't let us buy Safeway Stores several years ago.

KEN: That's a pretty good reason *to buy* Safeway Stores. (*laughter*)

NED: They thought they were making a good decision at that particular time. Just a casual remark by the customer about something he likes or doesn't like may influence the portfolio manager, and it may never go into the record. And yet he knows they don't like television stocks; they think they're evil; there are too many naked women and that sort of thing. (*laughter*) Let me see what else. There ain't no other. That's all I've got to say.

KEN: One more thing you have to consider—we talked about it before we broke for coffee—is the limited resources of talent that we all have. How much of that talent can we spend working on all this past history and making up these studies to show our customers and thinking of new ways to do it and making a nice-looking presentation? I know a fellow who was marvelous at doing all this, indeed, but think of the time he spent in making up charts of what had gone on in the past instead of focusing on what the future portfolio problems would be.

NED: It can be done easily on computers.

GLENN: I disagree with the word "easily," Ned.

NED: Not easily, but I mean we don't have to tie up a good investment man in calculating with a pencil.

GLENN: That's all right. You're going to have to tie up yourself or argue with the fellow who has charge of the time on the computer.

GUY: This is right.

NED: On small accounts, the chances are you don't want to make these calculations. If it's a $50,000 account, you can't afford to give the guy that sort of service.

GLENN: You treat all accounts equal——

Unfortunately, this remark was interrupted, and we shall never know exactly what the speaker wanted to say. It touches on the ethical question of whether large accounts should receive preferential treatment over smaller accounts. Obviously, they should not.

The weight of the seminarians' thinking was that performance should be measured primarily for purposes of internal improvement rather than for customer relations. Certainly, a trustee should be just as interested in how his small accounts perform as he is in the larger ones. A sampling of accounts by size should provide him with this information.

It is not certain that there is either a legal or ethical charge that the trustee measure the performance of his accounts. The law is silent on the question. At the same time, the capabilities of the professional trustee are now such that performance measurement will soon be a routine matter. The ethical trustee will attempt to measure all his weaknesses and mistakes in the continuing search for better investment performance.

NED: We are talking about half-million-dollar accounts and up. This eliminates a lot of this small stuff. I think, by and large, the customers with small accounts generally aren't the ones that come in and ask about performance.

KEN: Except for customer pressure, why don't you just calculate all these things on your common trust fund? It's a show account. Isn't that enough to give you an idea of the mistakes you're making or the things you're doing right? I think it is very important to use your common fund as a guinea pig on a great deal of this. In the first place, you can use it as a standard if you want to, and, in the second place, it would help open up possible questions you might have in organizational procedure.

GENE: I disagree, Ken. Let's talk about some of these consult accounts—the cotrustee account and that sort of thing—where they set up obstacles to doing what you think is best. How are you ever going to be able to show them what it costs the account if you don't have some way of measuring how their account is doing compared to an account that you run on your own?

GLENN: I think you have to do that, don't you? When the issue comes up, you have to go back and say, "Well, all right, we did this at your request, and this is the result." To keep a running performance record to guard against that, Gene, I just think you are spending too much time——

GENE: Well, no. It isn't a tough job to go back—I mean we are not going to go back. I think that would be an incredible job to go back and collect the data backward. But we have set up a data collection system that is not complicated and that we can use with the computer——

GLENN: On all accounts you do this?

GENE: Well, we are not doing it on all accounts initially, but we have the ability.

GLENN: It doesn't look so insurmountable, what you may do if you want to.

GENE: That's right. We are talking about, say, 400 accounts off the bat. You are talking about a few hours of computer time. I mean that's no joke. But it doesn't take an investment man's time, and part of our motivation, as Ned said, is that NABAC is going to come up with a system. If you don't set up the data collection system, then you are faced with a fantastic job if you ever want to go back. But at least start collecting the data as you go along in a way that you can use, and put that into the machine. Then when the system comes along that you think is the right system, at least you are a little ahead of the game.

VIC: That would be wonderful.

NED: This will permit us to exchange figures without showing the name of the account. I'd just give you 50 trust accounts, 50 pension funds, 50 profit sharing funds. So could 100 other banks. Then you could compare your results with 100 other banks.

GLENN: Backtracking just a little bit, I feel that we must take these comparisons not only among our accounts and with the averages but also with some of the leading mutual funds, and with other banks, as a monitor of our own performance—as an offset to some of the competitive statements that have been made that are not well founded but just poorly put together. You all run across some of your friends who may look at what ———— Fund has done and look at what my pension fund has done. You've got a balanced pension fund and ———— Fund has an all-stock fund. They [the customers] are taking [measuring] the pension fund with money coming in periodically, or monthly, perhaps over the last five years, against what was put in the ———— Fund five years ago. This is comparing oranges and apples.

NED: And on that pension fund you've got no control over contributions. I just calculated what it would have meant to one of our pension funds if $1 million received on January 30, 1962, had gotten lost in the mail for six months—the account would have been several hundred thousand dollars better off! (*laughter*)

GENE: This may sound like speculation, Ned, but you could have invested that money in bonds!

The word speculation here half humorously refers to an earlier discussion of a court case in which one of the three findings of the trial judge was that a reduction in common stocks and investment of the proceeds in bonds with the intent of repurchasing common stocks at a later date was speculative. None of the seminarians or committeemen considered shifts in the percentages in equities in fixed-income securities to be speculative. On the

contrary, they considered them to be an essential part of effective investment management.

NED: If you get $1 million, the chances are you are going to put
some of it in common stocks.

GENE: Well, I mean this is a decision the trustee has the ability to
make.

VIC: Speculation?

GENE: That's what I mean.

NICK: Not under our philosophy.

KEN: We are supposed to be talking about personal trusts. I think
it is very interesting that we've spent this much time on portfolio—
performance measurements of personal trusts. It hasn't been this big
a problem to us in personal accounts.

NED: It will be, though.

GIL: Val, under this heading of standards of comparison, last night
you were saying to me, over about a third drink, that perhaps a discussion of the standards of comparison with respect to the competition of
these high-performance funds might be exposed here in a little more
conversation. This is the appropriate time to throw that question at
Ned.

VAL: Well, of course, I think it comes in more with your pension
funds and institutional accounts. But I think—with this generation of
performance mutual funds—I think we are being pressured into a
short-term performance horizon, which results in some unwise investment practices, and if we could say something about that, and perhaps discourage quarterly performance records in an effort to match
this on a competitive basis, it might be desirable. It is long-term results that count, not three months. At least I'd like to hear what you
have to say about it.

GEORGE: In other words, you are asking us to evaluate nimbleness.

VAL: Exactly, and this is what some of our customers are asking
us to do. In fact, they are demanding.

Customers are aware of the various superior performance records of performance mutual funds during the previous two years. A subsequent discussion indicated a division of opinion on the proper time horizon for a
trustee. Some felt that the extremely short-term horizon used by some investment organizations was nothing more than old-fashioned speculation
based on quarter-to-quarter or year-to-year earnings gains, plus a heavy dose
of technical analysis. The doubters felt that such an investment approach

would ultimately lead to disaster. On the other hand, quite a number of the seminarians felt that the best investment performance could be achieved by a sharply reduced emphasis on fundamental analysis and an increased emphasis on those factors that tend to cause movements in stock prices over relatively short-term periods of time.

GEORGE: The customers see it.

VAL: They see it. That's right. But is this policy over the long term desirable or not? I mean is it leading to short-term investment decisions that are awfully hard to unwind? I guess that's what I'm saying.

GEORGE: I think you can appropriately ask the question of just how compensatory or defensive is long-term investing. I think a lot of us quite honestly use it as an excuse for a little bit of laziness, and I question the wisdom of it.

NICK: What do you mean by long term?

GEORGE: Five or ten years.

NICK: What do you mean by short term?

VAL: One quarter.

GEORGE: Six months and one day.

The speaker was referring to the period of time necessary for a holding to be considered a long-term capital gain, for which the tax rate is lower than for shorter periods of time. In effect, he was saying that the time horizon should be as short as practicable, giving consideration to the existing tax regulations.

GEORGE: I think this is a very serious question, because it is going to come up. Of course, you're talking about performance in pension funds. But this approach also gets involved in individual accounts and living trusts—the tendency to be alert. And all sorts of studies are being done now. We are not the only people doing it. I know many, many people who are doing it, and invariably they show that *activity* pays off. Activity pays off. You're not going to get away from it. You just can't. Trustees are going to live with it, and we had better be flexible and do more than just hire analysts and portfolio managers.

On this time horizon again, what is the shortest period of time you would be willing to put your reputation on the line? A potential customer comes in and says, "I want to put this account with you, and I'd like to take a look at it at the end of the year and see how you've done, and on the basis of that we'll see whether I continue with you or go somewhere else."

KEN: If he says that to you, you're probably not going to turn him down. You're going to say, "We don't think you can measure accurately in a year, but we hope that by the end of the year we will have convinced you of that."

GENE: It depends on the size. But with the startup cost of the account, you are going to lose money on the account if you lose it at the end of the year.

KEN: If he says he is going to do the same thing with your bank and the ———— [another bank], and at the end of the year if you have done better he will bring the whole thing over here, aren't you going to be in the competition? I think you are.

GEORGE: I think you will find that people have done that. We have had several that have. It's a quite reasonable approach. The people are willing to go beyond a year.

KEN: You are fairly close to the customer after about a year, so he'll let it go another year. It's only after four or five that you have any divergence, so then you're in the soup or you're OK.

NICK: What is the shortest period of time you feel is practical?

GENE: Three years.

NED: In making measurements of a portfolio, what reaction do you have at my thoughts of five years as a reasonable period of time?

GUY: I think it is a good measure.

GEORGE: Good.

GENE: I think you are going to be stuck with three years. I think that maybe five years is too long for some people.

VIC: We like five. The customer would rather have three if he is generous.

GREG: I would think the customer is going to be wanting to see it as you go along. We have one that we must do quarterly. We measure against 12 other accounts and some investment funds, and let the client name some that he wanted to pick. So this is a real challenge for every quarter. I think five years is a fair length of time. You get a real feel of your results.

KEN: Well, in most nongrowing accounts—personal accounts—this is quite easy to measure, isn't it?

GREG: Sure it is.

KEN: I mean, you don't need any complicated formulas for that.

At this point, the discussion shifted substantially to the general area of responsibility and decision making by portfolio managers, security analysts, the investment committee, and what limitations and flexibility should be given to each. We have therefore shifted a good deal of the dialogue to Chapter Four, simply because this was where the initial debate on the relative capacities and proper functions of security analysts and portfolio managers was first introduced.

The discussion did not touch on the measurement of the portfolio manager's performance. The points emphasized included the obvious problem that different portfolio managers have different sets of accounts to work with. One portfolio manager may have accounts that are aiming primarily for long-term growth, while another may have accounts whose objectives are principally the production of high income with great market stability. Comparison of their relative performance would be quite unfair on an overall return basis because of the difference in account objectives. It was also mentioned that the portfolio manager is often burdened with the assets that were originally deposited in the account. While it was generally accepted that every account is all cash in the sense that the trustee has the right to liquidate present holdings at any time, there are special problems in which sale of a security would result in very large capital gains taxes in addition to commissions, so the all-cash view does have exceptions.

Further along, we pick up a portion of the discussion that returns to the specific problem of measuring the performance of portfolios.

VIC: Ned mentioned a subject we haven't treated much, and that is the *standards of comparison* for use—a target account, some index, or some combination of indexes, or some concept of return. What is the general practice? We use a comparison of the common stock section against the Dow; that is about the limit of the comparisons we can make. And we started with exploring alternatives to that, and I would very much value any——

KEN: Don't start now. Wait until Dow catches up with S & P. (*laughter*)

VIC: I am not satisfied with the way we are measuring our performance. The only performance measurement we are doing is the performance of our common stocks against the Dow. And that doesn't satisfy me at all. What sort of things do you measure against? Ned gave some suggestions. I would like to know what you people do.

GEORGE: We use the three—the Standard and Poor's 500, the S & P 425, and the Dow Jones. For a while I equated them with our star-rated buy list, and it did remarkably well.

NED: Well, in using the system you use, shouldn't you use your star-rated buy list as your standard for measuring your portfolio manager? If he had a choice from those stocks only, that's his universe.

GEORGE: That's right. The only drawback to the point Gene had in mind—the tax factor, I think, is a very significant part in a taxable account, and it could be an important deterrent. It could be a very important deterrent.

GENE: In the buy list, you are switching the unattractive stocks off the list. I assume when the name goes off the list that no one is selling it.

GEORGE: No.

GENE: You are putting it into a hold category?

GEORGE: Yes, generally.

KEN: There are terrific biases in a bank as big as ———— [a large New York bank] on what you caused to happen because of your own buying of that stock. You could measure that too. That's big. You may not think it, but you look at the share of the volume you are taking, and you know it's been an influence on a stock that is newly on your buy list.

VIC: Do you use any indexes for bond measurement, George? Do you measure bond performance?

GEORGE: We do in certain accounts, but we haven't done too much of that because the biggest part has gone in private placements, and we have done so much better than any of the indexes.

Private placements typically yield from 0.25 percent to 1.75 percent more than publicly offered issues of similar quality and terms; the spread depends on the market conditions. It should be noted, however, that private placements are not publicly quoted, and therefore they are often overpriced when the market value is estimated on an investment review. Realistic pricing of private placements would show that they have declined in price more or less continuously for the past two decades.

VIC: Ken, what do you use?

KEN: In bonds?

VIC: No, in stocks.

KEN: We measure against the S & P 500. We also keep track of other common trust funds and mutual funds. We try not to pick the hottest one. (*laughter*)

VIC: Pick a few older, more seasoned ones. (*laughter*)

KEN: No, I think measuring against an actual fund rather than against some weighted index has a lot to say for it. That takes in commissions and market impact.

GREG: How many of you are measuring all of your private trusts that we're talking about?

KEN: All? (*pause*)

GENE: How many of you are measuring a quarter of them? (*laughter*) How many of you are measuring any more than you have been told to measure? (*laughter*)

NED: How many of you are measuring your common trust funds against some standard?

GLENN: Yes, we do that.

GUY: We are measuring our common stock trust funds. I don't think we are measuring our municipal or bond funds; we haven't done the municipal funds; we have done the balanced fund.

VAN: In this measurement thing, isn't it important to get a mutual fund that has the same *objectives* as the account, that is willing to accept the same *risks?* That's hard to do, but I think there's a fallacy in just measuring against the market, because you are not assuming the same risks in the individual account that are inherent in the market average.

GEORGE: In large accounts, you have a cross section pretty much representative of the 425 industrials.

GARY: How many stocks or individual issues would you have in a large account?

GEORGE: Between 50 and 75.

GREG: By large, you mean——

GEORGE: Oh, by large I am talking about something that goes over $10 million.

NED: Nobody has said much about measuring the risk at the same time they are measuring the performance, and I think this is the central element. How much risk would you take in order to accomplish something?

NICK: We don't even know what risk is, do we?

GEORGE: How do you define risk?

NED: I can't.

GIL: If you can't define it, you sure can't measure it.

NED: Well, I think there are certain things you can measure—the variability of return, volatility, the semivariance, the downward percentage swings as compared to some standard. They will be greater or less than that standard is. You could do some things mathematically, and you could identify those as being related to certain types of risk. You could measure variability of income in an income-oriented account and say, "What we've done in this account is better, or worse, than some standard might have been."

NICK: You are setting a mathematical definition?

NED: Yes, because the more acceptable definitions of risk, like "failure to meet the objectives of the account," we don't know how to handle mathematically.

GENE: An unhappy customer.

GLENN: It's the only answer, isn't it?

NED: Well, I think this unhappy customer thing deserves some debate. What are you trying to do with money? As I say, I rejected it immediately when I first heard it, but when I thought about it a little bit I was more willing to think there was some validity to the view.

GEORGE: Well, I've found that most customers who are happy stay happy until they've gone to somebody else. (*laughter*)

GIL: I'd like to know how to measure an unhappy customer. I think that would be an excellent statistical thing to work on.

GENE: It would be very closely correlated with the Dow Jones Average.

NED: It would be very closely correlated with the number of calls you got from the president of the bank. You could plot that index, I suppose.

VAL: How can you tell whether you have a good portfolio manager or not, if you are not measuring the performance of the accounts he is handling?

GEORGE: We've always been right on one factor, and that's the rate of renewal of new customers. It always works.

VIC: I get a feeling in talking about performance measurements that you are essentially looking at the performance of the common stock sector of the account, and yet most of the personal accounts that I'm familiar with are not all common stocks. Most of them are balanced accounts.

GEORGE: Commons are the side of the balance that pays off.

VIC: Yes, but you are looking to your overall return in the account. What can you measure that against? You can't do that very well against the S & P 500. I don't know whether you are meeting the customer's objectives. Are you doing a job for the customer? If all you are doing is finding out whether you picked good stocks for him, you are only doing part of the job.

GENE: In a lot of our pension accounts, we are measured against other trustees. We work hard at doing the best on the bond side, and the other people are too, and we just come out so close. Everybody is just very close in terms of the rate of return that you're getting.

VIC: Yes, but your ratio also has a factor in there. You may do well on the bond side and well on the stock side, but if you do, let's say you're 60 percent bonds and somebody else is only 30 percent bonds, and he may beat your ears in.

GEORGE: Well, that should be taken into account.

GENE: The overall account is what matters.

VIC: Well, this is what I am trying to get at. How do you get an overall measure of a portfolio's performance——

NICK: For a personal trust account?

VIC: Yes, which takes into account the bond side and the stock side and the mix of the two.

NICK: Why can't you simply measure it against the S & P Index? This, it seems to me, would equate out if one guy wanted to run 50 percent bonds and the other wanted 20 percent. This is a management decision and——

GEORGE: Don't you think that a well-managed balanced fund of 65–35 percent should do as well as any average?

GLENN: No.

NICK: No.

KEN: The manager is fighting with one hand behind his back.

GLENN: It makes it that much harder for him.

GEORGE: Yeah.

KEN: As I said earlier, ——— Fund [a well-managed mutual fund] at 50–50 hasn't done so well as the Dow at 100 percent over the last 10 years, but think how well it would have done if it were 100 percent.

GEORGE: But these people shouldn't be Dow conscious.

VAL: But if you are measuring only the common stock part of the funds, you are assuming that it is speculative to make any shift at all in the mix between bonds and stocks, and, therefore, in individual trusts you can't shift the mix from time to time.

VIC: But we settled that yesterday and said that we were quite willing to shift the mix, that we *ought* to shift.

VAL: If that is the case, then I don't see how you could measure the performance of an account without taking the mix change into consideration.

GEORGE: Right, my very point.

NICK: But don't you do this when you simply stack this account up against the average?

VAL: No.

NICK: Why not?

VAL: Because you don't give any consideration to the mix. The mix is a constant.

NICK: The mix is a discretionary matter. I may decide to have 50 percent bonds; you may decide to have more. Then I may change the mix.

GEORGE: It's a discretionary matter based on your client's requirements.

NICK: But for the same account, you and I might make a different decision about how we would have that account invested. Right?

GEORGE: I doubt that very much. I think if Widow Smith came up to both of us and told us that she was interested in reasonable preservation of her capital, maintenance of purchasing power over a long period of years, and the ability to call on specified funds at any given time without severe loss, there's no question how you and I would handle it. I bet you and I would come back with maybe a 2 or 3 percent variation between 35 and 40 percent bonds and the rest in stock.

VAL: You are assuming, Nick, that it's always the same percent in bonds.

NICK: No, no I don't. That's what I am arguing.

VIC: Nick is saying, as I understand it, you take the S & P 500 as a norm, and you measure against that whatever you have. Whatever you do in the bonds, whatever you do in the stocks. The thing you are measuring against is the S & P 500. Is that right?

NICK: That's exactly what I am saying.

VIC: What are the pros and cons of that?

KEN: You'd better be 100 percent in stocks or you're going to get whomped.

VIC: You are measuring the difference.

NICK: Right!

VIC: Admittedly, if you have 65 percent stocks versus 35 percent bonds, over a 5-year period you are not going to do so well as the S & P, but what you are really trying to measure is how much less well you do.

KEN: And how much more conservative you have been in doing just that little bit less. That's what you have to sell to your customer.

GARY: You have to consider income. Your bonds are going to give you that.

VIC: I am assuming we are looking at total returns. I can tell you one thing. Looking at total return of a balanced portfolio, if you are measuring it against a common stock index it doesn't help you much. You can't pick up enough in income from bonds to be able to beat an all-stock fund or index.

After another divergence, the seminarians returned to the question of performance comparison. The following point was raised as a result of some discussions during the previous evening, in which several of the seminarians agreed that certain industries, such as electric utilities, telephone companies, banks, and perhaps even oil stocks, had such well-protected dividends and such an excellent history of not reducing dividends that they might prove to be better long-term fixed-income securities than were bonds and preferred stocks. The argument was that a slight amount of income would be given up, but that growth of perhaps 5 percent a year could be expected, and the overall return might be in the neighborhood of 9 percent or 10 percent versus the 6 percent then available in the bond market. We start off with a comment by one of the seminarians to the effect that such a policy would make measurement of the common stock section of a portfolio more difficult because of this radical departure from the traditional view of what is and what is not a fixed-income security.

GLENN: Not taking issue with your idea of stocks over bonds, you commented yesterday that perhaps you would use utilities commons in lieu of bonds, because the record would be better. I wouldn't disagree with that, but would it foul up your performance comparisons because you are not using more stocks but you are using different kinds of stocks?

KEN: Of course, I don't think you can compare just stocks against stocks, although that is the way we like to do it. The comparison of stocks should be stable versus stable, growth versus growth, and the same for cyclicals and the cats and dogs [speculative stocks]. But that money you now have invested in bonds is available for stocks if you saw fit to put it there, so you had better do what we have just been saying; you have got to compare your whole portfolio against a stock index.

KEITH: That's Nick's point. It's also good to break down our industrials. We break down our utilities, and we compare these against the proper industry indexes.

GIL: This is all very interesting, but in the last 15 minutes or so we have drifted away from performance measures.

Are there any other observations or remarks that we ought to get in at this time? Gary, I'm terribly sorry I let this run over into discussion on a lot of the things you are going to take up.

GARY: I thought we could all go play golf.

GIL: That's fine. No, we'll come in to hear what you have to say, and then if——(*laughter*)

GARY: And then play golf. (*laughter*)

CHAPTER EIGHT

Ethics

During the formal sessions of the seminar, reference was made at various times to the subject of ethics. For example, in Chapter One an ethical problem is raised concerning the rights of the remainderman as opposed to the rights of the income beneficiary. In Chapters Three and Seven, ethical questions about second-class accounts arose but were not explored.

The dialogue of the seminar, however, represents only the taped sessions and none of the conversations that took place during the coffee breaks, the meals, the happy hour, and in the evening bull sessions among small groups of seminarians. These informal evening sessions sometimes lasted until quite late and produced some very interesting debates. If a single subject stood out in degree of intense interest and controversy, it was certainly the question of ethics. One ethical question was initiated before dinner and was still under discussion until 1 the next morning, with practically all the seminarians, the committeemen, the staff of the Institute, the moderator, and the observers putting in their 2 cents worth during the evening, sometimes with a good deal of heat.

It is unfortunate that some of this material was not available for use in the monograph. It is important especially for the reader to know that some highly ethical financial analysts were in total disagreement. A good deal more study will be necessary before a fully satisfactory set of rules of ethical conduct for investment people becomes available.

We can be sure, however, that the financial analysis profession must determine what is and what is not ethical behavior, and must discipline its own profession, or the Securities and Exchange Commission will do it.

The following dialogue is somewhat general in nature and occurred during the cleanup session on Saturday morning. Seminarians touched on conflict of interest, self-dealing, disclosure, and on the usefulness of specific rules on ethics.

Earlier questions on conflicts of interests involving interlocking director-ships and on the use of commissions for the benefit of accounts of the trustees have been transferred to this chapter.

The seminarians also raised the question of whether or not a higher standard of ethics is demanded by the trust relationship than for other investors.

Since all the seminarians were experienced trust men, they did not bother to discuss legal aspects of permissible behavior for trustees. These are pre-sented briefly in the Standards of the Trust Division of the American Bankers Association[1] and in somewhat greater detail in **Scott on Trusts.** These source materials are commended to the reader.

GIL: There has been a great stir, usually during coffee break and meals and after we have stopped the discussion for the day, about the matter of ethics in the profession and the behavior of each individual in the personal trust area. Perhaps we should say a few words about this. This has come up before, you'll remember, and we didn't do much with it. So let's bring that issue out again for a brief go-round, and see if we reach any worthwhile consensus on it. How about the ethical demands of the profession?

GLENN: The first thing I think you have to say is that a trust in-vestment officer has to conduct himself in such a manner at all times that it will not be to the detriment of his responsibility in accounts.

GENE: Right. That's true not only for the trust business, it's true for anybody in the investment business. We are professionals. We are getting paid by other people. We have an obligation to treat them for their own sake before we even think about anything that we might do for ourselves.

NED: I wonder if we trust people don't require even higher stan-dards than others in the investment advisory business. Isn't the trust business a little bit of a special area?

GENE: No, I don't think so.

NED: Our customers have a total dependence on us, as opposed to—

GENE: Ned, if you were in the brokerage business and you saw some of the people that your customers' men were dealing with—they are totally dependent, even more so. The relationship is the same.

KEITH: The ethics should be so high that no one group could be higher than the other.

GENE: If you are doing it, you are doing it. I don't see the——

---

1 See Appendix F.

KEITH: In one respect, we are more responsible than the broker. If the broker makes a mistake in trading a customer's security, he admits it. But he has no fund to draw on to make this thing hold. He made a bad trade or he did something——

GENE: It isn't his responsibility. The other guy——

KEITH: Yes, I know, but if we do this—whether it's an investment advisory account or a trust account—if we make a mistake we pay for it. It is a higher standard than you find in the brokerage business.

KEN: But the responsibility is forced on us.

GENE: Right.

KEN: That's just the nature of the business.

KEITH: What about the brokers when they make the same kind of mistake?

GENE: Someday, the lawyers will be after them the same way.

KEITH: OK. But there are two standards here at the moment. There shouldn't be.

VAL: There are some standards, but they're not ethical standards. It is just that the trustee is more heavily penalized. But the ethics are the same.

NED: We should separate the legal and the ethical, but I merely pose the question: Hasn't there developed out of the concept of the trust relationship a higher standard of ethical behavior, a leaning over backward to avoid any possible self-interest or self-dealing and that type of thing?

GENE: If you are saying that other areas in the investment business needn't be so ethical, you don't have to go that far. I think you are creating a false vision, because everybody should be leaning over backward to take the clearest possible course to favor the client first.

VIC: I don't think either Ned or Keith would disagree with that, nor would I, but I think the point they are making is that, pragmatically perhaps, the ethics in the trust area could develop to a higher degree. There is a greater sensitivity to them, and maybe only for the economic reason that you will pay for your mistakes. There is no doubt about that in the trust business.

KEITH: What about the confidential nature of the relationship? We don't tell anybody what we are buying and selling. It is between ourselves and the customer, but when we enter an order on behalf of the customer with a brokerage firm it is known immediately all over the firm and all over the Street. And they may even tell what account it is.

GLENN: How do they know?

KEITH: This is an ethical thing.

GLENN: How do they know, Keith?

KEITH: Oh, many times we will have allocated business by trust number, not name, but they know they got the business because so-and-so directed it.

KEN: And a year ago when they——

KEITH: And they say, "Oh, XYZ is buying such-and-such in their pension fund." Or, "The bank is buying it for XYZ." They have the trust number. And the brokers are not constrained to keep quiet about it.

GENE: There are brokers like that. Certainly to the extent that you know that happens, it influences where you place your orders, so that there is a good business reason for brokers not to act that way. But some of them do.

The discussion that follows revolves around the trading function and the allocation of commission business to brokerage firms.

GEORGE: We have a trading department, headed by a vice president.

GENE: And they handle blocks——

GEORGE: All blocks—they handle everything but private placements.

GENE: Does that include dividing orders among accounts—things like that?

GEORGE: Well, they have discretion; that's their responsibility.

GLENN: On this matter of the trading department, first, it seems to me that a trading department should have something to offer our trust customers that mutual funds and investment services don't have. This should be stressed, and it should be part of the trust investment department. Moreover, this is business that results from the activity in trust accounts. It seems to me appropriate that the trust investment division should control that business not for the benefit of the commercial side of the bank, although they do benefit incidentally, but in order to have available the best information from brokers' research staffs, which only the trust business can generate.

VIC: I think that ought to be in the record. Underlined and three exclamation points after it.

KEITH: In payment for investment services.

VIC: I think, also, one of the thoughts we have kicked around, although we have done nothing formally about it, is to tell those accounts where they insist on directing the business to a particular broker that their fee is higher than an account where we can direct the business.

KEN: We had better do it that way before it is done to you the other way. I had this happen the other day: "If we give you discretion we are not going to expect to pay you regular rates. We know what you are going to get out of this brokerage business, i.e., the deposits. We want a cut rate."

GENE: But Vic is right. Our fee, basic fee——

KEN: So was that customer right?

GENE: That deposit, or research material from the broker, is part of your compensation.

KEN: I don't think we ever thought about it when the fee schedule was being set up.

GENE: No, but it is with us today in terms of cost.

VIC: I would argue that—Nick has talked about this more than I have, but I agree with him fully—the trust investment fees for services rendered are astonishingly low, lower than in any other area. Yet, the customer says you should give him a further cut because you control the brokerage commission; I don't think he is right.

KEN: As soon as we can improve our performance to the point that we can brag about it, we can raise our fee.

VIC: That's right.

NED: One other point on this trading is that if you go back and analyze the trading job that is done by a professional trader as opposed to an individual who calls his cousin Joe who works at —— [a large retail broker], or whatever it is, you will generally find that the fee the trust department gets from that account is less than the dollars you save him in trading. Get out your pencil and paper and you will be astonished—just on municipal bonds and things of that sort.

NED: Third market——[2]

KEN: In accounts where we have to give business to a special broker, we always do it with a proviso that he gets it only if he can match the best price around.

GLENN: But some banks do not observe this.

NED: No, I'm talking about the customer who has no trust department account and handles his own securities through a broker. His

—————
[2] The third market is an off-the-stock-exchange market through which listed stocks can often be bought and sold at net prices more advantageous than through exchange members.

friend takes care of him—good buddies! You can pay our fees out of what we can save him.

NICK: I would go one step further than that, and I've thought this for years. I haven't seen a case tried on it, but I believe a good lawyer could win it. I think allocating brokerage business on the basis of deposits or any commercial bank relationship is a flagrant violation of fiduciary responsibility.

KEN: How should they be allocated?

NICK: They should be allocated in some manner to benefit that particular customer. To the extent that that account generates business, it should if at all possible be used to benefit the customer.

GLENN: You have a problem, then. Sure, you have to allocate a certain amount of business to compensate the brokers for research. We do it by having an annual round robin of analysts, who say, "I want to give this man $5,000 in commission, and this man $2,000, and this man $10,000." It seems to me that if we don't allocate from some of these account relationships the business will be given on personal relationships, which is even worse. And after all, we get a lot of free service. We get a lot of security quotations, the stock exchange board is provided by the brokers. I don't know how to compensate——

NICK: You are not paying them because they have cash in your bank.

GENE: You should set aside as much commission business as you need to compensate the brokers that you want to work with, but don't overcompensate them.

NICK: I don't see any justification for your taking your customer's brokerage business and using it for the benefit of the bank.

GENE: Because it's part of your fee. Because it is a part of the bank's fee.

VIC: Listen, I don't know how much brokerage you have for research, but my own experience has been that, by and large, banks do not nearly match the brokerage commissions that are allocated by the mutual funds. The service you get is what you pay for.

GENE: I don't agree, I think that mutual funds overpay.

VIC: Well, whether they overpay or not, they get the service.

GENE: OK. That doesn't mean we can't. You have to pay them, but it's your responsibility to get the service. When I was in the brokerage business we would service an account that gave us $5,000 more than an account that gave us $30,000 because they asked for it.

VIC: And the senior partner in charge of research didn't go down to that $5,000 account and put the bee on them three times a year to get it up to $30,000? I would be astonished if he didn't do that.

NICK: Gene, what would you do if you were put on the stand and you were asked by an attorney, "Explain to the jury how you justify this"?

GENE: The chairman of our board says this. Of all the commission business generated by the bank, which is a lot more than just in the trust department, enough is available to the trust department to pay for whatever services are needed to service our accounts. It is only over and above what the trust department says it needs that any business is allocated for balances.

GREG: The first obligation the trust department has if you have an order is to get the best price possible for the client, if you are either buying or selling.

GIL: You used the word "code" before, Gene. There is no ethical code, you said. It is just a matter, to some extent, of economic necessity. Should certain ethical principles be codified in your view?

GENE: To me, the thing an ethical code would do is to keep a guy from doing something that he didn't even realize was wrong. If a man wants to do something wrong, no code, nothing in the world, is going to keep him from doing it. He'll figure out a way to do it. We should write these things for the man who may be naïve, or just inexperienced, and who may wind up doing something that just seems to make sense to him. If you know other people are going to buy a stock, it sort of makes sense to buy it yourself. These codes are to prevent that, so that nobody is going to say, "Well, I didn't realize that. I shouldn't have done that."

KEN: Is the present C.F.A. code adequate?

GENE: It's pretty general. Most of us have some sort of set of rules for our own people.

GLENN: I have a difference of opinion in my own shop over investing for the analyst's own account in terms of what's appropriate and what is not appropriate.

VIC: I think we could all agree on the ethical concept of the customer's coming first, no self-dealing, and that sort of thing. I think the matter that came up in our discussion last night, and a matter that was warmly toasted, is that perhaps the application of this may vary, and it requires different rules for different trust departments, essentially depending on their size, complication of accounts, and so on. What might be reasonable for a small trust company might not be reasonable at all for a big one. The purchasing power of a big bank—the impact of a big bank's purchases—is much greater than that of a small one. This is one of the areas where when you get down to the specifics it becomes almost impossible to make up a standard. Is this statement I just made true? Would you argue that the same thing that is applicable to a large bank must also be applicable to a small one? There is no difference? That ethics are ethics and they are equally defined in specific cases for everyone?

GENE: No, I think there is just more responsibility, let's say, on big banks to have laid out clearly what is right and wrong. And to reinforce it because there is more temptation. There is more chance of abuse. Some analysts have more impact than others on the price of a stock. You've got a 20-share buyer, you know. He is not really going to get in your way.

GREG: It seems that ethics is the same whether it is a small bank or a large bank. You can't get away from this.

GLENN: Gene, that's what we were talking about, for example, last night. George here at his big bank wouldn't buy 100 shares of General Motors if they were going to put it on their buy list. I can't visualize 100 shares affecting the market one way or the other in General Motors. This is the kind of difference in size that we had in mind when we discussed it last night.

GREG: Well, I think you have to exercise judgment. You are measuring ethics. You can't dismiss judgment on whatever the factor is.

GENE: It really is a question of motivation. If the man is buying 100 shares of General Motors to scalp 3 points out of it because he knows some fund, or his own trust department, is going to be buying it, that is clearly wrong.

KEN: But if he is buying it because he believes the story that causes you to buy it, it may be all right.

GUY: I think it depends on a great many things. For instance, if Joe Dokes said, "Will you be a cotrustee under my will with the XYZ bank?" I would say no. But if this person happens to be related to me, if she were my sister and she lived in Kalamazoo, and the Kalamazoo Bank were the logical bank to take care of her affairs, I don't think I would have any hesitation about doing it.

GREG: Well, that is exercising judgment.

GLENN: I agree that these are matters of ethics and judgment, but what I think we are striving for is to see if we can have some kind of concensus on a guide, or code, for other analysts.

KEITH: Well—what might be a point of view in George's case—

the analyst may have followed General Motors for a long time, and all of a sudden he has decided it is an attractive stock, and it takes him some time to do his homework. He is enthusiastic about it. He buys 100 shares just for his own account. He goes to see George and says, "George, here are the reasons I think General Motors is attractive. I am so certain of this that I bought 100 shares of this in my own name." This is *disclosure*. Now, if this is disclosed and they are operating with his report, which obviously is not prepared with the idea of stimulating George to accept his report so that this fellow can make a profit out of 100 shares, it might be all right.

KEN: Well, let's take the case of a small company with the same situation applied but where you know that a large bank's buying is going to influence the price, and yet you are still buying for purely investment reasons. What then?

GENE: It is very difficult. What happens, again, if you own a stock in a small company, and you have owned it for some time, and it becomes particularly attractive? I mean, it is just a steal, then are you entirely——

KEITH: I think when you have disclosed your ownership, that puts the thing on the table——

GENE: That is only warning people that maybe your motives aren't the best.

KEN: Of course, I sometimes say that to my committee, and with emphasis, that I have owned this stock for two years——

GLENN: Last evening, somebody had the opinion that no analyst, no account manager, should own any stocks that are in his portfolios. This to me is going pretty far.

KEN: One of the fringe benefits in this business is that you have people doing research for you, I think.

GLENN: Right.

GENE: I want my analysts to be interested enough in the stock market so that they make an investment. I want this.

VIC: How about the issue that was particularly warm last night— no analyst should be permitted to purchase any stock on the current buy list.

GUY: I would certainly say no.

GLENN: I would say no.

GENE: I don't see the merit in that.

KEN: Well, from then on he will buy his 100 shares a week before he blasts it on the buy list.

GENE: There's a way around it.

VIC: Well, the point I think we made before is that if a man wants to be unethical it is extremely difficult to prevent him. If George's analyst came in to him, for example, and disclosed the information that he owned the stock, I would think that George would be put in a difficult decision position, because even though the analyst said to him, "I bought it, and I think we should buy it," but with no intention of benefiting by his bank's great purchasing power, at least in George's mind the question would be raised: "Is he telling me the truth?" And the next time he will kind of look at this fellow and wonder whether to believe him. You get into some extremely difficult decisions here, and I am saying that to prevent these sorts of things maybe you should be a little bit more rigid in your attitude. The thing that seemed to come out of the meeting last night was the point I made before. Each trustee has its own character and its own size, its own market impact, and what might be the right regulation for George's bank might not be the right regulation for Glenn's bank. I don't think you can draw up a rigid set of rules, Greg, that will be equally applicable to all sizes of departments.

GLENN: If you attempted to draw up a code that Gene said would be helpful for a naïve analyst who might go astray unknowingly, would it be so watered down as to not be meaningful?

GENE: I think the more you structure this, the more rules you lay out, the more you divert attention from the whole concept of ethics and the more you invite the wrong sort of thing. Just what Ken was saying. Someone's figuring out how to get around them and, you know, not infringing the rules but at the same time infringing the concept, infringing the question of ethics.

GIL: I was just handed the guidelines to the Code of Ethics that's in the C.F.A. program brochure, and paragraph two reads this way: "A Chartered Financial Analyst shall conduct himself in such manner that transactions for clients have priority over personal transactions, and such personal transactions shall not in any way operate adversely to the interest of the clients. Full disclosure should be made of any individual or firm interest in the specific securities recommended for purchase or sale." That's the paragraph in the C.F.A. Code.

KEN: We read to all of our people twice a year words very similar to those in the C.F.A. Code, so at least they can't say they haven't heard.

VIC: Does that mean the officers in the trust department must make known to clients their interest in any securities they own personally?

GENE: No, I think that part is aimed at brokers, because the broker does not make the decision. He just advises. The trust department makes the decision. If you are recommending a stock to somebody else, then you have to tell them what you own and where your interest lies. Maybe, Ned, that's what you are trying to differentiate. This is one differentiation. We are the decision makers, so that it is even more clear where there is a violation of this ethical code.

GREG: Why can't we in the record make reference to the C.F.A. Code of Ethics that you just referred to. I think this would be a good idea.[3]

GIL: All right, fine. I think that reaffirmation would be good, because there is no disagreement here as far as I can see.

GLENN: And are we satisfied that we should not try to amplify it?

GIL: Yes.

VIC: I think Gene made the best point. The more you try to structure it, the more you invite opportunity to get around it. You have to judge each case as it comes along. Otherwise, it gets like some of these state constitutions, which have a zillion different articles.

GREG: The only change would be if there were some special strictures related to our own trust area that didn't have so much application in other financial areas. I would think that for this beginning point reaffirmation is still the best course, and not try to amplify some special factors that relate to the professional field of trust investment management.

GIL: I think if we start distinguishing among members of the financial community we run into problems.

GLENN: Let's stay in our own backyard.

VAL: That's like a story an architect told me once. If you wanted to get a roof on your house and the contract said a roof that won't leak, it wouldn't leak. But if you started specifying exactly how the roof was to be made it probably would leak, because the contractor then could see loopholes showing how he could save some money.

Commercial banks usually have several members of the board of directors who represent local business firms and, in the large banks, national companies. The discussion that follows concerns the possible conflict-of-interest situations involving interlocking directorships.

GLENN: If you are through with that, I would like to ask a question of the group. I know this has mystified me, and perhaps deserves

---

[3] See Appendix G.

an explanation. We all know banks that will not buy securities of a company that has either an officer in their bank serving on the board of that company, or if an officer of the corporation is serving on the board of the bank. We know of other banks who are not concerned with this matter whatsoever and do not contact the director or executive of the corporation. Then, we know of a third group of banks who would send the report of their analytical department to the member of their board who might be the chief executive officer of the corporation, for his comment. Now here are three quite diverse views, and there doesn't seem to be any consensus. Is there any good thinking about this problem? It's not my problem; we don't have any national corporations represented on our board.

VIC: We have an interesting thing; it's funny in a way. Two of our officers are on the boards of two companies in both of which we hold stock. In the last bank examination of the trust department, we got gigged for one of them. The reason was very simple; the stock was under the cost. But we've never been gigged on the other. And we have a lot more of it than we have of this under-cost stock.

GLENN: You had no prohibition against buying stock of a company with one of your officers on the board?

VIC: No, sir. And the other one——

GLENN: Should you have?

VIC: I would be unhappy with it, because we buy and sell it. Let me put it this way, we don't permit that relationship to inhibit our making an investment decision.

GLENN: Do you go over the results of your studies with him and counsel him?

VIC: No.

GLENN: Do you send him a copy of your report, or a draft of it or whatever——

VIC: But our industry reviews go to their pension and profit sharing committee because we have their pension and profit sharing fund.

GENE: Yes.

VIC: But not to the directors. But the interesting thing is the gig that we got from the comptroller suggested that we should dispose of the stock——

KEN: Because it was under cost?

VIC: Yes. Well, it brought attention to the fact that there was a conflict of interest because of the dual board memberships——

KEN: No conflict of interest in the stock that had a profit?

Vic: Precisely. The thing I don't understand is why did we get gigged on the one that went down but not on the one that went up.

Glenn: There's a question on the bank examination report that I am sure you are aware of: "Interlocking directorships, or any directorships on your board, from what companies?" We don't get much comment on it, but there must be some point to having the question on the examination report.

Greg: One of our officers is on the board of a large utility, but we do not hesitate to buy their stock, and we dispose of it when the time comes.

Glenn: I think this is the more sophisticated approach. I find some very major banks who won't buy stock where there is a director relationship.

Van: They won't buy any director's stocks.

Guy: We have no hesitation about buying stocks of the large companies where we have a director when we think they should be bought. If there are major decisions involving one that has some directors on our trust committee, they ordinarily do not vote. They give us the benefit of their judgment in the meeting, however.

APPENDIX A

Selected investment aids

EXHIBIT I

Stock Diversification Inventory

Account No._____

Date_____

Cyclical Industries	Market Value	%	Stable Industries	Market Value	%
Durable & prod. gds.			Nondurables & svcs.		
Agricultural equip.	$_____	____	Brewing & distill.	$_____	____
Aircraft	_____	____	Containers	_____	____
Auto	_____	____	Drugs	_____	____
Building	_____	____	Entertainment	_____	____
Chemical	_____	____	Food, bev., & tob.	_____	____
Electrical	_____	____	Oil	_____	____
Industrial mach.	_____	____	Paper	_____	____
Office equipment	_____	____	Retail	_____	____
Steel	_____	____	Soaps	_____	____
Textile	_____	____	Miscellaneous	_____	____
Tire & rubber	_____	____	Total	$_____	____
Miscellaneous	_____	____			
Total	$_____	____	Financial		
			Banks & finance	_____	____
Raw materials			Fire insurance	_____	____
Aluminum	_____	____	Life insurance	_____	____
Coal	_____	____	Other	_____	____
Copper	_____	____	Total	$_____	____
Other metals	_____	____			
Total	$_____	____	Public utility		
			Gas	_____	____
Transportation			Electric	_____	____
Air transport	_____	____	Telephone	_____	____
Railroad & equip.	_____	____	Total	$_____	____
Total	$_____	____			
Total Cyclical	$_____	____	D.C.T.F.	$_____	____
			Total Stable	$_____	____
			Grand Total	$_____	____

EXHIBIT II

Common Stock Lists

(a) Guidance (date)

Company	Market (Date)	66-67 Range	Cash Dividend	Yield	1967E P/E	Earnings 1967E	Earnings 1966	Policy *

Total number of stocks on list:

*Hold
Working List quality, not added to contain size of list or prevent misunderstanding re industry emphasis (e.g., not too many rails, etc.).

Hold for income
Emphasis on holding unless the objective is clearly growth.

Switch for growth
Emphasis on switching unless income is the major objective.

Hold for cyclical gain
Should be retained unless too much risk for account.

Hold for price recovery
Price depressed, hold unless too much risk for account.

Hold for appreciation
Not for Working List quality, opportunity for further price appreciation apparent.

Consider sale
Sale indicated subject to account considerations.

(b) Selected Common Stocks Approved for Retention (date)

Policy	Current (date) Price	Dividend	Yield	Company Industry	1966	1967E	Earnings/Share Average Growth Rate 10 Years 1957/66	Average Growth Rate 5 Years Anticipated Future	P/E 1967 Earnings Estimate

Total number of stocks listed:

Symbols
HI
H2
H-Spec
R (review)

EXHIBIT II (Continued)

(c) Common Stocks Approved for Purchase (date)

Policy	Current (date) Price Dividend Yield	Company Industry	Earnings/Share		Average Growth Rate		P/E 1967 Earnings Estimate
	Price Dividend Yield	Company Industry	1966	1967E	10 Years 1957/66	5 Years Anticipated Future	Earnings Estimate

Total number of stocks listed:

Symbols
PI)
P2) General Purchase
P3)

MI)
M2) Management Accounts
M3)

SMI)
SM2) Special Management Accounts
Spec)

(d) Common Stock Working List (date)

Sym-bol	Industry Company	Market (Date)	66-67 Range	Cash Dividend	Yield	1967E P/E	Annual Earnings 1967E 1966 1965	Interim Earnings Months 1967 1966	% Change from 65-66 Hi (date)

Total number of common stocks on list:

Symbols
A   Most attractive
B   Reasonably valued
C   Fully priced
D   Defer purchase

I – over II% (growth)
2 – 8% to II%
3 – 5% to 8%
4 – 2% to 5%

Electric & Gas Utilities
3 – 5% to 6 1/2%
3+ – 6 1/2% to 8%

(S) Approval required

EXHIBIT III

List of Stocks for Investment Consideration

April 17, 1967

Stocks for Investment Consideration

In accordance with a recent Securities Committee decision, *Continental Telephone* has been added to the list with a rating of favorable. Its use should be confined to aggressive accounts able to absorb more than ordinary risk.

Florida Power & Light has been added to the list with a rating of favorable. Although a large rate reduction will restrict this year's earnings gain to modest proportions, the stock appears reasonably attractive in relation to longer term growth prospects.

The ratings on *General Motors* and *Ford* have been downgraded from neutral to unfavorable on the basis of the outlook for an extended period of lower earnings in the industry. Earnings estimates for both stocks have been reduced and it is estimated that first quarter earnings will be particularly poor. The stocks can be held generally although sales to raise cash or for reinvestment in special situations would be reasonable.

The rating on *Avon* is reduced to neutral with the latest increase in the P/E ratio.

Smith, Kline & French has been removed from the list because of uncertainties about the direction of its research and increasing competition in tranquilizers. A memorandum will be circulated shortly to the account managers.

X—Stock on Approved Purchase List	a—Actual
F—Fairly priced	e—Estimated
N—Neutral	s—Also pays stock dividend
U—Unattractive	y—Fiscal year ending in following year

		Market 4/13/67	Earnings Per Share (Fiscal Years) 1965	1966	1967 (E)	P/E 1967	Est. Annual Div.	Yield
Aerospace								
U	Boeing	83	$4.78	$4.13	$4.75	17.5	$1.20	1.5%
U	Lockheed	64	4.65	5.29	5.75	11.1	2.20	3.4
U	North Amer. Avia. (y)	47	5.43	5.75	5.10	9.2	2.80	6.0
U	United Aircraft	89	4.33	3.93	5.60	15.9	1.60	1.8
Airlines								
N	American Airlines	89	4.37	5.80	6.75	13.3	1.50	1.7
N	United Air Lines	76	3.27	4.25*	5.25	14.5	1.00	1.3
Automobiles								
U	Ford	51	6.33	5.63	4.50	11.3	2.40	4.7
UX	General Motors	77	7.41	6.24	5.00	15.4	4.00	5.2
Banks								
NX	Bank of America	54	3.57	3.97	4.25	12.7	2.20	4.1
FX	BT New York	63	4.33	4.86	5.15	12.2	2.60	4.1
FX	Chase Manhattan	61	4.40	4.71	5.00	12.4	2.20	3.6
F	Chemical Bank N.Y. Trust.	48	4.01	4.14	4.35	11.0	2.20	4.6
F	Citizens & Southern	41	2.12	2.46	2.70	15.2	1.00	2.4
FX	First National City	57	3.52	3.94	4.25	13.4	1.80	3.2
F	Wachovia Bank & Trust ...	42	2.12	2.39	2.65	15.8	.80	1.9
N	Western Bancorporation ..	32	2.00	2.16	2.30	13.9	1.10	3.4

* Before strike losses about $1.80 a share.

EXHIBIT IV

General Stock Lists

(a) Monthly Common Stock Statistical Report

Oct. 31, 1967

Avg. $ (62-66)	Growth Rate %	Avg. Ret. Cap. %	1966 Ret. Cap. %	Fis. Yr. End	2 Market Averages / 40 Industries / 336 Companies	10/31 1967	1967 Range	1966 $	Last 12 Mos. $	Std. 1967 Est. $	P/E Ratio 1967 Std.	Ind. Rate $	Yld. %	5 Yr. Avg. P/E	1967 P/E	From 12/62	From 12/66	From 9/67
1.00	10.2	5.9	5.9		Middle South Util.	21	30 20	1.19	1.23	1.28	16.1	.76	3.7	120	100	84	75	95
1.49	6.8	6.4	6.8		Minnesota P. & L.	21	27 21	1.69	1.62	1.70	12.4	1.10	5.2	87	77	73	76	101
1.64	14.5	6.8	6.6		Nevada Power	37	43 36	2.02	2.15	2.21	16.5	.92	2.5	128	102	98	87	103
1.19	10.8	6.3	6.1		Orange & Rockland Ut.	25	30 25	1.44	1.50	1.51	16.8	1.04	4.1	126	104	78	82	104
1.89	8.5	5.9	6.1		Pacific G. & E.	32	38 30	2.23	2.45	2.40	13.4	1.40	4.4	94	83	78	86	99
1.30	8.7	6.1	6.2		P. S. Colorado	20	27 20	1.52	1.56	1.60	12.6	1.00	5.0	109	78	75	77	97
2.06	12.6	6.3	7.1		P. S. Indiana	40	53 40	2.57	2.57	2.70	14.9	1.92	4.8	111	93	90	88	97
2.10	6.4	6.9	7.1		P. S. New Mexico	23	28 21	1.55	1.66	1.65	14.0	.90	3.9	113	87	62	80	94
2.20	6.4	6.5	6.7		P. S. Electric & Gas	30	38 30	2.39	2.43	2.51	12.0	1.54	5.1	93	74	65	80	100
.79	14.3	5.8	5.8		Sierra Pacific Power	15	21 15	.97	.99	1.05	14.7	.64	4.2	132	91	80	69	101
1.93	7.1	6.1	6.2		Southern Calif. Ed.	32	42 32	2.23	2.32	2.38	13.6	1.40	4.3	97	84	78	72	95
1.29	6.9	5.7	5.8		Southern Company	24	32 24	1.45	1.52	1.55	15.6	1.08	4.5	121	97	69	72	101
.72	3.9	6.8	6.8	8	Southwestern P. S.	13	17 13	.73	.73	.89	14.7	.64	4.5	139	91	56	76	93
.93	12.9	6.6	6.8		Tampa Electric	26	34 26	1.21	1.24	1.28	20.1	.68	2.7	151	125	89	78	101
2.16	7.1	7.9	7.9		Texas Util.	50	61 48	2.45	2.61	2.64	18.8	1.52	3.1	140	117	72	80	96
1.82	8.9	6.6	7.3		Toledo Edison	31	42 30	2.18	2.17	2.31	13.4	1.40	4.5	97	83	87	80	102
2.14	5.3	5.7	5.9		Utah P. & L.	30	37 30	2.39	2.40	2.49	12.2	1.60	5.3	94	75	59	80	97
1.78	7.8	6.5	6.3		Va. Electric & Power	40	50 38	2.07	2.12	2.23	17.9	1.36	3.4	136	111	73	78	97
					NAT GAS TRAN													
2.57	9.2	6.4	6.5		Amer. Natural Gas	36	43 36	3.03	3.12	3.17	11.5	1.90	5.2	89	71	65	83	98
2.09	3.4	6.9	7.0		Brooklyn Union	29	31 28	2.26	2.31	2.35	12.1	1.60	5.6	89	75	58	88	102
1.89	8.1	6.4	6.4		Columbia Gas	26	29 26	2.19	2.29	2.32	11.1	1.44	5.6	79	69	71	91	100
2.09	15.0	6.1	7.3		Consol Natural Gas	28	31 27	2.58	2.61	2.68	10.6	1.60	5.7	81	65	73	87	100
1.58	5.3	7.0	7.6	9	Laclede Gas	23	41 32	1.75	1.84	1.86	12.4	1.30	5.7	84	77	67	96	104
2.08	6.9	NA	NA		Northern Illinois Gas	32	54 46	2.33	2.46	2.50	12.7	1.52	4.8	117	79	61	82	97
2.97	7.8	NA	NA		Northern Natural Gas	49	40 32	3.42	3.70	3.54	13.9	2.40	4.9	100	86	84	99	106
2.18	9.1	NA	NA		Panhandle E. P. L.	33	39 33	2.54	2.63	2.74	11.9	1.60	4.9	92	74	73	86	99
2.39	8.8	7.3	7.7		Peoples Gas	35		2.73	2.79	2.85	12.3	1.96	5.6	90	76	68	89	105
					TEL. & TELEG.													
3.22	6.4	NA	NA		Amer. Tel. & Tel.	51	63 51	3.69	3.69	3.76	13.4	2.20	4.3	102	83	64	82	103
.68	38.7	NA	NA		Cont. Tel.	25	35 24	1.07	1.14	1.18	21.2	.60	2.4	NC	132	NA	92	97
1.62	16.9	NA	NA		Gen. Tel. & Elect.	42	55 41	2.16	2.20	2.29	18.2	1.40	3.4	119	113	137	86	95
.97	10.3	NA	NA		United Util.	27	33 25	1.16	1.23	1.25	21.6	.80	3.0	123	134	132	101	100
					Vending													
1.76	13.7	8.8	7.5	9	A. R. A.	75	80 52	2.22	2.40	2.58	29.0	.72	1.0	126	180	150	148	99
.79	86.1	7.3	10.9	9	Canteen	21	28 20	1.41	1.21	1.48	14.1	.80	3.9	130	87	108	100	91
1.14	20.4	13.8	14.0	6	Servomation	39	47 29	1.72	1.71	2.03	19.1	.40	1.0	105	119	171	129	104

Header groupings: "5 Years 1962-1966 Earnings" (Avg. $, Growth Rate %, Avg. Ret. Cap. %); "1966 Ret. Cap. %"; "Prices" (10/31/1967, 1967 Range); "Earnings" (1966, Last 12 Mos., Std. 1967 Est.); "P/E Ratio 1967 Std."; "Dividend" (Ind. Rate $, Yld. %); "Index Relative to D-J" (5 Yr. Avg. P/E, 1967 P/E) and "Price Change" (From 12/62, From 12/66, From 9/67).

EXHIBIT IV (cont'd.)

(b) Monthly Common Stock Price List

Oct. 31, 1967

Prices					Month End Prices 1967						Company	Market Action thru Oct. 31, 1967									
	1962-67 Range											Percentage Change						Prin. & Pr. Change Relative to the D-J			
1962 Dec.	High	Low	1965 Oct.	1966 Oct.	May	Jun.	Jul.	Aug.	Sep.	Oct.		1962-1967 High	Low	3 Mos	1 Yr	2 Yrs	5 Yrs	3 Mos	1 Yr	2 Yrs	5 Yrs
32	42	26	37	35	30	28	30	32	29	27	Louisville G. & E.	-35	6	-9	-23	-26	-16	94	71	81	62
18	30	13	27	25	26	23	23	23	23	21	Middle South Util.	-32	64	-12	-18	-23	-13	91	75	84	84
21	32	17	31	26	22	23	23	22	23	21	Minnesota P. & L.	-34	24	-11	-17	-32	-1	92	76	74	73
28	55	15	46	39	41	40	42	38	37	37	Nevada Power	-34	137	-12	-6	-20	32	90	87	88	98
24	35	18	32	29	29	35	28	27	26	25	Orange & Rockland Util.	-27	45	-8	-11	-13	6	95	82	88	98
32	40	25	37	34	34	35	34	34	34	32	Pacific G. & E.	-20	29	6	6	-13	1	97	86	95	75
27	35	19	37	34	34	35	34	34	34	20	P. S. Colorado	-42	5	-10	-16	-32	-24	92	77	75	56
33	55	24	55	49	46	48	47	46	45	40	P. S. Indiana	-27	69	-15	-17	-26	22	88	76	81	90
28	36	20	32	24	27	26	25	23	24	23	P. S. New Mexico	-35	14	-8	-4	-28	-16	94	80	79	62
35	44	25	41	38	35	35	33	33	32	30	P. S. Electric & Gas	-32	20	-8	-13	-35	-13	94	80	71	65
14	27	10	24	20	13	16	17	16	16	15	Sierra Pacific Power	-43	54	-9	-25	-19	8	94	69	88	80
31	43	23	40	38	33	37	39	35	35	32	Southern Calif. Ed.	-24	40	-17	-14	-31	6	86	79	75	78
26	35	19	35	31	23	27	27	25	25	24	Southern Company	-33	27	-9	-21	-40	-25	94	72	66	69
18	23	11	22	17	14	14	14	14	14	13	Southwestern P. S.	-42	15	-11	-21	-13	20	92	76	95	56
21	34	14	29	31	31	29	28	28	29	26	Tampa Electric	-25	78	-9	-17	-23	-3	91	78	84	89
51	68	37	65	58	57	54	56	55	52	50	Texas Util.	-27	34	-12	-15	-24	18	94	80	87	72
26	42	28	39	35	33	32	34	35	34	31	Toledo Edison	-26	53	-8	-13	-24	-21	97	80	83	87
38	46	31	40	35	32	32	32	31	31	30	Utah P. & L.	-34	8	-5	-13	-18	-8	93	78	87	59
40	53	31	50	47	45	42	42	44	43	40	Va. Electric & Power	-25	29	-10	-15	2	24	99	92	90	73
68	81	60	76	63	62	62	65	66	67	63	Nat. Gas Cos. Ind. Distrib.	-23	5	4	0	-19	-13	102	103	112	69
74	99	65	90	83	87	86	93	97	97	92	Nat. Gas Cos. Ind.-Pipeline	-7	42	1	11	-13	-21	95	83	95	92
42	67	45	52	40	38	39	38	39	39	36	Amer. Natural Gas	-46	19	-8	-10	-13	-4	99	88	88	65
36	46	26	35	30	29	29	30	29	30	29	Brooklyn Union	-38	71	-4	-4	-22	-1	99	91	85	58
27	34	22	30	26	27	27	27	28	27	26	Columbia Gas	-25	23	3	1	-12	-9	101	87	86	71
29	40	23	37	30	27	29	29	29	29	28	Consol. Natural Gas	-29	30	2	5	-34	-18	99	87	96	73
25	32	18	26	22	23	24	24	24	24	22	Laclede Gas	-28	3	7	5	-23	14	101	96	72	67
39	54	35	48	46	35	35	34	35	35	32	Northern Illinois Gas	-41	43	-1	-10	-20	-2	96	82	88	61
43	66	31	64	45	49	47	49	48	49	49	Northern Natural Gas	-25	47	5	8	-22	-6	104	99	88	84
33	44	35	41	36	35	34	35	33	35	33	Panhandle E. P. L.	-26	12	-1	-6	-23	-13	98	86	86	73
38	51	31	45	35	35	34	35	36	35	35	Peoples Gas	-30	8	-2	-3	-22	-2	104	89	86	68
26	34	23	32	27	27	28	26	25	25	25	Telephone Index	-27	3	-3	-10	-23	-6	100	85	86	70
58	75	49	66	56	55	57	52	51	52	51	Amer. Tel. & Tel.	-33	235	-15	-10	-11	-13	100	82	84	64
N.AP.	8*		23	25	31	29	31	27	29	25	Gen. Tel. & Elect.	-28	125	-11	-6	-11	N.AP.	87	92	97	N.AP.
23	35	19	46	44	47	47	47	48	46	42	Cont. Tel.	-24	144	-9	10	-10	85	92	86	99	137
15	33	11	30	25	31	29	29	30	28	27	United Util.	-19	108	-3	44	-11	78	94	101	97	132
22	44	18	31	26	36	37	38	39	39	37	Vending Machines Index	-17	168	4	62	19	67	100	132	130	124
37	80	28	45	46	65	71	72	69	80	75	A. R. A.	-6	113	-11	66	66	102	107	148	181	150
14	37	10	26	19	22	37	39	39	24	21	Canteen Corp.	-44	237	0	40	50	46	91	100	89	108
17	47	12	26	28	33	37	39	39	39	39	Servomation	-18	126	6	43	16	131	103	129	164	171
57	107	47	92	75	92	79	96	100	107	106	Capital Goods Index	-1	80	6	22	-2	86	109	131	127	138
54	86	46	85	68	77	79	83	82	85	83	Consumers Goods Index	-3	32	0	6	-9	54	102	112	107	114
68	89	59	85	74	73	79	83	80	82	78	High Grade Common Index	-12	255	-5	9	15	97	100	85	
55	182	49	112	98	143	161	177	171	177	174	Low Price Common Index	-4		-2	77	55	216	101	163	169	234

GENERAL NOTES

Stock prices have been adjusted for all stock dividends and stock splits.

† Adjusted for divestiture of General Motors common stock.

‡ General Motors stock added back.

N.AP. Not applicable.

PRICES

Stock prices are for respective month-ends.

Industry indexes are for the last Wednesday of the month.

1962-1967 range is the high and low price for years 1962 through 1967 to date.

* Indicates range since date of initial offering.

MARKET ACTION

Calculations are based on unrounded prices.

Prin. & Pr. (price) Change is an index of performance—each stock and S & P index compared with the Dow Jones Industrial Average.

EXHIBIT V

Company Analysis Summary

THE PROCTER & GAMBLE COMPANY

Procter & Gamble is the country's largest soap and detergent manufacturer, accounting for approximately 50 percent of total industry output. The company is also a leading producer of toothpaste, shortening, salad oil, prepared baking mixes, peanut butter, and household paper products. Among the well-known brand names utilized are: "Ivory," "Camay," "Dash," "Oxydol," "Duz," "Tide," "Spic and Span," "Cheer" and "Joy" soaps and detergents; "Crest" and "Gleem" toothpastes; "Crisco" and "Fluffo" shortenings; "Duncan Hines" cake-mixes; and "Charmin" paper towels and napkins. Research expenditures are not reported by the company; however, such expenditures are believed to be substantial based on the number of successful new products introduced since the end of World War II. Foreign earnings account for about 18.1 percent of total net earnings. In addition to fourteen domestic plants, factories are located in Canada, Puerto Rico and twelve foreign countries, including the six Common Market countries. In fiscal 1964, the company acquired J. A. Forger & Co., a major coffee producer. In April, 1967, the company was ordered by the Supreme Court to divest the Clorox Chemical Co. which was acquired in 1957.

Capitalization—Dec. 31, 1966	Outstanding -000-	Range 1967	Present Call	Price	Div. Rate	% Yield	Per 1968E
Long Term Debt	$42,398						
3⅞% Debs., Due 1968-81		Private Placement					
8% Pfd., Par $100	51,800 12 Shs.	89-86	102.30	89	—	4.94	—
Common, No Par	42,745 Shs.	168-168 85-69		168 84	— $2.20	4.8 2.6	— 19.5

Income—In $000,000—Fiscal Year Ends in June

	Net Sales	Oper. Income	% Oper. Inc. Mrgn.	Depr. & Amort.	Pretax Net	% Prof. Mrgn.	Net Inc.	% Ret. On Cap.	% Ret. Com. Equity	Adjusted for All Stock Splits & Divs. Per Share				
										Rptd. Earn.	Depr. & Amort.	Div.	Price Range	Hi-Lo Per
1968E	2,620.0	378.0	14.4	43.0	346.0	13.2	184.0	—	—	$4.30	$1.01	$ —	—	—
1967E	2,450.0	346.5	14.1	39.0	318.0	13.0	169.0	17.5	18.3	3.95	.91	2.10	—	—
1966	2,243.2	303.9	13.5	35.2	277.2	12.4	149.5	15.5	16.7	3.49	.82	1.93	77- 60	22- 17
1965	2,058.6	278.1	13.5	31.9	252.8	12.3	133.2	14.2	15.3	3.08	.74	1.80	82- 69	27- 22
1964	1,913.7	288.4	15.1	31.0	265.3	13.9	130.8	15.7	17.2	2.99	.71	1.68	87- 79	29- 26
1963	1,654.5	260.6	15.8	27.4	240.3	14.5	115.8	14.8	16.3	2.75	.65	1.55	81- 70	29- 25
1962	1,619.4	242.8	15.0	25.3	223.9	13.8	109.4	14.6	16.1	2.60	.60	1.45	92- 56	35- 22
1961	1,541.9	249.0	16.1	25.0	221.4	14.4	106.6	15.8	17.8	2.55	.60	1.33S	102- 67	40- 26
1960	1,441.5	219.1	15.2	23.1	194.6	13.5	98.1	15.8	17.8	2.36	.56	1.20	70- 41	30- 17
1959	1,368.8	188.7	13.8	22.2	165.6	12.1	81.7	13.9	16.1	1.97	.54	1.05	45- 36	23- 18
1958	1,295.2	173.2	13.4	20.1	151.5	11.7	73.2	13.5	15.8	1.78	.49	1.00	39- 27	22- 15
1957	1,156.4	160.4	13.9	22.1	136.5	11.8	67.8	15.9	16.4	1.70	.56	.93	28- 22	16- 13
1956	1,038.3	140.6	13.5	19.5	120.9	11.6	59.3	14.4	15.3	1.52	.50	.88S	27- 23	18- 15

Per Share Growth Rates

	5 yrs.	10 yrs.
Net Sales	7.3	6.3
Operating Income	3.6	6.8
Depr. & Amort.	6.7	4.8
Pre–Tax Net	3.9	7.6
Net Income	6.3	8.3
Reported Earnings	6.3	8.3
Dividends	7.6	8.6

— In $000,000 —

	1966	1965	1964	1963	1962
Capital Expenditures	92.4	64.8	44.2	67.3	56.7
Unconsol. Earnings	.0	.0	.0	.0	.0
Remitted Earnings	.0	.0	.0	.0	.0
Rents	7.0	6.5	5.0	4.0	3.8
Fixed Charges	6.2	6.3	5.8	5.3	5.0

Pro Forma Coverage on Latest Year Charges

	1966	1965	1964	1963	1962
Fixed Charges	25.1	22.5	22.1	19.6	18.5
F. C. & Rents	12.4	11.1	10.8	9.5	9.0
F. C., Rents & Pfd.	12.2	10.9	10.6	9.4	8.9

	Total Assets	Net Plant	Gross Plant	Other Liab.	Debt & M.I.	Pfd.	Common Equity	Total Capital
1966	1392.7	534.7	866.7	91.1	95.0	1.2	913.5	1009.7
1965	1337.2	487.0	792.0	71.5	105.6	2.3	894.7	1002.6
1964	1292.7	463.4	745.3	68.3	106.9	2.3	870.0	979.2

Other Ratios

	1966	5 yr. Average
Net Sales/Net Wkg. Capital	4.592	4.022
Net Sales/Gross Plant	2.588	2.532
Net Sales/Total Capital	2.222	2.027
Oper. Income/Gross Plant	.351	.367
Depr. & Amort./Gross Plant	.040	.040
Income Tax/Pre Tax Net	.461	.493
Dividends/Rptd. Earnings	.553	.564
Net & Fix Chge./Total Assets	.112	.106
Net & Fix Chge./Total Capital	.154	.143

Earnings Per Share

	1966	1965	1964	1963
1st Quarter	$ .98	$ .92	SF	$ .84
2nd Quarter	.79	.70	1.61	.65
3rd Quarter	.94	.81	.81	.71
4th Quarter	.76	.62	.57	.55
Year	$3.47	$3.05	$2.99	$2.75
Latest 12 Mos.	3.47	3.05	2.99	2.75

Balance Sheet—In $000,000—Fiscal Year Ends in June

	Cash & Equiv.	Inv.	Curr. Assets	Notes Pay.	Curr. Liab.	N.W.C.
1966	371.9	283.7	780.4	30.5	291.9	488.5
1965	400.6	265.0	784.3	23.5	263.1	521.2
1964	416.6	240.9	766.4	18.0	245.2	521.2

Balance Sheet Ratios

	1966	5 yr. Average
Curr. Asset/Curr. Liabilities	2.674	2.898
Cash & Rec./Curr. Liabilities	1.701	1.911
Total Capital/Debt & M.I.	10.629	8.955
Total Cap./Debt, M.I. & Pfd.	10.496	8.781
Long Term Debt/Net Plant	.178	.223
NWC/Debt & M.I.	5.142	4.512
NWC/Debt, M.I. & Pfd.	5.078	4.425
NWC/Common Share	9.172	8.545
Comm. Eqty/Common Share	21.357	19.412

Interim Figures

Sales $MM

	1966	1965	1964	1963
1st Quarter	558.4	523.1	SF	SF
2nd Quarter	531.3	486.8	954.9	826.7
3rd Quarter	591.8	527.8	SF	SF
4th Quarter	561.7	520.9	958.8	827.8
Year	2,243.2	2,058.6	1,913.7	1,654.5
Latest 12 Mos.	2,243.2	2,058.6	1,913.7	1,654.5

E—Estimate   A—Actual but not in calc.   AF—Annually Reported   NA—Not Available
S—Plus Stock   X—Includes Extra   SF—Semi-Annually Reported

EXHIBIT VI

Prospective Corporate Debt Issues

Est. Off. Dt.	Corporate Issuer	Type Issue	Type Offer	Amount (mil.)	Quality Mdy.	Quality S&P	Mat. Date	1st Ref. Date	Average Life (Yrs.) Max. Min.	Probable Yield	Comments
5-2	Tenneco	DEB	NEG	$ 50	Ba	BB	1987	1977	12.7	6.50%	
5-2	Mich. Wis. Pipe Line	FMB	Comp	45	A	BBB	1987	1967		6.25	
5-3	Henry I. Siegel	DEB	NEG	10	Baa	BBB	1987				
5-3	Union Pacific RR	Eq. Tr.	Comp	10	Aaa	AAA*	68/82	68/82		5.50	Municipal Scale
5-3	Central Ill. P.S.	FMB	Comp	15	Aa	AA	1997	1972		5.70	
5-3	Potomac Elect. Pwr.	FMB	Comp	35	Aa	AA	2002	1972		5.65	
5-4	P.S. of New Mexico	FMB	Comp	20	A	AA	1997	1972		5.75	
				$185							
5-9	Flying Tiger	Eq. Tr.	NEG	$ 10	Baa	BBB	1980	1980	7.5	6.00	
5-9	Cutler Hammer	DEB	NEG	20	A	A	1992	1977		5.65–5.70	Good Interest
5-9	Texas Electric Serv.	FMB	Comp	18	Aaa*	AAA	1997	1967			
5-10	So. Calif. Edison	FMB	Comp	80	Aa*	AA	1992	1972			
5-11	Ohio Power Co.	DEB	Comp	20	A	A	1997	1967			
5-11	Ohio Power Co.	FMB	Comp	50	Aa	AA	1997	1967			
				$198							
5-16	Interstate Pwr. Co.	FMB	Comp	$ 17	A*	A*	1997				
5-16	Kansas City P & L	FMB	Comp	30	Aaa*	AAA*	1997	1972			
5-16	TVA	REV	Comp	70	A	A	1992				
5-16	Textron, Inc.	DEB	NEG	100	Baa*	A*	1992				
5-17	Trane Co.	DEB	NEG	30			1992				
5-17	Conn. Light & Pwr.	FMB	Comp	30	Aaa*	AAA*	1992	1977	17.1	5.62–5.65	
5-17	Eastern Assoc. Coal	DEB	NEG	25			1987	1977			
5-17	Continental Air	Conv	NEG	30			1992	1967			
5-18	Trailer Train Co.	Eq. Tr.	NEG	48	Baa*	A*	1982	1982			
5-19	Kerr-McGee	Conv	NEG	96	Baa*	BBB*	1992	1967			Rights Offering
				$596							
5-22	Philadelphia El.	FMB	Comp	$ 75	Aaa*	AAA*	1997	1972			
5-23	Kentucky Power Co.	FMB	Comp	10	A*	A*	1997	1967			
5-23	Mich. Consolidated Gas	FMB	Comp	35	A*	A*					
5-24	Ches. & Potomac Tel.	DEB	Comp	60	Aaa*	AAA					
5-24	Burroughs	DEB	NEG	30	A	A*	1992	1977	16.8		
				$210							

Significant Issues without Firm Offer Dates

Est. Off. Dt.	Corporate Issuer	Type Issue	Type Offer	Amount (mil.)	Quality Mdy.	Quality S&P	Mat. Date	1st Ref. Date	Average Life (Yrs.) Max. Min.	Probable Yield	Comments
	Atlantic Richfield	DEB	NEG	$150	Aa*	AA*	1997	1977	19.0		

* Estimate.

Prepared 5-1-67

EXHIBIT VII

Bond List

Issues below have been approved for general programming but should not be purchased in individual amounts exceeding $25,000.

	Common-wealth	Dayton P & L	Shell Oil	Honeywell	(When Issued) Trane
Quality—Moody	Aaa	Aa	Aaa	A	A
S & P	AAA	AA	AAA	AA	AA
Type	FMB	FMB	DEB	DEB	DEB
Coupon	5.375%	5.625%	5.30%	5.60%	5.625% Est.
Maturity Date	4-1-97	5-1-97	3-15-92	3-1-92	5-1-92
Size (mil.)	$50	$40	$150	$60	$30
Industry classification	PU	PU	INDL	INDL	INDL
Years to Maturity					
Actual	30	30	25	25	25
Maximum average	30	Indet	18	17.6	17.1
Minimum average	30	Indet	12	13.3	NA
First date for—Refund	4-1-72	5-1-72	3-15-77	3-1-77	5-1-77
Call	Immed.	Immed.	Immed.	Immed.	NA
Price					Est.
Initial Offering	101.12	100.361	99.75	100.00	100.00
Current	97.75	100.361	98.75	100.75	100.00
Current Yield	5.50%	5.60%	5.37%	5.56%	5.625%
Adjusted Yield to Maturity					
Yield to					
Maturity	5.53%	5.60%	5.39%	5.55%	5.625%
Maximum average Life	5.53	Indet	5.41	5.54	5.625
Minimum average Life	5.53	Indet	5.44	5.52	5.625
Call in 5 years	6.78	6.41	6.25*	6.14*	NA*
Call in 10 years	5.97	5.87	5.65	5.71	NA
Rate at which refund is economic	4.625%	4.875%	4.55%	4.85%	4.875%

Issue Description

Commonwealth Edison Co. 5.375 percent First Mortgage Bonds Series Y due April 1, 1997.

Dayton Power and Light Company 5.625 percent First Mortgage Bonds due May 1, 1997.

Shell Oil Company 5.30 percent Debentures due March 15, 1992.

Honeywell Inc. 5.60 percent Sinking Fund Debentures due March 1, 1992.

Trane Co. (Preliminary) Debentures due May 1, 1992. All terms are subject to final negotiations expected to be completed May 17, 1967.

* Callable, but not refundable for five years.
NA—Not available.

5-1-67

EXHIBIT VIII

Analyst's Relative Performance Chart

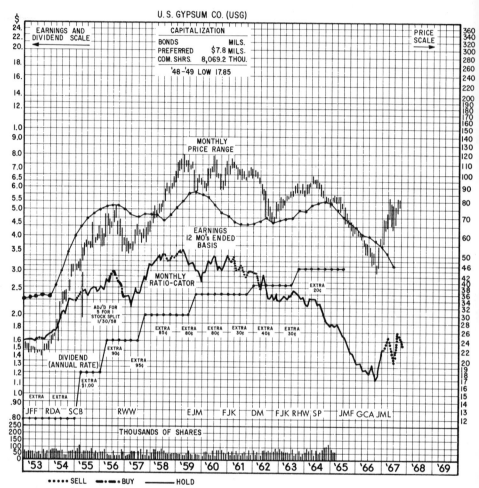

U.S. GYPSUM CO. (USG)

EARNINGS AND DIVIDEND SCALE

CAPITALIZATION

BONDS	MILS.
PREFERRED	$7.8 MILS.
COM. SHRS.	8,069.2 THOU.

'48-'49 LOW 17.85

PRICE SCALE

MONTHLY PRICE RANGE

EARNINGS 12 MO's ENDED BASIS

MONTHLY RATIO-CATOR

EXTRA 20¢

ADJ'D FOR 5 FOR 1 STOCK SPLIT 1/30/58

| EXTRA 85¢ | EXTRA 80¢ | EXTRA 80¢ | EXTRA 30¢ | EXTRA 40¢ | EXTRA 30¢ |

EXTRA 90¢

DIVIDEND (ANNUAL RATE)

EXTRA 95¢

EXTRA $1.00

EXTRA   EXTRA

JFF RDA SCB   RWW   EJM   FJK   DM   FJK RHW SP   JMF GCA JML

THOUSANDS OF SHARES

'53 '54 '55 '56 '57 '58 '59 '60 '61 '62 '63 '64 '65 '66 '67 '68 '69

••••• SELL   ••—•• BUY   ———— HOLD

EXHIBIT IX
Supplementary Investment Aids

Economic Forecasts: One Year (Quarterly)

Economic Forecasts: Three Year (Annually)

Industry Studies

Company Studies

General Stock List (Monthly)

Stock Sheets (Annually)

Trust Investment Committee Minutes (Daily)

Policy Memoranda (As required)

Current Investment List, or Buy-Sell List (Weekly or monthly)

Diversification Schedules (Semiannually or as required)

Security Codes

Master List of Bond Reserves

Master List of Stock Reserves

Corporate New Issue List (Weekly or biweekly)

Municipal New Issue List (Weekly or biweekly)

Corporate Bond Purchase List (Weekly)

New Deposit Schedule (Weekly)

Open Order List (Weekly)

Performance Graphs (Posted monthly)

APPENDIX B

Illustrative
bank trust department
organizations

EXHIBIT I

Bank X: Trust Department Organization

This bank has a large trust department with substantial holdings in mortgages and business interests in addition to its securities portfolio. There are separate investment and administrative divisions. The investment division is responsible for research and account administration. The administration division is divided into three operational teams.

There are four committees associated with the Investment Division:

Trust Committee of the Board—Meets semimonthly and considers matters of broad policy.

Investment Committee (securities)—Meets on Monday and Friday afternoon for a review of securities.

Investment Committee (accounts)—Meets each morning except Wednesday to review trust and advisory accounts. Each account analyst has a regular day to appear before the committee.

Investment Advisory Committee—Meets on Wednesday morning to review actions of the Investment Committees for the preceding week, to review actions taken by the common trust funds, and to take action on specific problems which could not be handled at the Investment Division level.

Bank X

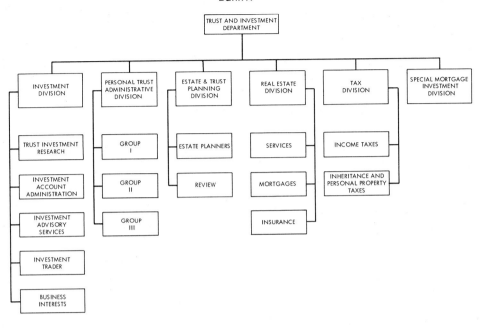

EXHIBIT II

Bank Y: Trust Department Organization and Account Supervision Procedures.

The organization charts, and the accompanying "Trust Account Supervision Procedures," describe the lines of responsibility and the method of operation of this trust company. Funds supervised are large in relation to the number of people in the organization, and consist in most part of securities of well-known corporations and public issuers.

The Investment Department, which is separate from the Trust Department, has responsibility also for supervising the Common Funds, Pension Accounts, and certain corporate and individual agency accounts.

All contact with customers is ordinarily through the trust administrative officers, who are given a degree of investment discretion through an approved purchase list. Beyond this, investment matters are referred to one or more members of the Investment Committee.

The Investment Committee acts also as the Review Committee for trust accounts, and sets general investment policies. Other committees, appointed by the heads of the Trust and Investment Departments, review securities, real estate and mortgages, and estates.

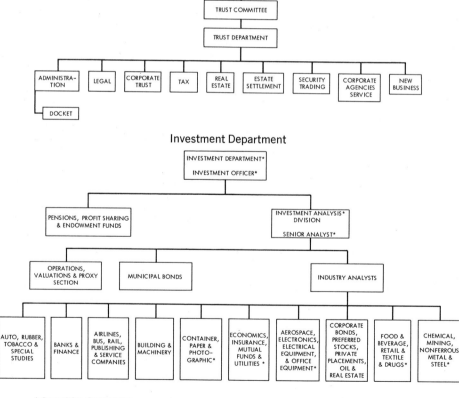

Trust Department

Investment Department

* Securities Committee.

January 1, 1967

Trust Account Supervision Procedures
Introduction

Certain changes in the manner of supervision of the Trust Department's accounts were made to streamline operations and to give the Account Managers more latitude in operating their accounts. There has been no change, however, in group judgment being brought to bear on major problems and in setting policies. Various revisions have taken place and are included in this statement.

Investment Committee

The Investment Committee, appointed annually by the Trust Committee and subject to directions from the Trust Committee, sets general investment policies. It reviews at least annually all trust accounts where we have investment responsibility, as well as all miscellaneous assets and notes.

Securities Committee

The membership of this Committee is selected by the Vice Presidents in charge of the Trust and Investment Departments. The purpose of this Committee is to review annually all securities acquired or held in a fiduciary capacity for which there may be any investment responsibility. Generally, these reviews will be made by the industry analyst at meetings of the Committee.

Reports prepared by the Investment Analysis Division, which may include those received from outside sources, will be reviewed by the Securities Committee who as a group will decide on purchase, retention, or sale unless it is determined the Investment Committee shall make the decision. After the decisions have been reached, the reports will be routed to the Account Managers for their information and/or action.

A monthly summary of the actions of the Securities Committee is supplied to the account managers.

Trust Real Estate and Mortgage Committee

The membership of this Committee is selected by the Vice Presidents in charge of the Trust and Investment Departments. The purpose of this Committee is to review at last annually all real estate and mortgages held in a fiduciary capacity for which there may be any responsibility, to pass upon all major expenditures and improvements to be made to real estate, and to pass upon the disposition of such real estate.

Estate Settlement Committee

The membership of this Committee is selected by the Vice Presidents in charge of the Trust and Investment Departments. The purpose of this Committee is to review at least annually all estates in the course of settlement and to pass on policy questions and written reports of the Estate Settlement officers.

Operating Rules for Account Managers

Account Managers will receive periodically a list entitled "Stocks for Investment Consideration," on which certain securities are marked to indicate they are on the "Approved Purchase List." Account Managers will do normal buying from the Approved Purchase List without consultation provided they are satisfied as to their choices and the amounts being invested are not so large that consultation is desirable. Account Managers will keep in mind, of course, that all securities on the Approved Purchase List are not necessarily prudent investments at all times or for every account.

Where consultation as to investment action is desirable, the Account Manager will discuss his problem with a staff member of the Investment Committee, who will assist in the decision or who will decide because of the importance of the problem that further consultation with the staff or Investment Committee is called for. In the latter cases, a detailed memorandum will be prepared.

Account Managers will follow the same consultation procedure with respect to general sales recommendations of the Securities Committee and other investment changes deemed desirable by the Account Managers.

Approved Lists

The Approved Purchase List for common stock purchases is prepared by the Investment Department Analysts and is approved by the staff. Municipal and corporate bonds rate "AA" or higher are considered to be approved for purchase, subject to a reasonable amount being held in several responsibility accounts and subject to satisfactory prices, yields, and call features. From time to time specific lists may be supplied to the Account Managers. Special approval similar to that detailed above can be obtained by consultation with the staff.

Equity Participations in Trusts

The Investment Committee will determine general investment limits for equity purchases within which the Account Managers will operate.

New Accounts

An initial review of each new trust or estate is to be prepared by the Account Manager to whom it is assigned. The memorandum to be reviewed by the appropriate Committee will contain the important background information, changes currently recommended, and the general investment policy suggested for future operations.

Review of Accounts

The respective Account Managers will be present at the meetings of the various Committees to furnish necessary background information and to answer questions.

The Account Managers will be expected on their own initiative to examine from time to time the accounts under their supervision and to make recommendations for their improvement.

Vice President

EXHIBIT III

Bank Z: Organization of the Trust Department Function

In this particular bank the Investment Department is separate from the Trust Department, and is responsible for all of the bank's activities involving securities, with the exception of those which might be held in the Loan and Discount Department. The Investment Department is divided into the Bond Department, with its usual list of functions, and a Trust Investment Research Division.

For trust investment purposes, the only connection with the Bond Department is the use of the municipal trader and the government trader of the Bond Department for transactions in municipal and governmental securities and subscription to U.S. Treasury Bills.

The first chart shows that Trust Investment Research has been divided in five major groups.

The *Portfolio Management* group is led by a division chief who supervises a number of portfolio managers. Since this bank operates a statewide branch system, the portfolio manager may be assigned to work on the portfolios of one or two administrative units of the main office, but very likely will also be assigned one or more branch offices. The head of the Trust Department's Pension and Profit-Sharing Administrative Unit is a former investment man and handles portfolio management of all pension and profit-sharing accounts. While he is not under the supervision of the Portfolio Management chief, he is shown in this section because of his portfolio management function.

The *Security Analysis* Division is headed by another investment officer. He supervises all of the experienced security analysts, who are assigned specific industries. Securities analyst trainees are not in this division. One of the industry analysts is a part-time economist. The head of the Investment Department also contributes economic knowledge.

The *Trading* function is guided by the Chief Trader. He is assisted by two experienced traders in his own division, and by the municipal trader and the government and agency bond trader of the bank's Bond Department. He also supervises certain clerical and operational work within the department.

The *Training and Special Projects* Officer is involved in two major areas. First, he has at least two security analyst trainees under his supervision at all times, and is responsible for teaching them not only the rudiments of security analysis, but an understanding of general Trust Department functions and all of the specialized areas of the Trust Investment Research Division. Second, he is in charge of all special research projects, and is assisted in this area by a mathematician and a computer programmer.

The *Investment Counselling* Division is directly under the supervision of the Trust Investment Research Head. Formerly, this division had been a part of the Trust Department, but its growth has been such as to justify a separate identity.

The second chart outlines the major committees in the Trust Department, and indicates the flow of information or action taken within the investment function. The *Board of Directors* appoints the members of the *Trust Committee*. These members consist of directors and officers of the Trust Department, the Investment Department and from the commercial bank. The Trust Committee is concerned with the general operation of the Trust Department and the various legal problems involving specific trust accounts.

The Trust Investment Policy Committee consists of the head of the Trust Department, the head of the Investment Department, the head of the Trust Investment

Research Division, and three senior Trust Department officers, all of whom have considerable investment experience. The Trust Investment Policy Committee has the duty of determining investment policies for the Trust Department and the review of actions taken, to determine whether or not they conform to policy. The measurement of performance is reported to this Committee. The Committee also conducts the initial review of each new trust account and suggests general investment strategy for the particular account.

Investment Department by Functions

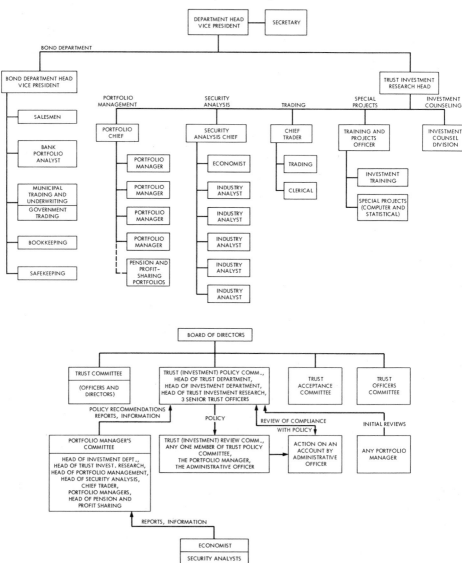

A flow of company and industry reports, as well as economic and market information, comes from the economists and the security analysts. These are first reviewed by the *Portfolio Manager's Committee* which meets weekly. The Committee consists of the head of the Investment Department, the head of the Trust Investment Research Division, the head of the Portfolio Management Division, the chief trader, all portfolio managers, and the head of the Pension and Profit-Sharing Division of the Trust Department (who is also a Portfolio Manager for his division). The Portfolio Manager's Committee summarizes its conclusions and passes them along to the Trust Investment Policy Committee with specific policy recommendations.

The Trust Investment Policy Committee publishes its policy decisions in the form of minutes. These minutes are often expanded by additional memoranda from the Portfolio Manager's Committee, from the economist, or from the security analysts.

The application of policy to specific accounts is carried out by a *Trust Investment Review Committee.* This Committee consists of any one member of the Trust Investment Policy Committee plus the administrative officer and the Portfolio Manager of the account. It should be pointed out that account considerations are always considered and may amend policy if they are of overriding importance. However, the portfolio manager is still responsible for the performance of his accounts where there is a deviation from the framework of policy.

The minutes of the Trust Investment Review Committee are the basis for action in a specific account. These actions are subsequently recorded in the minutes of the Trust Investment Policy Committee and are reviewed for conformity with policy. In addition, the performance of accounts is reviewed. It is hoped that the sophistication of these performance measurement efforts will rise substantially in order to strengthen the effectiveness of the organization.

Two additional committees in the Trust Department are the *Trust Acceptance Committee,* which accepts or rejects new accounts, and the *Trust Officer's Committee,* which reviews administrative and operational procedures and problems.

APPENDIX C

Selected material from
Regulation 9

(Title 12, Chapter 1, Part 9, Comptroller of the Currency)
April 5, 1963

§ 9.7—Administration of fiduciary powers.

(*a*)(1) The board of directors is responsible for the proper exercise of fiduciary powers by the bank. All matters pertinent thereto, including the determination of policies, the investment and disposition of property held in a fiduciary capacity, and the direction and review of the actions of all officers, employees, and committees utilized by the bank in the exercise of its fiduciary powers, are the responsibility of the board. In discharging this responsibility, the board of directors may assign, by action duly entered in the minutes, the administration of such of the bank's fiduciary powers as it may consider proper to assign to such director(s), officer(s), employee(s) or committee(s) as it may designate.

(2) No fiduciary account shall be accepted without the prior approval of the board, or of the director(s), officer(s) or committee(s) to whom the board may have designated the performance of that responsibility. A written record shall be made of such acceptances and of the relinquishment or closing out of all fiduciary accounts. Upon the acceptance of an account for which the bank has investment responsibilities a prompt review of the assets shall be made. The board shall also ensure that at least once during every calendar year thereafter, and within 15 months of the last review, all the assets held in or for each fiduciary account where the bank has investment responsibilities are reviewed to determine the advisability of retaining or disposing of such assets.

(*b*) All officers and employees taking part in the operation of the trust department shall be adequately bonded.

(*c*) Every national bank exercising fiduciary powers shall designate, employ or retain legal counsel who shall be readily available to pass upon fiduciary matters and to advise the bank and its trust department.

(*d*) The trust department may utilize personnel and facilities of other departments of the bank, and other departments of the bank may utilize the personnel and facilities of the trust department, as long as the separate identity of the trust department is preserved.

Bank trust departments

EXHIBIT I

Trust Departments in the United States

	1962	1961	1960	1955	1950	1947
Insured state nonmember banks..	1,153	1,100	1,066	887	870	819
State member banks............	575*	600	598	639	636	607
National banks	1,786†	1,763	1,738	1,727	1,774	1,429
Uninsured state banks.	175‡	–	–	–	–	121
Totals	3,689	3,463	3,402	3,253	3,280	2,976

* Nearly one half have trust assets of less than $1 million; 30% have trust assets of less than $100,000.

† Of these, 236 were inactive at the end of 1962.

‡ Approximate number, including some with more than $100 million of trust assets, as well as many very small departments.

Sources: 1947—a survey by Gilbert T. Stephenson, then Director of Trust Research, The Stonier Graduate School of Banking. Other years—Federal Deposit Insurance Corporation, Board of Governors of the Federal Reserve System, the Comptroller of Currency.

EXHIBIT II

Trust Department Assets According to Trust Department Size
(Dollar amounts in millions)

Trust Department Size	Number of Banks	Assets of Employee Benefit Accounts	Other Trust Assets	Total Trust Assets
Less than $10	1,110	$ 179	$ 2,067	$ 2,246
10 to 99.9	350	1,418	10,310	11,728
100 to 499.9	88	3,136	17,640	20,776
Over 500	26	23,835	30,935	54,770
Total	1,574	$28,568	$60,952	$89,520

Source: Stanley Silverberg, "Bank Trust Investments in 1965," *The National Banking Review*, 2, June, 1966, p. 489.

EXHIBIT III

Trust Assets of National Banks by States
(Dollar amounts in millions)

	Number of Banks Having Accounts	Employee Benefit Accounts	Other Trust Accounts	Total Trust Accounts
United States	1,574	$28,568	$60,952	$89,520
Alabama	27	118	735	853
Alaska	4	4	6	10
Arizona	2	21	430	451
Arkansas	26	12	224	236
California	17	1,804	5,831	7,635
Colorado	27	95	1,161	1,256
Connecticut	13	242	1,474	1,716
Delaware	1	*	*	*
District of Columbia†	6	205	1,019	1,224
Florida	65	196	2,052	2,248
Georgia	24	153	911	1,064
Idaho	3	9	36	45
Illinois	135	4,774	4,647	9,421
Indiana	88	243	1,752	1,995
Iowa	39	37	328	365
Kansas	37	23	325	348
Kentucky	51	25	254	279
Louisiana	18	64	193	257
Maine	16	21	201	222
Maryland	10	71	469	540
Massachusetts	56	901	2,194	3,095
Michigan	30	2,485	1,591	4,076
Minnesota	19	554	1,396	1,950
Mississippi	18	21	142	163
Missouri	28	581	1,942	2,523
Montana	11	3	43	46
Nebraska	17	57	417	474
Nevada	2	5	118	123
New Hampshire	21	4	120	124
New Jersey	81	106	1,105	1,211
New Mexico	14	8	178	185
New York	82	9,045	8,524	17,569
North Carolina	17	112	561	673
North Dakota	6	6	39	45
Ohio	50	972	3,137	4,109
Oklahoma	34	141	467	608
Oregon	2	128	522	650
Pennsylvania	153	3,726	8,233	11,959
Rhode Island	2	73	288	361
South Carolina	9	63	297	360
South Dakota	9	9	50	59
Tennessee	25	86	1,397	1,483
Texas	129	822	2,962	3,784
Utah	2	49	96	145
Vermont	12	4	36	41
Virginia	54	121	1,277	1,398
Washington	10	201	989	1,190
West Virginia	32	13	250	263
Wisconsin	32	153	501	654
Wyoming	12	2	33	35

* Less than $500,000.
† Includes national and nonnational banks in the District of Columbia.

Source: Stanley Silverberg, "Bank Trust Investments in 1965," *The National Banking Review*, 2, June, 1966, p. 490.

APPENDIX E

Selected bibliography on model building, portfolio selection, and measuring performance*

Model Building and Portfolio Selection

ALCHIAN, ARMEN A. "The Role of Securities in the Optimal Allocation of Risk-Bearing," *Review of Economic Studies* (April, 1964), pp. 91–96.

————. "Comment on the Portfolio Approach to the Demand for Money and Other Assets," *Review of Economics and Statistics* (Supplement, February, 1963), pp. 24–27.

————. "Liquidity Preference, Degree of Risk Aversion and the Expected Utility Hypothesis." Unpublished paper, 1967.

BAUMOL, WILLIAM J. "Mathematical Analysis of Portfolio Selection," *Financial Analysts Journal* (September-October, 1966), pp. 95–99.

CLARKSON, GEOFFREY P. E. "Trust Investment: A Study in Decision-Making," Pittsburgh, Pa.: Graduate School of Industrial Administration, Carnegie Institute of Technology, November, 1960. (Mimeographed.)

————, AND MELTZER, ALLAN H. "Portfolio Selection: A Heuristic Approach," *Journal of Finance* (December, 1960), pp. 465–80.

COHEN, KALMAN J., AND POGUE, JERRY A. "An Empirical Evaluation of Alternative Portfolio-Selection Models," *Journal of Business* (April, 1967), pp. 166–93.

* For further bibliographical references see Shannon P. Pratt, "Bibliography on Risks and Rates of Return for Common Stocks," *Financial Analysts Journal,* (May–June, 1968), pp. 151–66.

248

DUESENBERRY, JAMES S. "The Portfolio Approach to the Demand for Money and Other Assets," *Review of Economics and Statistics* (Supplement, February, 1963), pp. 9–24; followed by ARROW, KENNETH J., "Comment," pp. 24–27; CAGAN, PHILIP, "Comment," pp. 27–29; and FRIEND, IRWIN, "Comment," pp. 29–31.

EDWARDS, WARD. "The Theory of Decision Making," *Psychological Bulletin* (July, 1954), pp. 380–417.

FAMA, EUGENE F., AND ROLL, RICHARD. "Some Properties of Symmetric Stable Distributions." Center for Mathematical Studies in Business and Economics, University of Chicago, January, 1967.

FRIEND, IRWIN, AND VICKERS, DOUGLAS. "Portfolio Selection and Investment Performance," *Journal of Finance* (September, 1965), pp. 391–415.

———. "Portfolio Balance—The Demand for Money, Bonds, and Stock," *Southern Economic Journal* (October, 1962), pp. 71–76.

HEISTERBERG, ROBERT. "A Utility Earnings Growth Model," *Financial Analysts Journal* (January-February, 1967), pp. 116–19.

MAINE, ROBERT F. "My Attitude Toward Institutional Investment Attitudes," *The Analysts Journal* (Supplement, 2nd Quarter, 1948), pp. 31–36.

———. "Portfolio Selection," *Journal of Finance* (March, 1952), pp. 77–91.

MICHAELSEN, JACOB B., AND GOSHAY, ROBERT C. "Portfolio Selection in Financial Intermediaries: A New Approach," *Journal of Financial and Quantitative Analysis* (June, 1967), pp. 166–99.

MIDLER, JOSEPH L. "A Dynamic Portfolio Selection Model." Proceedings of the Seminar on the Analysis of Security Prices, University of Chicago, November 4–5, 1965.

MORRIS, WILLIAM T. "Diversification," *Management Science* (July, 1958), pp. 382–91.

RENSHAW, EDWARD F. "Portfolio Balance Models in Perspective: Some Generalizations That Can Be Derived from the Two-Asset Cast," *Journal of Financial and Quantitative Analysis* (June, 1967), pp. 123–49.

———. "Portfolio Analysis," *Journal of Financial and Quantitative Analysis* (June, 1967), pp. 76–84.

———. "Reply," (to Bierwag and Grove), *Journal of Finance* (March, 1965), pp. 94–95.

SHARPE, WILLIAM F. "A Simplified Model for Portfolio Analysis," *Management Science* (January, 1963), pp. 277–93.

———. "Addendum to A Simplified Model for Portfolio Analysis," *Management Science* (April, 1963), p. 498.

TIECHROEW, DANIEL; ROBICHEK, ALEXANDER A.; AND MONTALBANO, MICHAEL. "An Analysis of Criteria for Investment and Financing Decisions Under Certainty," *Management Science* (November, 1965), pp. 151–79.

TINTNER, GERHARD. "A Contribution to the Non-Static Theory of Choice," *Quarterly Journal of Economics* (February, 1942), pp. 274–306.

TOBIN, JAMES. "Liquidity Preference as Behavior Towards Risk," *Review of Economic Studies* (February, 1958), pp. 65–86.

————. "The Theory of Portfolio Selection," Chapter 3 in unpublished manuscript on monetary theory.

TREYNOR, JACK L. "How to Rate Management of Investment Funds," *Harvard Business Review* (January-February, 1965), pp. 63 ff.

WALLINGFORD, BUCKNER A. "A Survey and Comparison of Portfolio Selection Models," *Journal of Financial and Quantitative Analysis* (June, 1967), pp. 85–106.

Measuring Performance

ANTLIFF, JOHN C., AND FREUND, WILLIAM C. "Some Basic Research into Historical Results under Pension Plans with Benefits Based on Common Stock Performance," *Journal of Finance* (May, 1967), pp. 169–91.

BLOCK, FRANK E. "Risk and Performance," *Financial Analysts Journal* (March-April, 1966), pp. 65–74.

BOWER, RICHARD S., AND WILLIAMSON, J. PETER. "Measuring Pension Fund Performance: Another Comment," *Financial Analysts Journal* (May-June, 1966), pp. 143–49.

COHEN, KALMAN J., AND ELTON, EDWIN J. "Inter-Temporal Portfolio Analysis Based on Stimulation of Joint Returns." Pittsburgh, Pa.: Graduate School of Industrial Administration, Carnegie Institute of Technology, revised February, 1967.

————. "Returns to Speculators: Telser Versus Keynes," *Journal of Political Economy* (August, 1960), pp. 396–404; followed by TELSER, LESTER G., "Reply," pp. 405–12; and COOTNER, PAUL H., "Rejoinder," pp. 415–18.

DIETZ, PETER O. "Pension Fund Investment Performance—What Method to Use When," *Financial Analysts Journal* (January-February, 1966), pp. 83–86.

————. "Growth Stocks and the Petersburg Paradox," *Journal of Finance* (September, 1957), pp. 348–63.

EITEMAN, WILFORD J. "Yield on Common Stock Investments," *The Analysts Journal* (February, 1957), pp. 13–14.

FISHER, LAWRENCE. "An Algorithm for Finding Exact Rates of Return," *Journal of Business* (Supplement, January, 1966), pp. 111–18.

————, AND LORIE, JAMES H. "Rates of Return on Investments in Common Stocks," *Journal of Business* (January, 1964), pp. 1–17.

————. "Rate of Return on Common Stocks," *Financial Analysts Journal* (September, 1960), pp. 47–50.

MARKOWITZ, HARRY M.   "The Optimization of a Quadratic Function Subject to Linear Constraints," *Naval Research Logistics Quarterly* (March and June, 1956), pp. 111–33.

————.   "Portfolio Selection," *Journal of Finance* (March, 1952), pp. 77–91.

————.   "The Utility of Wealth," *Journal of Political Economy* (April, 1952), pp. 151–58.

McQUOWN, J. A.   "The Nature, Measurement, and Meaning of Investment Performance," paper presented at the Seminar on the Analysis of Security Prices, University of Chicago, May 9, 1966.

MILLER, MERTON H., AND MODIGLIANI, FRANCO.   "Dividend Policy, Growth and the Valuation of Shares," *Journal of Business* (October, 1961.)

MODIGLIANI, FRANCO, AND MILLER, MERTON H.   "The Cost of Capital, Corporation Finance and the Theory of Investment," *American Economic Review* (June, 1958), pp. 261–97.

————.   "The Cost of Capital, Corporation Finance and the Theory of Investment: Reply," *American Economic Review* (September, 1959), pp. 655–69.

Books and Pamphlets

BALL, RICHARD E. (ed.).   *Readings in Investments.* Boston: Allyn and Bacon, Inc., 1965.

BIERMAN, HAROLD, JR., AND SMIDT, SEYMOUR.   *The Capital Budgeting Decision.* 2d ed. New York: The Macmillan Co., 1966.

CHASE, RICHARD H., JR. *et al.*   *Computer Applications in Investment Analysis.* Hanover, N.H.: Trustees of Dartmouth College, 1966.

CLARKSON, GEOFFREY P. E.   *Portfolio Selection: A Simulation of Trust Investment.* Englewood Cliffs, N.J.: Prentice-Hall, Inc., 1962.

COHEN, JEROME B., AND ZINBERG, EDWARD D.   *Investment Analysis and Portfolio Management.* Homewood, Ill.: Richard D. Irwin, Inc., 1967.

COOTNER, PAUL H., AND HOLLAND, DANIEL M.   *Risk and Rate of Return.* Rev. ed.; Cambridge, Mass.: Massachusetts Institute of Technology, 1964.

DIETZ, PETER O.   "Evaluating the Investment Performance of Noninsured Pension Funds." Unpublished Ph.D. dissertation, Columbia University, 1965. Abstracted in *Journal of Finance* (December, 1965), pp. 720–21.

————.   *Pension Funds: Measuring Investment Performance.* New York: The Free Press, 1966.

FREDRIKSON, E. BRUCE (ed.).   *Frontiers of Investment Analysis.* Scranton, Pa.: International Textbook Co., 1965.

MARKOWITZ, HARRY M.   *Portfolio Selection: Efficient Diversification of Investments.* New York: John Wiley & Sons, Inc., 1959.

SOLDOFSKY, ROBERT M., AND MURPHY, JAMES T.   *Growth Yields on Common Stock: Theory and Tables*. Iowa City, Iowa: Bureau of Business and Economic Research, State University of Iowa, 1963.

WU, HSIU-KWANG, AND ZAKON, ALAN J. (eds.).   *Elements of Investments: Selected Readings*. New York: Holt, Rinehart & Winston, Inc., 1965.

APPENDIX F

A statement of principles
of trust institutions

This statement was adopted by the Executive Committee of the Trust Division, American Bankers Association on April 10, 1933, and approved by the Executive Council of the American Bankers Association on April 11, 1933.

FOREWORD

This Statement of Principles has been formulated in order that the fundamental principles of institutions engaged in trust business may be restated and thereby become better understood and recognized by the public, as well as by trust institutions, themselves, and in order that it may serve as a guide for trust institutions.

In the conduct of their business trust institutions are governed by the cardinal principle that is common to all fiduciary relationships—namely, fidelity. Policies predicated upon this principle have for their objectives its expression in terms of safety, good management, and personal service. Practices developed under these policies are designed to promote efficiency in administration and operation.

The fact that the services performed by trust institutions have become an integral part of the social and economic structure of the United States makes the principles of such institutions a matter of public interest.

ARTICLE I
DEFINITION OF TERMS

Section 1. Trust Institutions.—Trust institutions are corporations engaged in trust business under authority of law. They embrace not only trust companies that are engaged in trust business exclusively but also trust departments of other corporations.

Section 2. Trust Business.—Trust business is the business of settling estates, administering trusts and performing agencies in all appropriate cases for individuals; partnerships; associations; business corporations; public, educational, social, recreational, and charitable institutions; and units of government. It is advisable that a trust institution should limit the functions of its trust department to such services.

ARTICLE II
ACCEPTANCE OF TRUST BUSINESS

A trust institution is under no obligation, either moral or legal, to accept all business that is offered.

Section 1. Personal Trust Business.—With respect to the acceptance of personal trust business the two determining factors are these: Is trust service needed, and can the service be rendered properly? In personal trusts and agencies, the relationship is private, and the trust institution is responsible to those only who have or may have a financial interest in the account.

Section 2. Corporate Trust Business.—In considering the acceptance of a corporate trust or agency the trust institution should be satisfied that the company concerned is in good standing and that the enterprise is of a proper nature.

ARTICLE III
ADMINISTRATION OF TRUST BUSINESS

Section 1. Personal Trusts.—In the administration of its personal trust business, a trust institution should strive at all times to render unexceptionable business and financial service, but it should also be careful to render equally good personal service to beneficiaries. The first duty of a trust institution is to carry out the wishes of the creator of a trust as expressed in the trust instrument. Sympathetic, tactful, personal relationships with immediate beneficiaries are essential to the performance of this duty, keeping in mind also the interest of ultimate beneficiaries. It should be the policy of trust institutions that all personal trusts should be under the direct supervision of and that beneficiaries should be brought into direct contact with the administrative or senior officers of the trust department.

Section 2. Confidential Relationships.—Personal trust service is of a confidential nature and the confidences reposed in a trust department by a customer should never be revealed except when required by law.

Section 3. Fundamental Duties of Trustees.—It is the duty of a trustee to administer a trust solely in the interest of the beneficiaries without permitting the intrusion of interests of the trustee or third parties that may in any way conflict with the interests of the trust; to keep and render accurate accounts with respect to the administration of the trust; to acquaint the beneficiaries with all material facts in connection with the trust; and, in administering the trust, to exercise the care a prudent man familiar with such matters would exercise as trustee of the property of others, adhering to the rule that the trustee is primarily a conserver.

Section 4. Corporate Trust Business.—In the administration of corporate trusts and agencies the trust institution should render the same fine quality of service as it renders in the administration of personal trusts and agencies. Promptness, accuracy, and protection are fundamental requirements of efficient corporate trust service. The terms of the trust instrument should be carried out with scrupulous care and with particular attention to the duties imposed therein upon the trustee for the protection of the security-holders.

ARTICLE IV

OPERATION OF TRUST DEPARTMENTS

Section 1. Separation of Trust Properties.—The properties of each trust should be kept separate from those of all other trusts and separate also from the properties of the trust institution itself.

Section 2. Investment of Trust Funds.—The investment function of a trustee is care and management of property, not mere safekeeping at one extreme or speculation at the other. A trust institution should devote to its trust investments all the care and skill that it has or can reasonably acquire. The responsibility for the investment of trust funds should not be reposed in an individual officer or employee of a trust department. All investments should be made, retained or sold only upon the authority of an investment committee composed of capable and experienced officers or directors of the institution.

When the trust instrument definitely states the investment powers of the trustee, the terms of the instrument must be followed faithfully. If it should become unlawful or impossible or against public policy to follow literally the terms of the trust instrument, the trustee should promptly seek the guidance of the court about varying or interpreting the terms of the instrument and should not act on its own responsibility in this respect except in the face of an emergency, when the guidance of the court beforehand could not be obtained. If the trust instrument is silent about trust investments or if it expressly leaves the selection and retention of trust investments to the judgment and discretion of the trustee, the latter should be governed by considerations of the safety of principal and dependability of income and not by hope or expectation of unusual gain through speculation. *However, a trustee should not be content with safety of principal alone to the disregard of the reasonable income requirements of the beneficiaries.*

It is a fundamental principle that a trustee should not have any personal financial interest, direct or indirect, in the trust investments, bought for or sold to the trusts of which it is trustee, and that it should not purchase for itself any securities or other property from any of its trusts. Accordingly, it follows that a trust institution should not buy for or sell to its estates or trusts any securities or other property in which it, or its affiliate, has any personal financial interest, and should not purchase for itself, or its affiliate, any securities or other property from its estates or trusts.

ARTICLE V
COMPENSATION FOR TRUST SERVICE

Section 1.—A trust institution is entitled to reasonable compensation for its services. Compensation should be determined on the basis of the cost of the service rendered and the responsibilities assumed. Minimum fees in any community for trust services should be uniform and applied uniformly and impartially to all customers alike.

ARTICLE VI
PROMOTIONAL EFFORT

Section 1. Advertising.—A trust institution has the same right as any other business enterprise to advertise its trust service in appropriate ways. Its advertisements should be dignified and not overstate or overemphasize the qualifications of the trust institutions. There should be no implication that legal services will be rendered. There should be no reflection, expressed or implied, upon other trust institutions or individuals, and the advertisements of all trust institutions should be mutually helpful.

Section 2. Personal Representation.—The propriety of having personal representatives of trust departments is based upon the same principle at that of advertising. Trust business is so individual and distinctive that the customer cannot always obtain from printed matter all he wishes to know about the protection and management the trust institution will give his estate and the services it will render his beneficiaries.

Section 3. New Trust Department.—A corporation should not enter the trust field except with a full appreciation of the responsibilities involved. A new trust department should be established only if there is enough potential trust business within the trade area of the institution to justify the proper personnel and equipment.

Section 4. Entering Corporate Trust Field.—Since the need for trust and agency services to corporations, outside of the centers of population, is much more limited than is that of trust and agency services to individuals, a trust institution should hesitate to enter the corporate trust or agency field unless an actual demand for such services is evident, and the institution is specially equipped to render such service.

ARTICLE VII
RELATIONSHIPS

Section 1. With Public.—Although a trust department is a distinctly private institution in its relations with its customers, it is affected with a public interest in its relations with the community. In its relations with the public a trust institution should be ready and willing to give full information about its own financial responsibility, its staff and equipment, and the safeguards thrown around trust business.

Section 2. With Bar.—Attorneys-at-law constitute a professional group that perform essential functions in relation to trust business, and have a community of interest with trust institutions in the common end of service to the public. The maintenance of harmonious relations between trust institutions and members of the bar is in the best interests of both, and of the public as well. It is a fundamental principle of this relationship that trust institutions should not engage in the practice of law.

Section 3. With Life Underwriters.—Life underwriters also constitute a group having a community of interest with trust institutions in the common purpose of public service. Cooperation between trust institutions and life underwriters is productive of the best mutual service to the public. It is a principle of this cooperation that trust institutions should not engage in the business of selling life insurance.

APPENDIX G

Chartered Financial Analysts code of ethics and guidelines to the code of ethics

CODE OF ETHICS

Whereas, the profession of financial analysis has evolved because of the increasing public need for competent, objective and trustworthy advice with regard to investments and financial management; and

Whereas, those engaged in this profession have joined together in an organization known as the Financial Analysts Federation; and

Whereas, despite a wide diversity of interest among analysts employed by banks, brokers and security dealers, investment advisory organizations, financial relations counselors, insurance companies, investment companies, investment trusts, pension trusts and other institutional investors and corporate bodies, there are nevertheless certain fundamental standards of conduct which should be common to all engaged in the profession of financial analysis and accepted and maintained by them;

Whereas, the Financial Analysts Federation on May 20, 1962 duly adopted a Code of Ethics and Standards as a guide for those who practice the profession of financial analysis;

Now, therefore, we, the Trustees of the Institute of Chartered Financial Analysts, DO, this 14th day of March, Nineteen Hundred and Sixty-Four;

Adopt as a Code of Ethics for the Institute of Chartered Financial Analysts the Code of Ethics and Standards of the Financial Analysts Federation together with a set of "Guidelines" or interpretations of the Code such as may guide those members of the profession who have been awarded the designation of Chartered Financial Analyst:

I. Responsibility to the Public

The general public has the right to expect of the professional financial analyst technical competence and ability, honesty and a high degree of integrity, objectivity in opinions expressed, and avoidance of exaggeration and misrepresentation. Moreover, the financial analyst should not resort to misleading and high pressure sales methods in solicitation of business, including extravagant claims and flamboyant advertising.

II. Responsibility to Customers, Clients and Employers

Customers, clients or employers of the analyst should expect and receive strict, undivided fidelity and loyalty to their particular interests, maintenance of complete confidence respecting their private affairs, and diligent and judicious effort in handling their business. Customers and clients are entitled to a clear understanding of the source of compensation received by the analyst or his organization in connection with services rendered to them. Customers, clients or employers are entitled to full disclosure respecting any conflict of interest on the part of the analyst and the analyst should not enter into any business arrangement which might impair his ability to render unbiased and objective advice.

III. Responsibility to Corporate Management and Other Sources of Information

Corporations and others furnishing information to analysts have a right to expect of the professional analyst that any material so furnished will be reported accurately and not used in an inappropriate way or for any unfair personal advantage of the analyst. Information given to analysts by management on a confidential basis should be treated as such.

IV. Responsibility to Associates and Fellow Analysts

Associated and fellow analysts are entitled to expect of the analyst a high standard of professional conduct in all matters pertaining to competition with others in the field, relations with professional organizations, use of material, and terms and conditions of employment within his own organization. Every effort should be exerted to maintain unimpaired the professional status of the analyst in all aspects of his business relationships, and to uphold the honor and maintain the dignity of the profession.

GUIDELINES TO THE CODE OF ETHICS

1. The Chartered Financial Analyst shall maintain high standards of conduct in all aspects of his relationships with the public, customers, clients, employers, employees and associates and corporate management and other

sources of information, and shall give meticulous consideration to both the letter and spirit of the law and cooperate fully with regulation by government agencies, stock exchanges and industry groups.

2. The Chartered Financial Analyst shall conduct himself in such manner that transactions for clients have priority over personal transactions and such personal transactions shall not in any way operate adversely to the interests of clients. Full disclosure should be made of any individual or firm interest in the specific securities recommended for purchase or sale.

3. The Chartered Financial Analyst shall not undertake independent practice in competition with his employer.

4. The Chartered Financial Analyst shall not pay fees or commissions to others for recommending his service unless such payment is fully disclosed to the public or the client.

5. The Chartered Financial Analyst shall exercise care in borrowing from material prepared by other analysts, giving full credit where due, and being extremely careful to avoid plagiarism.

6. While the Chartered Financial Analyst is encouraged to display his diploma and to use the C.F.A. designation in a dignified and appropriate manner in keeping with the customary procedure of other similar professional designations, he shall not use it to draw attention to his personal professional attainments or services through the media of paid newspaper or journal advertisements.

7. Violations of the Code of Ethics or "Guidelines" will be regarded as cause for termination by appropriate action of the Board of Trustees of the Institute of the Chartered Financial Analyst's right to use the C.F.A. designation.